PHILOSOPHIES
OF EXCLUSION

Liberal Political Theory
and Immigration

PHILLIP COLE

EDINBURGH
University Press

Edinburgh University Press Ltd
22 George Square, Edinburgh

Typeset in Bembo
by Pioneer Associates Ltd, Perthshire, and
printed and bound in Great Britain by
MPG Books Ltd, Bodmin

A CIP Record for this book is available
from the British Library

ISBN 0 7486 1219 X (paperback)

CONTENTS

ACKNOWLEDGEMENTS

This book could not have been written without the research leave funded by the Arts and Humanities Research Board and the School of Humanities and Cultural Studies at Middlesex University. Equally important was the prior period of leave arranged through the cooperation of my colleagues in the Philosophy group at Middlesex. I am grateful to all for their support and encouragement.

I have drawn on material previously published elsewhere: 'The Limits of Inclusion: Liberal Theory and Immigration', in *Soundings*, Issue 10, Autumn 1998; 'Members and Strangers: Walzer on Immigration' in *Liberalism and Social Justice: International Perspectives* edited by Edward Garrett, Gideon Calder and Jess Shannon; 'Invisible Differences? Liberal Nationalism and Immigration' in *Ethics and Justice*, volume 2, nos 3 and 4, October 1999, pp. 85–93; and 'Embracing the Nation', in *Res Publica*, volume VI, Number 2, pp. 1–21. I am grateful to editors and referees for their invaluable feedback, and for permission to reproduce that material here.

Azzedine Haddour, Bob Brecher and Paul Gilbert read parts of the book at various stages: thanks for their constructive criticism. Audiences at a number of conferences also gave me extremely helpful comments: Rethinking Citizenship: Critical Perspectives for the 21st Century, at the University of Leeds, June 1999; The Liberal Order: The Future for Social Justice?, at Palacky University, Olomouc, Czech Republic, July 1999; and Nationalism, Identity and Minority Rights, at the University of Bristol, September 1999.

Thanks also to Jane Feore at Edinburgh University Press for her initial enthusiasm for the idea of the book before she moved on to other things; and to Nicola Carr for her subsequent patience and understanding as 'deadlines' came and went without any visible results apart from my apologies.

During the research leave my partner and I had to move 'house' twice, which of course has a certain irony given the subject of the book. If I write another text I will take great care over its subject matter. Thanks to the good friends who gave help and sustenance, physical and emotional, during that unpredictable process. I literally do not know what we would have done without them.

Finally, thanks to Roshi Naidoo for, above all her other support, the clarity of her vision. Without it, I would have lost my way.

FOREWORD

While I was writing this book, the publishers asked me if I could suggest an illustration for the front cover. This seemed a welcome diversion from my computer screen, and so I explored picture collections for a suitable image, something that would capture the issue of immigration. In my mind I could see something dramatic signifying exclusion – a painting of city walls with massive gates closed against besieging hordes, or a black and white photograph of barbed-wire fences and people with guns keeping out bedraggled travellers. I was searching for something spectacular or stark, which would signify one or other of the poles around which discussions of immigration gather – that liberal democratic states are justified in erecting firm barriers against teeming masses that would drain them dry, or that they are jealously guarding their privileges against the weak and helpless.

In the end, though, I came across an image that was completely at odds with my expectations. It was of a man with a bucket of white paint and a brush, bending over as he set out a white line down the middle of a street; in the background a few onlookers watched him in what I took to be bemusement. The photograph was taken in Berlin in 1947, and was of a British official marking out the boundary between east and west Berlin, to discourage Soviet police from pursuing black marketeers into the western sector. What struck me about the picture was precisely its lack of drama; what it signified for me was the banality of borders – and while I am not in a position to know what was in the minds of the onlookers, I like to think it was bemusement, because that is what I take to be the appropriate reaction when political borders are asserted.

In the end, of course, Berlin was divided by a wall, complete with barbed wire and men with guns. But that wall no longer exists and the boundary that both sides in the dispute were anxious to mark has been swept away both physically and in people's consciousnesses; and the fact remains that the vast majority of borders throughout the globe are not marked with walls or wire – they are boundaries that exist only within the imagination, represented as lines of a specific colour on pieces of paper. Sometimes the imagination is inspired by geographical features, but very often it is not. Whether we mark them with paint, wire, walls or only on maps, borders remain imagined constructs, and what is banal about them is their arbitrariness. Even in those cases where a state finds itself bounded by the sea, the fact remains that its political borders lie somewhere out at sea, beneath the ocean.

Of course, it may be replied that what is arbitrary here, and therefore banal, is the *fixing* of a border in a particular physical place, as the example of ocean boundaries shows; but the state boundary itself takes many forms, and the issue of immigration focuses, not on physical borders, but on a body of rules and laws that govern admission. Those boundaries are regarded as highly significant in political practice, and it is fundamentally misguided to describe them as banal. However, it is the whole round of boundary fixing that strikes me as banal, not merely the painting of a line on the ground: the whole body of rules and regulations and customs and mythologies that surround a national identity when it comes to membership of a state are bemusing. And while it is undeniable that people do attach great significance to these boundaries in political practice, the question is whether they ought to – and in political philosophy it is never enough to assert that they just do. Unfortunately, as we shall see, most of the work in political philosophy that does address the question of membership boundaries – especially that which approaches the issue from the stance of liberal nationalism – treads an uneasy path between the assertion that people just do attach significance to (national) boundaries, and the assertion that they ought to.

Again, it could be replied that political philosophy has to begin at some level of political practice; it has to start somewhere, and I would not argue with such an assertion. Indeed much of Chapter 2 is taken up with the demand that political philosophy take a more realistic view of the international order. And so it could be argued that, given the centrality of state boundaries in political practice, political philosophy must proceed on the assumption that such borders are legitimate. But this particular assertion of reality does not stand up. If we take political philosophy to be a normative discourse, then to take state boundaries to be legitimate is to take them to be ethical and rational elements of political practice. And yet what is being demanded of us here is that we must begin with a realistic view of the actual political order, and if we do that then we must surely accept that national borders as we find them practised are far from rationally and ethically unproblematic. However, the claim might be that it is the *idea* of state borders that has rational and ethical legitimacy, even if borders as they are practised fail to meet those standards. But if this is the claim, then those who make it are surely obliged to show how such an idea can have normative legitimacy, rather than assume that it does. And so while it is correct to say that political philosophy has to start somewhere, to say that it must start with the assumption of the legitimacy of state borders is to let far too much slip past the critical scrutiny that political philosophy demands. And so the starting point in this text is to demand that state boundaries as such must be shown to be rationally and ethically defensible if they are to play a legitimate role in political practice.

It should be made clear, once more, that the boundaries I am concerned with are boundaries of membership, rather than simply how and why borders are fixed in particular places. Practices of membership are broader than the mere drawing of a boundary around a territory, in that membership of a modern state does not coincide with territorial borders: one does not lose one's membership when one leaves the territory nor gain it when one enters. Territorial borders are, of course, important in many ways, but their relationship to member-ship boundaries is at a distance. They are one place where membership is policed, but not the only place, and sometimes play no policing role at all. One way in which one can often gain membership of a state is to be born within its borders, but in some cases this is not enough, and in others it isn't necessary at all. And so the precise question being explored here is what can morally justify the exclusive membership practices of modern states. The question is narrowed by putting it to liberal political philosophy in particular. There are two reasons for doing this. First, normative political philosophy at present simply is predominantly liberal political philosophy. Second, it is states that describe themselves as liberal democracies that play the leading role in shaping a global immigration regime. My claim is that liberal theory faces particular problems when it comes to the justification of exclusive membership. Many writers, we shall see, concede that, given its commitment to the moral equality of human beings as such, and therefore its abhorrence of arbitrary divisions between people, liberal theory should reject exclusive membership in principle and so oppose immigration restrictions in practice. But, having conceded this, they proceed to search for a justification for exclusion, often on the grounds that as it is such a widely accepted practice in liberal democratic states, a justification must be possible. But, as we shall see, this poses liberal theory with particular difficulties. The purpose of this book is to explore those difficulties. In doing so I hope we will learn something important about the membership of political communities, and also about liberal political philosophy itself.

Two things need to be said at this stage. First, this book does not address the question of refugees and asylum seekers in any great depth. To grant someone asylum is to say that their needs outweigh the limits imposed by our membership practices, and this is to assume that these practices have some degree of legitimacy. The question addressed here begins at a more fundamental level, asking how anybody, regardless of their circumstances, can legitimately be excluded from our political community. Second, it would be foolish of me not to point out that this book is set against the tide of current developments. States that describe themselves as liberal democracies are making their membership more and more exclusive: some European states have in effect banned immigration altogether, and the refugee and asylum system is under assault. The newspapers contain reports from around the world, especially from Europe, of anti-immigration movements both at street level and in political parties. During the week of writing this foreword there have been attacks on immigrants in Spain, the far-right Freedom Party has been elected to a share in political power in Austria after running on a strongly anti-immigration programme, and in the United Kingdom the Labour government has anxiously asserted that it is tougher on immigration and asylum seekers than the previous Conservative government. In political philosophy itself, the fact is that the issue of immigration has received very little attention, and there is more or less a consensus among those who do address it that, at least at some basic level, exclusive membership is justifiable. All this might indicate that I have chosen a topic for research that does not bear the weight of the attention I have paid it. On the other hand, the level of anger and violence that surrounds the question of immigration in practice, and the level of complacent and slipshod argument that surrounds it at the level of theory, may indicate that political philosophy should address it as a matter of urgency.

However, when liberal political philosophy *does* address the issue of membership, my argument is that it is forced to address some deeply disturbing problems about itself.

Chapter 1

INTRODUCTION:
LIBERAL PHILOSOPHY
AND MIGRATION

———·᠁ᠬᠬᠬᠬᡕᠥᠬᠬᠬᠬ·———

SECTION 1: INTRODUCTION

The mass movement of people across the globe constitutes a major feature of contemporary world politics. Whatever the causes of that movement – usually characterised as war, famine, economic hardship, political repression, climate change[1] – the governments of western capitalist states see this 'torrent of people in flight'[2] as a serious threat to their stability. Whether this perception is true or not – and we examine what empirical evidence there is for such a view in Chapter 2 – it may well be true that the scale and nature of this migration calls for a radical re-shaping of both political theory and practice, not for the sake of economic stability but for the sake of political, social and economic justice.

This re-shaped political theory has to make sense of the mass movement of people within two contexts. The first is economic globalisation: deregulation of the world economic order, and the relative decline in national autonomy over economic issues. This development is seen as at least one of the factors behind contemporary international migration, as people attempt to follow the flow of wealth to its centres; and yet at the same time those centres – western capitalist nation-states – are exerting strict control over immigration. The second context for

1

this new political perspective is that relationships between states and peoples must be understood against what is now a postcolonial world: a world that has been radically shaped by European colonialism and which is still living through its consequences. And so, not only does the global migration of peoples call for a re-shaping of the political order, it calls for a re-shaping of political theory itself; because liberal political philosophy, supposedly triumphant over other ideologies, cannot cope with this phenomenon within its own theoretical limits.

The point at which this fatal tension is expressed is at the borders of the liberal nation-state, and the practices of immigration control and naturalisation law. With its universalist commitment to the moral equality of humanity, liberal theory cannot coherently justify these practices of exclusion, which constitute 'outsiders' on grounds any recognisable liberal theory would condemn as arbitrary. And yet at the same time the liberal project depends upon those practices: the existence of a liberal polity made up of free and equal citizens rests upon the existence of outsiders who are refused a share of the goods of the liberal community. Liberal political philosophy maintains the appearance of coherence at the level of theory through the strategy of concealment. The vast majority of works in liberal theory do not address the question of national belonging and political membership, and only remain plausible on the assumption that the question has been answered in a way that satisfies liberal principles; but this assumption remains highly questionable. If the question of membership is made explicit, it becomes clear that there is an irresolvable contradiction between liberal theory's apparent universalism and its concealed particularism.

Liberal political theory is committed to the moral equality of persons: all persons carry equal moral weight. The liberal project aims to realise this principle in practice, expressed in the ideal of democratic citizenship. In a liberal polity all are at the same time equally subjects and sovereigns; they are equally subject to the law and at the same time those laws must be their expression of their sovereign will as citizens. However, in order to have a sustainable liberal polity consisting of free and equal citizens, some would argue that borders are required to make a clear distinction between those who are entitled to participate in that political community and those who are not – between insiders and outsiders. However, how can this distinction be sustained in the face of the principle of the moral equality of persons? How can the gap between citizens and outsiders be made in a way that does not appeal to features that liberal political philosophy would normally dismiss as arbitrary? It could therefore be argued that there is a serious gap between the legal and social practices of immigration and natural-isation in those states that describe themselves as liberal democracies, and the fundamental commitments of a recognisable liberal political theory. How serious that gap is depends upon whether there is a plausible justification of exclusive membership practices that embodies the principle of moral equality. However, the argument is not simply between liberal theory and practice, for the question of membership raises difficult questions for liberal theory's understanding of itself. As I suggested above, there is a tension, if not an outright contradiction, between the liberal principle of moral equality and the perceived need for closure of liberal polities.

SECTION 2: THE PRINCIPLE OF EQUALITY AND THE NEED FOR MEMBERSHIP

A central assumption of the argument is that a recognisable liberal political theory has at its centre the commitment to the moral equality of persons. A second assumption is that there is a strand of communi-tarian political theory which shares this assumption, and which can therefore be seen as liberal communitarianism; this form of commu-nitarianism has to be examined, because it provides many of the strongest justifications for membership practices.[3] This assumption of moral equality is one that many commentators of liberal theory would confirm. Amy Gutmann argues that what distinguishes modern political theory from ancient or classical theories is a commitment to individ-ualism, and that the belief in human equality has its source in this individualism. An assumption of human equality is therefore the 'uni-fying theme of liberalism', although 'no single postulate of human equality is to be found in classical liberal theory'.[4] Will Kymlicka takes the 'duty to treat people with equal consideration' as the basic principle upon which political theories can be critically assessed.[5] For example, what is attractive about utilitarianism as a moral theory is its 'deepest principle',[6] that is: 'Each person has an equal moral standing, each person matters as much as any other'.[7] Kymlicka takes seriously Ronald Dworkin's view that every plausible political theory is based upon equality as the ultimate political value: 'A theory is egalitarian in this sense if it accepts that the interests of each member of the community matter, and matter equally.'[8] Kymlicka recognises that the principle of moral equality is extremely abstract, and therefore cannot act as the basis of any theory of justice; but 'Each theory of justice is not *deduced from* the ideal of equality, but rather *aspires* to it, and each theory can be judged by how well it succeeds in that aspiration.'[9] Therefore, while in one sense it is difficult to ground a notion of moral equality, it seems intuitively indispensable to a recognisable liberal theory. Michael Walzer faces up to this problem when he says he does not know what characteristics make us equal, but:

> The answer has to do with our recognition of one another as human beings, members of the same species, and what we recognize are bodies and minds and feelings and hopes and maybe even souls. For the purposes of this book, I assume the recognition. We are different and we are also manifestly alike.[10]

Liberal political theory therefore has this assumption of moral equality at its centre. But there remains a tension at the level of theory between the principle of equality and what is perceived as a need for membership.

Walzer and others argue that the existence of liberal democratic communities depends upon exclusive membership practices: without borders that control immigration and naturalisation, political *communities* could not exist. A world without borders would either be a world of economic anarchism or it would be a global state. Neither option is attractive: the first would be an absence of anything that could be recognised as a political community, with all the benefits that brings; the second would be a state bureaucracy on a scale never experienced before, with all the dangers that brings. Therefore, in order to sustain political units on a scale that encourages the existence of communities without excessive state bureaucracy, borders are needed. Liberal political theory has been concerned with the problem of social justice, the distribution of welfare, without being overly concerned with the problem of who gets included in that distribution in the first place – and yet the question of who is entitled to membership of the community becomes crucial. As Walzer argues: 'The community itself is a good – conceivably the most important good – that gets distributed.'[11] And so while the liberal democratic project is driven by the principle of equality, the success of that project depends upon organised political communities, with a level of cohesiveness and commitment among their members. The achievability of the ideals that lie behind the principle of equality therefore rests upon practices of membership. And so while it may seem, at first sight, that there is a contradiction between the principle of equality and exclusive membership practices, they are in fact inseparable.

However, pointing out that the practical achievability of the liberal project depends upon exclusive membership practices does not solve the dilemma: it makes it sharper. Those practices must be such that they embody the principle of equality, or at the very least do not undermine it; such that if we cannot arrive at such a set of practices, then the liberal project is not practically achievable at all, because it is fundamentally contradictory. Liberal theory recognises the moral equality of all persons, and yet the practices of citizenship and democracy it deduces from that principle contradict it. And so the challenge for liberal, and liberal communitarian, theorists is clear: they must outline practices of membership that do not contradict the principle of equality. This is especially challenging for those who argue that notions of 'nationality' or 'national identity' are essential for the cohesiveness of political communities.[12] Walzer, for example, appeals to the notion of a shared identity as being essential if political communities are going to achieve their purposes. That identity, for Walzer, is based upon a shared understanding of who 'we' are, based upon common meanings, language, history and culture; these 'produce a collective consciousness'.[13] For Walzer, political communities depend upon a 'sense of relatedness and mutuality';[14] they are 'communities of character', consisting of people 'with some special commitment to one another and some special sense of their common life'.[15]

Appeals to such notions are especially problematic for the liberal theorist, because another characteristic element of liberal philosophy is what could be described as the rationality principle. This is the assumption that all human beings are in principle equally capable of rational thought, and that all political problems are therefore, in principle, capable of a rational solution: appeal to non-rational or arbitrary criteria for 'solving' problems is therefore ruled out. The concern to eliminate arbitrariness from social and political practices leads John Rawls to condemn as unfair any distribution of resources which rests upon what he sees as the arbitrary properties of 'social starting positions, natural advantages and historical contingencies';[16] these, for Rawls, are the 'fundamental' inequalities.[17] The arbitrary nature of resource distributions under capitalism therefore becomes the central problem for liberal theories of social justice.[18] If we see the membership problem as a question of distribution, then the same concerns about arbitrariness arise, especially if we are worried about natural and historical contingencies. Can an idea of national identity be arrived at which does not appeal to these sorts of properties?

There are four possible positions the liberal theorist could occupy here:

1. There are no non-arbitrary criteria for settling the membership question, and there is therefore no rational solution to it. The only liberal position is therefore to have no membership restrictions. The challenge for theorists taking this position is, of course, to show how political communities can be sustained without membership restrictions.

2. There are non-arbitrary criteria for settling the membership question, and therefore there is a rational solution to it: membership restrictions can be rationally justified. However, the notion of a common identity, such as a 'national' identity, is arbitrary, and so has no role to play in that solution. The challenge for theorists who take this position is to identify the non-arbitrary criteria which will act as the basis for membership.

3. The membership question cannot be settled without an appeal to some notion of shared identity, such as a 'national' identity. However, a notion of national identity can be arrived at which is non-arbitrary. Therefore the notion of a national identity, or a nationality, can play a role in the liberal solution to the problem. The challenge for theorists taking this position is to show how non-arbitrary conceptions of national identity, nationality or nationalism can be constructed.

4. There are no non-arbitrary criteria for settling the membership question, but it must nonetheless be settled: the open-borders option is not acceptable. Also, it can only be settled by appeal to notions of national identity, nationality or nationalism, although these remain contingent matters. The need for political community overrides the need for rational criteria for membership, and so the membership question has to be settled by appeal to contingent criteria. The challenge for theorists taking this position is to show how they can appeal to such notions and at the same time keep a moral and political distance from ideologies of nation and nationhood which they themselves would condemn as racist.

Any theorist working on the membership problem within a liberal framework must take one of these positions, and while all of the positions face difficult challenges, the main one is to show how the practices of membership they propose embody the principle of moral equality. While liberal communitarians could plausibly drop the rationality principle, they would not abandon the equality principle, and so still face the same challenge.

SECTION 3: EXCLUSIVE CITIZENSHIP

The revival of the concept of citizenship within western political theory has been remarkable,[19] especially within politics that regard themselves as radical. However, citizenship has an internal and external dimension, and the external dimension has been largely overlooked. Internally, the question has been how to ensure that all members of the community can actively be citizens in a meaningful sense, and it has been answered in terms of structures and policies that empower all to be equally active participants. Externally, the question is who will be admitted as a member of the community, and in political philosophy this has been interpreted as being a thin, legalistic issue (in practice, of course, it becomes a very complex legalistic issue, especially the case with the United Kingdom's nationality law). The focus of most contemporary political philosophy has therefore been on the first question, of empowerment. Will Kymlicka and Wayne Norman, in an important survey of current work on citizenship, illustrate the point. They make a distinction between citizenship-as-desirable-activity and citizenship-as-legal-status, where the former means that 'the extent and quality of one's citizenship is a function of one's participation', and the latter is 'a full membership' of the community in a purely legal sense.[20] They argue that the two concepts should not be conflated, and that most theorists are concerned with citizenship-as-desirable-activity:

> [T]hese authors are generally concerned with the requirements of being a 'good citizen'. But we should expect a theory of the good citizen to be relatively independent of the legal question of what it is to be a citizen, just as a theory of the good person is distinct from the metaphysical (or legal) question of what it is to be a person.[21]

If Kymlicka and Norman are correct, political philosophers can proceed with constructing theories of good citizenship based upon participation, and, with a clear conscience, leave the question of citizenship-as-legal-status for the lawyers: the two questions can be disconnected.

However, Kymlicka and Norman are too quick here, and the distinction between the person/good person shows why. For Kymlicka and Norman, there seems to be a moral problem of what it is to be a good person which is separable from a legal and/or metaphysical problem of what it is to be a person. But surely it is not true that the concept of a person is simply a legal and/or metaphysical concept: it is a profoundly *moral* concept, in that personhood itself is a status that carries moral significance whether or not one is a *good* person. That someone is a person is generally considered to impose moral constraints in the form of rights and responsibilities held by persons generally, not merely good persons. Similarly, surely the idea of citizenship is a moral concept independent of what makes a *good* citizen; because, once more, that someone is a citizen is considered to impose moral constraints in the form of rights and responsibilities held by citizens in general, whether or not one is a good citizen. And so the difference between citizenship-as-legal-status and citizenship-as-desirable-activity cannot be that one is a moral concept and the other is not: they must be different in some other sense, but still in a sense sufficiently important to justify setting the former aside. One difference Kymlicka and Norman pick out is that in general the former is a 'thin' concept while the latter is 'thick': but if the problems raised in this introduction are genuine, then citizenship-as-legal-status seems to have gained considerable 'thickness'.

The argument of this book is that the two questions are inseparable, and to construct a theory of internal membership without addressing the question of admittance is a fatally flawed project. It can only remain plausible on the assumption that the question of admittance has been settled in a way that is compatible with the principles of equality embodied in the structures of internal membership; but this assumption is highly problematic. The reality is that, at the level of theory, the institution of citizenship cuts in two directions: first, it makes a distinction between *members* and *outsiders* by drawing a boundary *around* the community; and second, it makes a distinction between *citizens* and *subjects* by drawing a boundary *within* the community. In any liberal polity the internal boundary cuts across the individual, in that all members are *both* subjects and citizens: they are subject to the law, but also sovereign over it by virtue of their democratic citizenship. In the ideal liberal polity, there are none who are purely sovereign (above the law) and none who are purely subject to it. This, of course, is not to ignore the problem of those considered incapable of participating as citizens by virtue of the lack of rational powers required, such as children; but in the ideal liberal polity this category is kept minimal. In an important sense, the citizens/outsiders boundary is a distinction between people: those who are admitted as members and those who are not; while the citizens/subjects boundary is a distinction, not between people, but between *activities*: the public activity of the citizen and the private activity of the subject. Again, in the ideal liberal polity, no members are confined *only* to the private sphere.

The problem comes when we realise that these two distinctions are inextricably entangled: the citizens/outsiders boundary is written into the citizens/subjects boundary, and this is why the question of internal membership cannot be separated from the question of admittance. The point of the citizens/outsiders boundary is to constitute and exclude outsiders – but from what? Not necessarily from the territorial boundaries of the liberal state; it is not important to the liberal state that outsiders are excluded from its geographical space (of course many are excluded in this way but the point is whether this can be justified on liberal grounds). Rather, what is crucial is that outsiders are excluded from *participation* in certain activities. If the citizen is entitled to participate in the most valued activities of the community, then the non-citizen must be excluded from those activities. They are outsiders in this vital sense: they are permitted to enter the private realm of the state, but are excluded from the public realm; they can be subjects of the law, but not sovereigns over it. And so the citizens/outsiders boundary is as much connected to activity as the citizens/subjects boundary: the border that is policed falls in exactly the same place.

Why should this matter? In fact it raises a number of tensions for the formation of a political community. First, it creates a category of persons who are not recognised by liberal theory, who are purely subject to the law with no sovereignty over it. Where their presence is long term, in the form of 'guest workers' for example, this is particularly discomforting, especially for the 'guests'. This can be seen in practice in the European Union, where citizens of member states have a superior status over non-EU nationals. Frances Webber comments that the way the European Union was built created a two-tier workforce, in which 'guest workers remain hostage to the "host" community', while citizens of member states have freedom of movement; and even in their 'host' community, guest workers 'did not have any rights worth speaking of'.[22] Michael Spencer points out that non-EU nationals:

> are reliant on national laws only, which in many cases relegate
> them to second-class status with minimal rights in such areas as

protection from discrimination and access to social security, health and welfare benefits.[23]

For Michael Walzer, this raises a painful problem at the level of theory. In effect, argues Walzer, this approach sets up two stages in the admissions process: (1) letting someone cross the territorial boundary; and (2) naturalisation.[24] This creates a distinction between the economic nature of the community and its political nature:

> As a place to live, it is open to anyone who can find work; as a forum or assembly, as a nation or a people, it is closed except to those who meet the requirements set by the present members.[25]

But these two visions of the state cannot co-exist, and so the arrangement fails on a point of justice:

> Men and women are either subject to the state's authority or they are not; and if they are subject, they must be given a say, and ultimately an equal say, in what that authority does.[26]

For Walzer, anybody who is subject to a law must also be sovereign over it: any situation that creates a class of people who are subjects only is manifestly unjust from a liberal point of view, a clear contradiction of the liberal democratic project; but this is exactly what liberal democratic states currently allow to happen. The existence of 'resident aliens', in whatever form they take, raises profound problems for liberal theory.

The second problem is that while the citizens/subjects and citizens/outsiders boundaries draw their distinctions in separate ways, they police them in the same location. The citizens/subjects boundary is based on a distinction between activities, not people: those activities proper to the public sphere of political citizenship. The citizens/outsiders boundary is based on a distinction between people, but in practice it is policed through controlling activities: outsiders cannot participate in the public activities definitive of citizenship. This creates potential dangers for certain groups of full members of the political community. As the boundaries between citizens/subjects and citizens/outsiders coincide, the way the external boundary is policed will have an impact on the way the internal boundary is policed. In effect, any group which shares characteristics with those identified as outsiders will themselves be in a vulnerable position. Their membership will be constantly questioned; they will be subjected to forms of surveillance from which other members are free, and their access to the public sphere of citizenship will become hazardous. If the external boundary of the community is policed by criteria based on 'race', however indirectly, then those members who share the criteria will be subjected to racism, from other groups and individuals who refuse to identify with them, and from institutions. The institutional racism is inevitable, as the external boundary is increasingly policed at access points to public goods such as social security and education; and so members of these groups will find it increasingly difficult to gain access to public institutions, as institutions such as those associated with the welfare state are used as a site of immigration control.[27]

The political community can therefore only be confident that its public realm is open to all its members in an inclusive way if it can be equally confident that its external boundary is not closed to others in an exclusive way. This is going to be especially problematic for those who wish to answer the membership question by appeal to 'national identity'. The policing of the external boundary of the state therefore has profound internal implications, and the problems of immigration and naturalisation cannot be set aside, as Kymlicka and Norman suggest.[28]

It should now be clear why the membership question has the potential to injure fatally the liberal democratic project. Practices of exclusion cannot be coherently justified within the terms of a recognisable liberal political theory, and yet the practical realisation of the liberal project depends upon those practices: the achievability of a liberal political polity made up of free and equal citizens rests upon the exclusion of others. And, finally, the exclusion of outsiders necessary to establish free and equal citizenship for insiders will, in practice, make free and equal citizenship for all an impossibility. The migration of peoples therefore calls for a re-shaping of the political order, and a re-shaping of political theory itself.

SECTION 4: CONCLUSION

Whatever the correct way forward, the claim remains that exclusive membership practices raise deeply disturbing questions for liberal political philosophy. The dilemma for liberal theory is how it can achieve coherence between its internal principles and external principles – by internal principles I mean those that govern its treatment of its own citizens; by external principles I mean those that govern its treatment of non-citizens, for example applicants for immigration. The liberal dilemma as I have described it is how to ensure that both these sets of principles are consistent with core liberal values such as the moral equality of persons. One obvious way to achieve this coherence is to have a policy of completely open borders, with no immigration constraints whatever. Most liberal theorists would not want to adopt this option, and instead attempt to justify some degree of immigration control, which, of course, amounts to a practice of exclusive membership. Their task is to justify those practices and show that the liberal coherence remains in place. My claim is that it is not possible to achieve this coherence, and the result is that in both theory and practice liberal theorists and states apply non-liberal if not illiberal principles to outsiders. I examine three responses to this dilemma. The first is to argue that the principle of the moral equality of persons has a more limited role to play than is supposed by this criticism, and can be overridden by more local principles. The priority of these local principles over the global principle of equality can be justified by appeal to special relations that hold between members of a particular liberal polity that are stronger than the relations that hold between persons as such. These local relations get their ethical content from a theory of community, and so this approach has a communitarian element to it. I examine the most important statement of this approach in Chapter 4 when I look at the arguments presented by Michael Walzer. One criticism of it may be that one needs to share with others far more than a mere location within a territory in order to constitute something that can genuinely be called a 'community', and these shared elements would have to be capable of outweighing the ethical significance of shared humanity. It is not at all obvious that the elements that Walzer and others identify as being shared within a political community are genuinely shared in the sense needed, and even if they are, that they *can* morally justify treating 'insiders' more favourably than 'outsiders': *do* these features (for example language, history, culture) morally outweigh shared humanity? Other theorists take this approach further and appeal to the idea of 'nationality' to provide the ethical framework that constitutes a community; but once more it remains unclear that those elements they identify as constituting a nationality are shared in the sense needed, and even if they are, that they carry greater ethical significance than shared humanity. I examine this form of liberal nationalism in Chapters 5 and 6, when I will look at the arguments of David Miller and Yael Tamir.

The second option is to argue that the liberal dilemma can be diffused without appeals to ideas of the community or the nation, but by appeal to values more central to the liberal tradition such as order, equality, welfare and so on. These arguments, then, confront the criticism directly rather than via non-liberal notions of community and national identity, and assert that there can be a liberal coherence between internal and external principles other than a policy of completely open borders. The problem here is to show how the liberal state can distinguish between 'insiders' and 'outsiders' without appealing to some feature that is morally arbitrary from a liberal point of view: where one is born or who one's parents happen to be are not things under one's control, and therefore under the central liberal theories of justice should not determine where one stands in the distribution of any good, and that surely includes the good of membership. I examine liberal egalitarian arguments that attempt to justify the division between members and non-members in Chapter 7.

The third option is to accept the claim that this liberal coherence cannot be achieved, and that exclusive membership practices are necessarily non-liberal or illiberal, but to assert that this should not matter from a liberal point of view. One can remain a liberal, and indeed an egalitarian liberal, and defend even the most severe of immigration constraints. This is because the international situation rules out the need to apply liberal principles at this level: the only ethical obligation that falls upon liberal states is to do whatever is in their interests and the interests of their citizens. I examine this 'Hobbesian' response in Chapter 8.

My own view is that, in the end, if the open borders option is rejected, the Hobbesian response is inevitable: and so in a sense, this part of the book is a journey through liberal argument to show how, in the end, it has to reach what is a deeply pessimistic conclusion. It is deeply pessimistic because it means that political philosophy under-stood as a normative discourse – and this is what I take liberal political philosophy to be – comes to an end at the national border. At the international level, there can be no ethical principles as there is, in effect, a Hobbesian state of nature here. Those liberal theories which implicitly or explicitly outline systems of distributive justice within the boundaries of a single state are, in the end, absolutely correct: liberal theories of justice are necessarily confined to national borders. Therefore any immigration policy, because it deals with outsiders, need only be informed by whatever the state believes to be in its best interests, and a liberal democratic state is therefore under no ethical obligation to have anything that can be described as a liberal immi-gration policy. We have come to the end of political philosophy.

The Hobbesian argument, I claim, makes two assumptions that can be questioned: first, that the international order *is* a Hobbesian state of nature; and, second, a particular theory of sovereignty according to which a sovereign state has unlimited power over its affairs. These two assumptions lead us to a position which seriously underestimates the possibilities for international justice. There is already a rudimentary framework of international justice in place, with codes of international human rights and courts of international law. There are, therefore, grounds for supposing that the Hobbesian conclusion is too pessimistic, and that states can be held to be under an obligation to treat 'outsiders' according to moral principles; and therefore that an immigration policy must be ethical, not merely an expression of state interest. We are left, once more, with the question of what an ethical immigration policy would look like. But the way out of the Hobbesian conclusion is not merely a recognition of the possibility for international justice: it is also the recognition of history. The relations between states and the borders between them are the product of a history, and that history gives rise to ethical conclusions: for example there may have been a colonial relationship between the two states. Too often liberal political philosophy is written against the background of a fictional history in which colonial exploitation never occurred. But once we bring this historical element into our considerations, it has a profound impact upon our ethical reasoning concerning migration. It is therefore inadequate to insert an international dimension into a 'traditional' and therefore ahistorical liberal framework; we have to move forward to a postcolonial perspective, a perspective that recognises that colonial power and exploitation have fundamentally shaped the world. The final chapter of the book seeks to develop these ways forward for political philosophy.

At the end of that exercise, I may not have offered a solution to the question of immigration that many people find satisfactory. But this work has a triple purpose. The first and most ambitious is to propose some sort of solution to the immigration dilemma for those who consider themselves to be egalitarians. The second is to expose what I take to be inadequate and sometimes deeply disturbing approaches to immigration taken by some liberal theorists, and the even more disturbing approaches taken by states that describe themselves as 'liberal democracies'. The third is to use the question of membership to learn something important about the limitations of liberal political philosophy, and to explore ways in which political philosophy can be transformed to break free of those limits, and find a version of it that is more adequate for the contemporary world, and which can play a positive role in bringing about justice in that world. So, if at the end

14

of the day I am judged to have failed in that first and most ambitious aim, I hope that I have at least succeeded in the remaining objectives, and that these are worth striving for.

NOTES

1. We shall see in Chapter 2 that these characterisations are somewhat inaccurate.
2. The phrase is taken from M. Teitelbaum and M. Weiner (eds) (1995), *Threatened Peoples, Threatened Borders: World Migration and US Policy* p. 29.
3. For example D. Miller (1995), *On Nationality* and M. Walzer (1983), *Spheres of Justice: A Defence of Pluralism and Equality*.
4. A. Gutmann (1980), *Liberal Equality*, p. 18.
5. W. Kymlicka (1990), *Contemporary Political Philosophy: An Introduction*, p. 34.
6. Kymlicka (1990), p. 36.
7. Kymlicka (1990), p. 37.
8. Kymlicka (1990), p. 4.
9. Kymlicka (1990), p. 44.
10. Walzer (1983), p. xii.
11. Walzer (1983), p. 29.
12. For example see D. Miller (1995), and Y. Tamir (1993), *Liberal Nationalism*.
13. Walzer (1983), p. 28.
14. Walzer (1983), p. 50.
15. Walzer (1983), p. 62. The term 'communities of character' is derived from Otto Bauer; see T. Bottomore and P. Goode (eds) (1978), *Austro-Marxism*, p. 105.
16. J. Rawls (1978), 'The Basic Structure as Subject', in A. Goldman and J. Kim (eds), *Values and Morals*, p. 56.
17. Rawls (1978).
18. See Kymlicka (1990), pp. 85–6.
19. See G. Andrews (ed.) (1991), *Citizenship* and W. Kymlicka and W. Norman (1994), 'Return of the Citizen: A Survey of Recent Work on Citizenship Theory', *Ethics*, 104 (January), pp. 352–81.
20. Kymlicka and Norman (1994), p. 353.
21. Kymlicka and Norman (1994), p. 353.
22. F. Webber (1991), 'From Ethnocentrism to Euro-racism', in *Europe: Variations on a Theme of Racism, Race and Class*, vol. 32, No. 3, p. 12.
23. M. Spencer (1990), *1992 And All That: Civil Liberties in the Balance*, p. 45.
24. Walzer (1983), p. 52.
25. Walzer (1983), p. 58.
26. Walzer (1983), p. 61.
27. See P. Gordon (1989), *Citizenship for some? Race and Government Policy 1979–1989*, pp. 7–8, and R. Lister (1990), *The Exclusive Society – Citizenship and the Poor*, p. 53.
28. Kymlicka and Norman (1994), p. 353, note 3.

Chapter 2

THE 'CRISIS' OF MIGRATION

SECTION 1: INTRODUCTION

The philosophical debate concerning immigration takes place against a particular background, and it is important to explore it in some depth as it determines, to a large extent, the shape of the debate. One concern is that the arguments within liberal political philosophy take place against a background which is largely the product of the liberal imagination, rather than one that bears much relation to political realities. The features of this imagined global order are that it comprises independent and autonomous nation-states with clear national identities; that they have immigration regulations that are transparent, rational and based upon these identities; and that people move around the globe for one of two reasons: seeking shelter from political persecution or an economically better way of life.

This imagined order fails to represent adequately the reality of the political order, or to respect the historical background to it. The fact is that the political order is highly regionalised and globalised, such that nation-states act within the confines of regional and global regulations and agreements. Also, people migrate throughout the globe for a range of complex reasons, many of them to do with historical connections between countries and regions; one of the major factors leading to migration from one country to another is past military occupation, for example. Finally, the regulations surrounding immigration vary widely in their rationality and transparency – and those who

16

wish to argue in defence of such regulations from a liberal point of view have to come to terms with the fact that the vast majority of immigration restrictions had their origins in racist ideologies and mythologies, and many still express racist 'concerns' however indirectly.

The purpose of this chapter is to display the gap between liberal theory's imagined global order and the reality. In Section 2 below I examine the processes of globalisation and regionalisation that are dominating the political order at present, and which raise profound questions for how we should regard political communities in political philosophy. In Section 3 I look at the historical story behind global migration, and the implications of its current levels for the political order. And in Section 4 I examine a range of migration regulations, to understand better their complexity and their relationship to racist ideologies.

SECTION 2: THE GLOBAL ORDER

The global order of the liberal imagination is one in which individual nation-states are regarded as free and equal entities, with sovereign power over their internal affairs. We can see this order at work when we look at David Miller's account of the international duties that constrain what states can do.[1] He identifies five such duties: (1) To abstain from materially harming other states, e.g. through pollution; (2) not to exploit states that are vulnerable to actions in a one-sided way, e.g. through economic exploitation; (3) the duty to comply with international agreements; (4) duties of reciprocity, e.g. coming to each other's assistance in times of natural disaster; and (5) the duty to ensure the fair distribution of resources. This last duty is based on the observation that states cannot be autonomous unless they are economically viable. This does not, however, entail global equality of nations, rather that 'resource transfers should be made so as to allow each national community to reach a threshold of viability, giving it an economic base from which national self-determination can meaningfully be exercised'.[2]

The background of this framework of international duties is, for Miller, 'a world in which nation-states are self-determining, but respect the self-determination of others through obligations of non-interference and in some cases of aid'.[3] But, importantly, there is no formal obligation to aid poorer states: 'international obligations should be seen as humanitarian except in cases where people's basic rights were put at risk and it was not feasible for their own national state to protect them'.[4] This constraint is entailed by respect for self-determination:

17

> To respect the autonomy of other nations also involves treating them as responsible for decisions they may make about resource use, economic growth, environmental protection, and so forth. As a result of these decisions, living standards in different countries may vary substantially, and one cannot then justify redistribution by appeal to egalitarian principles of justice.[5]

We can see from this that behind Miller's position is an assumption that nation-states, in a liberal world order, have the right to self-determination as an expression of respect for their autonomy or sovereignty. This 'sovereignty principle' means that individual states have the complete right to determine internal matters, such as immigration regulations, without external interference or constraint. There are three questions we can raise concerning this sovereignty principle. (1) Is it philosophically coherent, from a liberal viewpoint? (2) Has it played a central role in the history of liberal political thought? (3) Does it reflect the realities of the global political order? I will address the first question in Section 4 of Chapter 8, where I will argue that it is difficult to find a coherent philosophical argument for the sovereignty principle within liberal theory. In this section, I will confine myself to the second and third questions, and suggest that Miller's picture of the international order fails to reflect the reality of globalisation and regionalisation; and that, indeed, there are good 'realist' and ethical reasons to suppose that the sorts of issues he confines to the sovereign authority of the individual state – resource use, economic growth, environmental protection – should be handled at a more regional or global level.

The global order of the liberal imagination is often characterised as 'Westphalian'. Stephen Krasner argues that, although the Peace of Westphalia of 1648 has 'virtually nothing' to do with the Westphalian model of state sovereignty,[6] the doctrine, which actually emerges towards the end of the eighteenth century, has come to be known by this name. The model sees sovereignty as 'territoriality and the exclusion of external actors from domestic authority structures'.[7] According to this view, 'states exist in specific territories, within which domestic political authorities are the sole arbiters of legitimate behaviour'.[8] However, Krasner points out that:

> The norm of autonomy, the core of Westphalian sovereignty, has been challenged by alternatives including human rights, minority rights, fiscal responsibility, and the maintenance of international stability.[9]

18

Krasner goes further, arguing that Westphalian and international legal sovereignty – and especially the former – 'have always been violated'.[10] And so:

> Violations of Westphalian sovereignty have been almost routine in international politics even though observers have been blinded to their frequency by the assumption that the Westphalian model has been operative.[11]

What is remarkable, then, is 'the extent to which relations between rulers and ruled have been subject to external pressures or authority structures'.[12] And so the growth of human-rights frameworks since the second world war should not be seen as a fundamental break with the past – rather: 'Understood more generally as a problem of the relations between rulers and ruled, human rights are but one more incarnation of a long-standing concern in the international system.'[13] Krasner concludes:

> The right, or ability, of the state apparatus to exercise full authority within its own territorial borders has never been consistently established in practice and has been persistently challenged in theory.[14]

Whatever the virtues of Krasner's view that Westphalian sovereignty has never been an accurate picture of international relations, the contemporary processes of globalisation and regionalisation certainly show it to be of limited application today.

David Held, Anthony McGrew, David Goldblatt and Jonathan Perraton have produced a thorough examination of the contemporary global order,[15] and conclude that it is 'marked by a deterritorialization of politics, rule and governance'.[16] While under the Westphalian model – and, in my view, under liberal political philosophy's view – political communities are seen as 'ultimately the people in a fixed, territorially based community',[17] the growing reality is 'the extension of political power and political activity across the boundaries of the modern nation-state'.[18] While state governments are still the major actors in the global order, there has been a dramatic growth in the number of intergovernmental organisations (IGOs), international agencies, and quasi-supranational institutions (for example, the European Union). There has also been a growth in multi-national corporations, power groups and other sorts of organisations, and subnational groups who also act in the international arena. The result is that 'the global arena can now be conceived of as a polyarchic "mixed actor system" in which political authority and sources of political action are widely diffused'.[19]

The Westphalian model gives rise to a rather narrow conception of legitimate international concerns – mainly defence and security; but in the contemporary order a range of complex issues are seen as needing international solutions:

> Pollution, drugs, human rights and terrorism are among an increasing number of transnational policy issues which cut across territorial jurisdictions and existing global political alignments, and which demand international cooperation for their effective resolution.[20]

Held and his co-writers therefore talk in terms of 'global governance', and the existence of 'international regimes' which cover these issues. While the power of the nation-state may not have been eroded as much as some may think, the fact remains that they increasingly have to act within these international regulatory regimes which themselves are made up of a variety of actors.[21] 'National government is locked into an array of global, regional and multilateral systems of governance.'[22]

One important area where nation-states are becoming increasingly enmeshed at the international level is the law: 'the proportion of national legislation which reflects or incorporates international legal standards has increased significantly during the century'.[23] The Westphalian model can no longer account for these developments, as international law increasingly covers matters not traditionally understood as subjects for international concern, and increasingly involves agencies not recognised by the Westphalian model. The establishment of the United Nations Tribunal in the Hague, in the Netherlands, to prosecute those 'responsible for serious violations of international law' in the former Yugoslavia, and of a second tribunal in Arusha, Tanzania, to look at charges of genocide in Rwanda,[24] has brought the notions of 'war crime' and 'crimes against humanity' into sharp focus.[25] There are movements towards the establishment of a permanent international criminal court through the July 1998 Rome Statute. That statute has so far been signed by eighty-nine states, but so far ratified by only four. The court will come into existence in the Hague once the statute has been ratified by sixty states. The United States has not as yet signed the statute, and such problems show that the movements towards greater scope for international law and justice face difficult problems – and yet the progress made so far cannot be dismissed.[26]

The United Nations, of course, represents another aspect of the globalised order. Although the UN Charter is made up of individual states, they are increasingly interlinked and constrained by the UN framework.[27] And one of the most important aspects of the UN is the framework of international human rights that it has established, such that there is now a regime of human rights at the global, regional and national levels. Held and his co-writers comment:

> In regional and international law, accordingly, there has been a gradual shift – albeit unevenly experienced and reinforced – away from the principle that state sovereignty must be safeguarded irrespective of its consequences for individuals, groups and organizations. Respect for the autonomy of the subject, and for an extensive range of human rights, creates a new set of ordering principles in political affairs which can delimit and curtail the principle of effective state power.[28]

Perhaps the most interesting area of concern is the environment. Under the Westphalian model, 'the earth, sea and air were recognized as phenomena legitimately falling under the sovereign authority of states'[29] – they were embodied within the territory. However, the UN Charter of 1967 refers to 'the common heritage of mankind', and this is interpreted as:

> a device to exclude a state or private right of appropriation over certain resources and to permit the development of those resources, where appropriate, for the benefit of all, with due regard paid to environmental protection.[30]

It may be replied that this global order – of increased globalisation and regionalisation – is the product of the imagination of certain academic writers, and what matters is how nation-states imagine themselves. The suspicion is that they see themselves as sovereign bodies as conceived under the Westphalian model, and this should determine how we understand the global order. However, there is evidence that the governments of nation-states do conceive of themselves as increasingly 'enmeshed' in the way described here, and that they see this as a source of empowerment rather than merely constraint. For example the Labour Party in the United Kingdom has issued a consultation document for its members, in which it sets out its understanding of Britain's place in the global order.[31] There, it is set out how the Labour government of Britain conceives itself as being at the centre of international decision-making through its membership of intergovernmental organisations, such as the International

Monetary Fund, the World Bank, the World Trade Organisation, the G8, the Organisation for Security and Cooperation in Europe, the Council of Europe, the European Union, the United Nations and the Commonwealth. The document claims that it is vital to strengthen Britain's role within this framework, as:

> Globalisation involves the whole spectrum of social, political and economic activities across frontiers. It has increased our mutual dependence, breaking down barriers, opening sources of infor- mation and enriching our culture. It has also speeded up the world in which we now live, with new modes of transport and communication resulting in goods, capital, people and ideas moving more rapidly. Several other, less benign activities have however also increased as a result of globalisation, with dangerous elements taking advantage of global integration – the drugs trade, terrorist groups and the traffic of nuclear materials have all been globalised.[32]

The document emphasises the importance of being integrated within global and regional organisations in order to tackle these problems. For example, at the regional level the European Union is seen increasingly as the focus in 'the fight against cross-border crime and drugs',[33] with the formation of Europol in 1998 in order to share intelligence on drug trafficking, terrorism and other issues. At the international level, the document identifies the following set of problems that need international solutions:

> war and conflict; mass migration; the violation of human rights; international crime, terrorism and the illicit drug trade; the spread of health pandemics, like HIV/AIDs; environmental degradation; and rapid population growth.[34]

On the environment in particular, the document notes:

> In the new century, we face a range of global environmental challenges – climate change, the depletion of the ozone layer, threats to biodiversity, acute water shortages – to name but a few. These are challenges we need to tackle together – as one global community – or not at all.[35]

The question of the environment perhaps best illustrates the problems with David Miller's conception of the world order. We have already seen that respect for the autonomy of other nation-states 'involves treating them as responsible for decisions they may make about resource use, economic growth, environmental protection, and so forth'.[36] The only international duty that Miller identifies concerning the environment is to abstain from materially harming other states, for example through pollution. And yet this negative approach seems to assume that no positive international action is needed in order to tackle environmental concerns – that if individual states simply stop polluting each other's territory, there is no international issue here; one assumes that if they continue to pollute their own territory, other states have no right to interfere. The point that pollution does not respect national boundaries is not at issue here – Miller is clearly aware of that, and a duty constraining states from polluting each other's territory would, indeed, involve a radical re-assessment of environmental practices. What is at issue is the notion that environmental problems can be solved by sovereign, negative actions alone, that no positive international action is required. All the evidence presented at the Kyoto environmental summit in 1997 pointed out that the level of environmental damage was such that positive and concerted international action was needed if it was to be reversed; for example, the need to reduce industrial gas emissions.[37] In the absence of such action, global warming is predicted to increase around 3 degrees celsius by 2100.[38] This must lead to the suspicion that Miller's conception of international issues – such that they can be solved through nation-states acting in isolation, and through predominantly negative international duties – is impoverished.

Increasing globalisation and regionalisation have important implications for how we are to understand political communities. They can no longer be seen as 'discrete worlds'.[39] Rather:

> Political communities today are locked into a diversity of processes and structures which range in and through them, linking and fragmenting them into complex constellations.[40]

Therefore:

> The assumption that one can understand the nature and possibilities of political community by referring merely to national structures and mechanisms of political power is clearly anachronistic.[41]

And one of the elements of political thought that has to be questioned is that there is a clear 'inside' and 'outside' of the political community that can give rise to clear boundaries between members and non-members. So many important issues that need to be faced transcend the boundaries of nation-states – health issues such as AIDS, the environment, financial stability, control of drugs – that the idea of the proper democratic 'constituency' is now being transformed. 'At issue is the nature of the political community – how should the proper boundaries of a political community be drawn in a more regional and global order?'[42] In the face of this, we cannot meaningfully tackle the question of freedom of international movement within boundaries which claim their legitimacy from the Westphalian order of things.

SECTION 3: THE MOVEMENT OF PEOPLES

Another element of our picture of the global order which is, of course, of fundamental importance to the question of international freedom of movement is how people actually *do* migrate. What are the historical patterns of global migration and are there any contemporary patterns emerging? Here, the liberal imagination works in contradictory ways: from the fact that very few liberal political theorists have addressed the question of migration, we can conclude that we exist in a world order in which people stay where they are born, and if they move do so in minimal numbers. On the other hand, where liberal theorists *do* address the question, they conceive it in catastrophic terms: masses of people are flowing towards liberal democratic states, which must protect themselves if they are to survive this onslaught (see Chapter 8, especially Section 2, for this 'catastrophe prediction' within liberal political philosophy). In fact, the International Organisation for Migration (IOM) reported that around 120 million people were on the move in 1994, but this is less than 2 per cent of the global population,[43] which means, of course, that 98 per cent stay put. This seems to indicate that the reality lies somewhere between the two extremes of the liberal imagination: significant numbers of people do migrate across the globe, but still the overwhelming majority do not. However, this report excluded *internally* migrating and displaced peoples, which, according to the IOM, would increase the figure tenfold; and it is also significant that this figure has increased from estimates of 1.7 per cent in 1990. Still, as Philip L. Martin points out, while the numbers on the move are significant:

> [I]t should be emphasized that most people do not migrate despite ever more incentives to do so. The industrial democracies are not being overrun by a tidal wave of migrants.[44]

Therefore the sense of panic that is informing the rhetoric of state governments concerning immigration has little basis in fact. Still, according to Emek M. Ucarer, the official view still has an 'apocalyptical element',[45] and therefore the emphasis is on restriction:

> Current policies in the receiving countries are framed almost exclusively in restrictive terms that emphasize controlling migratory inflows.[46]

For Stephen Castles and Mark J. Miller it is important to note that migration has 'been part of human history from the earliest times'.[47] Ucarer sees this as a paradox:

> [I]f various waves of migration were indeed the building blocks of civilizations throughout history, how is it that migration today is largely seen as a threat, and why are migrants looked upon as being responsible for many of the social ills of the receiving societies?[48]

However, Castles and Miller do believe contemporary migrations to be distinct, because of 'their global scope, their centrality to domestic and international politics and their enormous economic and social consequences'.[49] They understand contemporary migration within the context of globalisation; it is an important element within that process: 'International migration is part of a transnational revolution that is reshaping societies and politics around the globe.'[50] They see this as a largely benign process, but acknowledge that it is not inevitably so: it can give rise to tension and conflict.

David Held and his co-writers identify four periods of migration: pre-modern – up to 1500; early modern – from 1500 to 1760; modern – from 1760 to 1945; and contemporary – from 1945. Each of these periods has seen significant levels of migration, but of distinct kinds.[51] While pre-modern migration was immense in scale, it was regional rather than global; global mass migration occurs in the modern period. The early modern and modern periods saw three distinct phases of global migration.[52] The first came with European expansion from 1492, when there was rapid European expansion into America and Oceania. This reached its peak between 1850 and 1914, when between 46 and 50 million people left Europe for those regions. This form of migration only came to a halt in 1914 with the commencement of the first world war.

The second form of mass global migration during this period was the slave trade, which lasted 400 years from the mid-sixteenth to the mid-nineteenth centuries, but was at its height during the eighteenth century. Although figures are controversial Held suggests that between

9 and 12 million people were taken from Africa to the Americas and other regions during this period. The third element was the Asian diaspora, which began in the mid-nineteenth century at the end of the slave trade, with mass migration of Asian labour to replace slave labour. There was large-scale movement from India, China, Japan and Java to north America and to the European colonies throughout the globe. Figures are unclear but massive numbers were involved: for example between 1815 and 1914 around 12 million people left China in a vast wave of migration. In all perhaps 35 million people were on the move, around 12 million permanently.

This period of global migration came to a halt in 1914, and movement remained low in the interwar period.[53] However the postwar settlement in 1945 saw the beginning of a new age of migration, but this time with different flows. Now the labour shortages were not within European colonies, but within European nation-states themselves, and so the 1950s and 1960s saw overseas labour recruitment with guest workers entering states such as Belgium, Germany and Switzerland, and migration from ex-colonies to France, Britain and the Netherlands. Australia and north America remained the focus of mass migration, but now from south America, the Asia-Pacific and the Caribbean. In the mid-1970s an economic downturn saw immigration restrictions tightened in Europe, but the transatlantic flows continued to be reversed, with migration increasing from Argentina and Brazil to Spain, Portugal and Italy.[54] Migration to north America and Australia continued to escalate.

The two great ages of migration have, therefore, been from 1880 to 1920, and between 1945 to the present day. During that first period, around 30 million people migrated to the United States, while during the latter period it has been around 35 million.[55] However, although the numbers are around the same, the intensity was greater during the earlier period, when we take into account that the US population in 1900 was around 75 million and in 1990 it was around 248 million. Therefore 'we can reasonably conclude that contemporary migrations to the USA, while of similar absolute intensity, are of lesser relative intensity than those experienced at the end of the 19th century'.[56] However, the story for European nations is different; for some immigration is around three times what it was from 1880 to 1920, with population increasing far more slowly than in the United States.

However, even if – in the case of the United States for example – contemporary migration is relatively less intense than that experienced at the end of the nineteenth century in terms of numbers, its implications must be different given the existence of extensive welfare systems and a different form of economic organisation.[57] Here, once more, the liberal imagination comes into play: it seems to see immigrants as always involving a cost to the receiving state (see Chapter 3, Section 2, for such an account, and Chapter 8, Section 2), and yet the evidence suggests that matters are more complex. Held and his co-authors state:

> Conventional xenophobic wisdom has argued that the conse-
> quences ... are uniformly negative for host welfare states.
> Immigrants crowd out the indigenous poor and working class
> from the bottom end of the job market, overburden already
> dilapidated welfare systems and generally constitute an overall
> drain on the public finances. However the evidence, such as it is,
> does not support this position.[58]

For example, the fact is that population growth in the west is either negligible or in decline, and there is a major shift in the age structures of populations, with growing demands on welfare services and pensions. Immigration has made a 'significant contribution' to population growth and therefore alleviated some of these problems.[59] And so: 'in the few systematic studies of the contribution of immigrants to welfare through taxes paid set against the benefits received, no conclusive evidence exists to suggest that benefits received outweigh contributions'.[60] In fact, 'in Western Europe and Canada the impact of immigrants on the welfare state may actually be positive'.[61] In the case of the United States, Peter Schuck points out that the USA has a relatively low population density compared with Europe, and the density of cities has been falling throughout the twentieth century. He states:

> [W]e are in most important respects a far better society than we
> were before these immigrants arrived. Their contribution to this
> progress is striking in the growth of the economy, the expansion
> of civil rights and social tolerance, and the revitalization of many
> urban neighbourhoods. Moreover, these immigrants bear little
> blame for the great exception to this progress: the increase in the
> social pathology afflicting some inner-city subcultures.[62]

Elliott Robert Barkan also argues that most anti-immigration studies in the United States have 'seriously underestimated the taxes immigrants actually pay, directly and indirectly, and significantly overestimated the service costs of immigrants'.[63] A report by the anti-immigration

Carrying Capacity Network put the annual costs to government at $42.5 billion, but in 1994 the Urban Institute of Washington DC claimed this over-estimated costs by $71.2 billion. Barkan comments:

> Such studies critical of immigration's impact have also usually omitted the contributions of immigrant-owned business . . . They have likewise ignored the extent to which immigrants stimulate other, related sectors of the economy both as entrepreneurs and as consumers.[64]

The Urban Institute concluded that immigrants 'create more jobs than they themselves fill and recent immigrants from abroad create as much employment growth as internal migrants from other areas of the United States'.[65] Anton Kuijsten[66] points to Julian Simon's work on immigration to North America,[67] which concludes that:

> [T]he presence of immigrants is good for the migrants themselves, good for the community through their large net contribution to the public coffers, and at least not bad for the individual natives.[68]

The question is whether this also applies to Europe, and Kuijsten takes the Netherlands as a case study. While the data is complex, he concludes that 'it is not self-evident that [the] balance will always be negative, as is often suggested'.[69] It is therefore too simplistic to assume that people who immigrate always impose a cost on the receiving state; it depends on a complexity of factors which possibly defy prediction. And so basing arguments for immigration controls upon catastrophe predictions is a dubious and dangerous move for political philosophy.

Another important factor in understanding global migration is comprehending what factors determine such movement. Liberal political philosophy, where it addresses this question at all, seems to see international migration as predominantly determined by push–pull factors. Castles and Miller characterise such views as push–pull theories, 'because they perceive the causes of migration to lie in a combination of "push factors", impelling people to leave the areas of origin, and "pull factors", attracting them to certain receiving countries'.[70] They condemn such theories as individualistic and ahistorical.[71] According to such a view, there has to be some attraction within the receiving country, and some negative feature of the country of departure, and this is characterised in economic terms – people migrate based on an economic cost–benefit basis.[72] This theory would predict, therefore, that the poorest people would seek to move to the richest parts of the globe, but the available evidence does not support this. Rather, the evidence shows:

> that it is rarely the poorest people from the least-developed countries who move to the richest countries; more frequently the migrants are people of intermediate social status from areas which are undergoing economic and social change.[73]

And so 'the idea of individual migrants who make free choices' in order to 'maximize their well being' is 'so far from historical reality that it has little explanatory value'.[74]

Castles and Miller favour migration systems theory, which emphasises 'international relations, political economy, collective action and institutional factors'.[75]

> Migration systems theory suggests that migratory movements generally arise from the existence of prior links between sending and receiving countries based on colonisation, political influence, trade, investment or cultural ties.[76]

The leading sources of immigration to the United States are currently Vietnam, the Dominican Republic, Mexico, Korea and the Philippines – all countries the United States has invaded and occupied or culturally dominated.[77] For Great Britain, major sources of migration are India, Pakistan and Bangladesh – all former colonial possessions. Similar movements are from Martinique to France, Surinam to the Netherlands, and Algeria to France. A major factor in shaping global migration is, therefore, the historical relationship between the sending and receiving country, and the overly individualistic and ahistorical picture that liberal political philosophy presents is, once more, misleading.

Liberal political theory, then, presents us with a picture of global migration which is highly inaccurate. While it works on the basis that people stay put, it imagines that hordes of people are on the move – and these people are predominantly on the move for economic reasons, based on a cost–benefit analysis, and they will inevitably have a negative impact on receiving states. The reality is that, while significant numbers of people are on the move, the vast majority stay where they are born – those who do migrate do so because of a complex set of factors, but mostly because of the historical relationships between sending and receiving states; and historically migrants have contributed benefits to those receiving states, politically, economically and culturally. Our consideration of the morality of immigration control has to take place against this understanding of global movements.

SECTION 4: REGULATION

The large-scale, bureaucratic regulation of membership now taken to be an essential element of state sovereignty is a relatively recent phenomenon. Richard Plender outlines the classic view of freedom of movement as expressed by Francesco de Vitoria: 'It was permissible from the beginning of the world, when everything was in common, for anyone to set forth and travel wheresoever he would.'[78] This view could be found up until the end of the nineteenth century, when a movement grew towards the restriction of movement as a response to Chinese labour migrating westwards. What follows is the 'enactment of racially and culturally exclusive immigration laws':[79] the Chinese Exclusion Act in the United States in 1882; the Chinese Immigration Act in Canada in 1885; and Australia's Immigration Restriction Act of 1901. The rise of immigration laws at the end of the nineteenth century, therefore, was based on racism, and the laws themselves were explicitly based on racist theories and mythologies. The history of immigration control ever since has been one of institutionalised racism at the border. Francis Fukuyama says of those states he describes as 'posthistorical' (liberal democracies):

> [T]hey have had difficulty formulating any just principle of excluding foreigners that does not seem racist or nationalist, thereby violating those universal principles of right to which they as liberal democracies are committed. All developed democracies have imposed limits on immigration at one time or another, but this has usually been done, so to speak, with a bad conscience.[80]

Robert A. Huttenback provides a detailed examination of racist immigration controls throughout the British empire between 1830 and 1910,[81] focusing on the self-governing colonies of Australia, New Zealand, Canada and Natal in South Africa. He describes a situation in which the imperial authorities were in conflict with the self-governing colonies over their wishes to employ explicitly racist immigration restrictions aimed at free 'coloured' migrants. A policy was needed that would not involve 'shattering the fragile hypocrisy surrounding the imperial philosophy of equality'.[82] In Natal in 1897, Act 14 was introduced which introduced two tests: first, a property qualification ($£25$), and, second, an education test focusing on language ability, which was to be administered at the discretion of immigration officials.[83] This was 'to be administered in such a way that Europeans were to be judged eligible to enter Natal while all Indians were not'.[84] The Natal prime minister declared in 1897:

> It never occurred to me for a single minute that it should ever be applied to English immigrants . . . Can you imagine anything more mad for a Government than that it should apply to English immigrants? The object of the bill is to deal with Asiatic immigrants.[85]

And so the governor of Natal could inform the United Kingdom government that 'the main object of the proposed law is to prevent Natal from being flooded by undesirable immigrants from India', and at the same time the imperial government could reassure its Indian subjects that 'the Immigration Restriction Act . . . does not affect British Indians as such'.[86] The Natal formula was seized upon as the solution to the empire's problems, and was adopted throughout the self-governing colonies,[87] and was embodied in the white Australia policy of 1901.[88] Huttenback makes it clear that: 'Racial hatred was the vital driving force behind legislation',[89] along with a profound fear of miscegenation.[90]

The white Australia policy itself is, of course, a primary example of racist exclusion, and it is also an illustration of how immigration rules work alongside internal exclusions of 'native' peoples. James Jupp points out that:

> White Australia cannot be understood simply as a restrictive immigration policy. It was central to building a white British Australia from which all others would be excluded, whether recent Chinese immigrants or the original Aboriginal inhabitants.[91]

The Immigration Restriction Act remained in force from 1901 to 1958, and was part of a framework of colonial, commonwealth and state law 'to prevent anyone from contributing to Australian nation-building who was not of European descent and appearance'.[92] Therefore people defined as 'aboriginal natives' of Australia, Asia, Africa and the Pacific Islands were to be excluded from citizenship. As a policy it 'was almost completely effective between the 1890s and the 1960s as a form of immigrant exclusion'.[93] And, says Jupp, however the exclusionary regulations were framed, and whatever the official justifications for them: 'White Australia was overwhelmingly racist in its motivation and in the definitions it used'.[94]

Before addressing the question of whether this racism is still an issue within immigration regulation, we need to survey current practices.

Immigration and citizenship regulations are enormously complex and varied, and it is difficult to generalise about them without grossly oversimplifying how they work. However, while remaining aware of this danger, we can say that they seem to share a set of general characteristics. In the first place, there are usually two levels of admission to a state: residency and citizenship; one can take up permanent residency within a state and still never acquire the status of citizen; in such situations, the difference between residents and citizens is usually expressed in terms of political rights. T. Hammar expresses this as a distinction between citizens and 'denizens' – the latter being people with legal permanent residence but not full citizenship.[95] According to Hammar, half the foreign population in western Europe in 1987 were denizens of this kind.

Citizenship itself can be acquired in two distinct ways: (1) by birth and (2) by immigration. Citizenship by birth can itself be acquired in two ways: (1a) by being born within the territory of the state, regardless of the status of one's parents (*juis soli*); or (1b) by being born to parents, at least one of whom is a citizen of the state (*juis sanguinis*). Citizenship by immigration can also be acquired in two ways: (2a) by acquiring a relationship with someone who is already a citizen, for example through marriage; and (2b) through length of residence within the state as a denizen. There are other exceptional ways of acquiring citizenship: for example, under Austrian law, 'aliens' who become employed as professors at an Austrian university automatically become citizens, and their spouse and children may also, if they wish.[96]

All four main methods, of course, admit of wide variety. *Juis soli*, for example, can be revised by re-defining what counts as the state's territory, and former colonial powers have a history of such revisions. For example, the United Kingdom granted citizenship by *juis soli* to anybody born within its colonial territories and independent member states of the Commonwealth until 1948 – in effect all were British subjects and all were entitled to entry to the United Kingdom. The 1948 Nationality Act created citizenship of the United Kingdom and Colonies, which could be acquired by British subjects under certain conditions, and while at first right of entry into the United Kingdom itself remained automatic for all British subjects, this opened the way to future restrictions: Commonwealth citizens lost their automatic right of entry in 1962, and United Kingdom and Commonwealth citizens theirs in 1968. One oddity about British nationality and immigration law was that, during this period, they parted company such that British citizenship did not bring automatic right of entry. They were brought back into line when the United Kingdom finally abolished *juis soli* altogether in 1981.[97]

Juis sanguinis can also be manipulated by re-defining how many parents must count, whether they must themselves be citizens or merely denizens, and whether they themselves are citizens by birth or immigration. It may even be that the 'countback' reaches to further generations, such as grandparents. The United Kingdom introduced the 'patriality' clause in 1971, under which Commonwealth citizens were free to enter the United Kingdom with indefinite leave to stay (which itself brings the possibility of acquiring UK citizenship) only if they could show that one grandparent was born in the United Kingdom.[98] Both methods of citizenship by immigration can obviously be manipulated in various ways: the specific relationship through which one can acquire citizenship can be varied, and the length of residency needed before one can be considered for citizenship can of course be altered.

The immigrant, in effect, has three boundaries to cross in order to acquire full membership of the state: first, they have to cross the border into the state territory; second, they must gain access to residency within the state; and, third, they must gain access to citizenship itself. Achieving any one of these 'crossings' carries no guarantee of success at the next stage. Emek M. Ucarer comments:

> Generally speaking, it is invariably the case that only some people are allowed in, and, of those, only some are granted civil and political rights. Historically, there has not necessarily been a linear path from resident alien status to citizenship.[99]

We can also see that the state, through its unlimited power to manipulate the four conditions of citizenship, can closely control the character of its membership. Jules L. Coleman and Sarah K. Harding make a distinction between those states that have a concern with preserving some kind of cultural identity, and those that do not:

> [T]hose nations which focus on cultural integration attribute citizenship solely on the basis of parentage, typically an indication of cultural affiliations, whereas most of the other countries attribute citizenship in other circumstances.[100]

They identify Japan, Germany and Israel as examples of the first kind, and Canada, the United States and Sweden as examples of the second, with the United Kingdom and France lying somewhere in between. Another dimension they draw attention to is the extent to which under some practices citizenship is acquired as a matter of right once certain conditions are met, and the extent to which it remains at the state's discretion; again, states which are concerned to control the 'character' of their citizens are more likely to retain discretionary control over citizenship (for example, the United Kingdom). Emek M. Ucarer makes much the same distinction, between states which regard themselves as immigration countries and those that do not.[101] The United States, Canada and Australia belong in the former group, and characteristically have policies to encourage integration and assimilation; they have 'extended citizenship and commensurate civil and political rights fairly readily'.[102] In contrast, western European states belong in the latter category, and 'their policy objectives have been to stabilize inflows, to limit long-term stays, to discourage permanent residence, and to withhold citizenship and its prerogatives'.[103] However, the relevance of this distinction is blurring, as even the traditional countries of immigration 'are having second thoughts'.[104]

The concern I expressed at the beginning of this section was over the extent to which all immigration regulation has its roots in racist ideology, and whether we are now in a position to set this concern aside. It may be that even though the initial frameworks of immigration control put in place at the end of the nineteenth and the beginning of the twentieth centuries were expressions of racism, they have now been sufficiently reformed and liberalised so that we can now consider the justice of immigration practices without focusing on the question of racism. The United States gives grounds for some optimism here. In 1921 the Emergency Quota Act introduced race-based exclusions, which were strengthened in 1924 and 1929. Elliott Robert Barkan comments: 'America had effectively blocked the way of particular Europeans and others whom they deemed less desirable.'[105] But in 1965 the Immigration and Nationality Act abandoned national origin quotas,[106] and instead introduced a system of visas based on non-racialised categories. The main groups were family-based, employment-based and 'diversity' immigrants. However, there is still some concern over how these categories work in relation to race issues, as each has its own priorities – within the family category it is unmarried sons and daughters of US citizens, and under the employment category it is people with 'extraordinary' abilities.[107] Peter Schuck allows that racism 'plays a less significant role than it did before 1965',[108] but points out that 'three decades after the national origins quotas were repealed, we still select most immigrants according to their national origins'.[109] As the case of the Natal formula shows, it is clearly possible to have admissions criteria that make no explicit reference to race, but still work to exclude certain racial groups.

The United States, then, is an example of a state moving away from a racist immigration framework (setting aside the qualifications expressed above). The United Kingdom, in contrast, provides an example where the state has moved from an open policy on immigration to an increasingly racialised regulatory framework. We have already seen how the United Kingdom's citizenship and immigration laws came apart between 1948 and 1981, such that citizenship, paradoxically, carried no right of entry into the United Kingdom for some groups. The 1981 Nationality Act was designed to solve this paradox, but in doing so brought into being some of the most complex citizenship anywhere in the world. The 1981 Act formally created different levels of belonging to Britain:

i/   British citizenship.
ii/   British Dependent Territories Citizenship (BDTC).
iii/   British Overseas Citizenship (BOC).
iv/   British National (Overseas).
v/   British Subject.
vi/   British Protected Person.
vii/   Commonwealth Citizen.
viii/ Citizens of Eire.

Only category i/ had automatic right of entry to the UK: the other classifications are more or less hierarchical in their degree of belonging to Britain. The effect of European Union law is that EU nationals leap-frog to second place when it comes to right of entry, over two classifications of British citizens.

As we have seen the object of the 1981 Act was to bring British nationality into line with the immigration Acts passed between 1962 and 1971, which had created a situation in which Britain was refusing entry to its own citizens while admitting non-citizens: many full UK citizens had no right of entry. The 1981 Nationality Act solved the problem by taking full citizenship away from those groups, who 'happened' to be predominantly black. Ann Owers comments:

> [N]ationality law was to do with cutting down the possibility of immigration, especially black immigration. This priority meant that much of the Nationality Act merely codified and petrified British immigration law. Its provisions are dominated by a fear of who might be able to come here.[110]

But rather than simply strip UK citizenship from the former UK and Commonwealth citizens who had been deprived of entry rights under the immigration laws, the 1981 Act did give them a form of British citizenship, but a degraded form – the classifications of BDTC and BOC were created, a British citizenship that gave no right of entry to Britain. Vaughan Bevan comments:

> Whilst BDTC and BOC perpetuate, in formal terms, the UK's Commonwealth responsibilities, they are virtually meaningless in municipal law, since they carry no right of entry into the UK. . . . They are cosmetic concepts designed to mollify local and international opinion.[111]

Kathleen Paul summarises the British experience: 'In this process, formal definitions of citizenship increasingly, have had less influence than racialized images of national identity.'[112]

SECTION 5: CONCLUSION

The reality is that we are faced by a vast array of immigration regulations, which have their historical origins in deeply racist ideologies and commitments which were still explicitly shaping regulations in the 1960s. While some countries have moved away from restrictions based on national origins, others have moved in that direction, however much they may avoid expressing regulations in explicitly racist terms. Given the centrality of migration within the international framework, it remains remarkable that immigration control remains an anarchic system, with each state determining its own set of rules. Ucarer comments:

> In an increasingly interdependent world, this norm of jurisdiction over territory seems to be one of the last holdouts of sovereignty. But, it surely makes an ominous task of efforts to deal in a multilateral manner with transnational issues like migration.[113]

There is, therefore, no global migration regime.[114] However:

> [O]ne of the first steps toward coping with the mass movement of poor people today is to begin to look at the world differently and perhaps to reconsider time-honoured doctrines like sovereignty and traditional entities like nation states.[115]

There seem to be three alternatives to the system of state anarchy. The first is an alternative anarchy of complete freedom of movement,

leaving the issue to individual choice. The second is a system of international regulation based on standards of justice, ensuring that all state
regulations meet a common standard. The third is a weaker system of
an international code, with unenforceable provisions. However, liberal
political philosophy seems to be hostile to any of these alternatives
because of its commitment to a state's right to determine its membership. One point worth making is that this commitment to state
sovereignty over the membership question has an impact on another
issue that liberal theory often takes a different view of, and that is
the right of asylum for refugees. What needs to be realised is that the
international framework that governs asylum and the rights of
refugees is itself exceedingly fragile and under pressure, precisely
because of the question of state sovereignty over membership.

The relevant United Nations' treaties are the Convention and the
Protocol relating to the Status of Refugees.[116] The Convention of
1951 governs the status of refugees in receiving states, rather than
rights to admission or asylum;[117] it therefore regulates their access to
certain goods once they are lawfully within the receiving state:

> The treaty deals with *status* for populations already in place and
> accepted. It does not create obligations for admission, nor for
> granting full residence rights to those who may be within the
> territory and are able to establish that they are refugees.[118]

D. A. Martin points out that under traditional international law, asylum
is not a right of individuals, but a right of states: 'States, in their discretion, may provide asylum to those they choose to shelter; they do
not thereby commit a wrong against any other state.'[119] Therefore the
Universal Declaration of Human Rights and the 1951 Convention were
both worded to avoid conflicting with this notion.[120] This means that
someone seeking refuge within a state may meet the Convention
definition, but not be lawfully in the state of refuge[121] – this status is
at the discretion of the receiving state. 'Thus at the global level it
remains the case that no treaty guarantees asylum; no individual right
of asylum exists.'[122] It also remains the case that the Convention only
protects the status of those who are granted asylum: those who have
entered the state and are having their cases considered have no protection except at the discretion of the receiving state. The Convention
therefore offers no protection to asylum *seekers*. In 1997 the United
Kingdom government abolished certain welfare entitlements to a wide
range of asylum seekers, putting them at risk of destitution.[123] This was
overturned in the High Court which ruled that local authorities had

a duty to provide assistance to asylum seekers who were without any other means of support, a decision confirmed by the High Court in 1997. The present government are seeking a new system, based on the belief that:

> [P]eople who have not established their right to be in the UK should not have access to welfare provision on the same basis as those whose citizenship or status here gives them an entitlement to benefits when in need. Any support for asylum seekers should operate on a separate basis, with provision offered as a last resort to those who have no other means.[124]

Under the proposed new system:

> Support will . . . be available only where it is clearly necessary while an application is awaiting decision or appeal. Accommodation, in such circumstances, will be provided on a no choice basis, with no cash payment for this purpose being made to the asylum seeker. Other basic needs will also be met where there is a genuine risk of hardship.[125]

The new measures include provision for detention of asylum seekers in detention centres, where there is need to clarify identity or the basis of the claim; or where there is reasonable belief that the applicant will not keep the terms of their temporary admission.[126] Detention is at the discretion of immigration officers.

It is clear, therefore, that the 1951 Convention is designed to protect the status of successful applicants for asylum; the anomaly is that those *seeking* asylum have no such protection – their status is entirely at the discretion of the receiving state. The 1967 United Nations Protocol added nothing to the Convention provisions in this respect: it was concerned to establish the definition of 'refugee' – that is, anyone who:

> . . . owing to a well-founded fear of being persecuted for reasons of race, religion, nationality, membership of a particular social group or political opinion, is outside the country of his nationality and is unable or, owing to such fear, is unwilling to avail himself of the protection of that country; or who, not having a nationality and being outside the country of his former habitual residence, is unable or, owing to such fear, is unwilling to return to it.[127]

During the 1980s and 1990s states have moved to extending asylum only to those who meet the Convention definition, and even then are adopting an 'increasingly restrictive interpretation of the Convention definition' itself.[128] Martin comments that: 'These developments make it hard to muster optimism for further progressive developments in the 1990s and beyond.'[129]

The assumption of the state's right to control its membership is therefore having an adverse impact upon a group that liberal political philosophy would seek to protect, and yet its desire for international protection is irreconcilable with the sovereignty assumption. Somehow we need to progress beyond this obstacle, but we can only do this by coming to understand why liberal theorists are so hostile to a system of freedom of movement that removes regulation from state control. The next chapter explores a set of arguments against this liberalisation.

NOTES

1. D. Miller (1995), *On Nationality*, pp. 104–8.
2. Miller (1995), p. 106.
3. Miller (1995), p. 107.
4. Miller (1995), p. 108.
5. Miller (1995), p. 108.
6. S. D. Krasner (1999), *Sovereignty: Organized Hypocrisy*, p. 20.
7. Krasner (1999), p. 20.
8. Krasner (1999), p. 20.
9. Krasner (1999), p. 8.
10. Krasner (1999), p. 24.
11. Krasner (1999), p. 28.
12. Krasner (1999), p. 28.
13. Krasner (1999), p. 125.
14. Krasner (1999), p. 51.
15. D. Held, A. McGrew, D. Goldblatt and J. Perraton (1999), *Global Transformations: Politics, Economics and Culture*.
16. Held et al. (1999), p. 32.
17. Held et al. (1999), p. 49.
18. Held et al. (1999), p. 49.
19. Held et al. (1999), p. 50.
20. Held et al. (1999), p. 50.
21. Held et al. (1999), pp. 51-2.
22. Held et al. (1999), p. 55.
23. Held et al. (1999), p. 57.
24. For an extremely valuable and detailed study of the events in Rwanda, see G. Prunier (1995), *The Rwanda Crisis 1959–1994: History of a Genocide*.
25. The United Nations Security Council declared its intention to establish

the first international war crimes tribunal since Nuremberg and Tokyo in United Nations Security Council Resolution 808 on 22 February 1993. The International Criminal Tribunal for the Former Yugoslavia was formally established by United Nations Security Council Resolution 827 on 25 May 1993. The International Criminal Tribunal for Rwanda was established by United Nations Security Council Resolution 955 (8 November 1994).

26. See *The Guardian* newspaper, 18 November 1999: 'International court to try war crimes'.
27. Held et al. (1999), p. 63.
28. Held et al. (1999), p. 69.
29. Held et al. (1999), p. 73.
30. Held et al. (1999), p. 64.
31. *Britain in the World* (2000), second-year consultation document, published by the Labour Party.
32. *Britain in the World* (2000), p. 7.
33. *Britain in the World* (2000), p. 11.
34. *Britain in the World* (2000), p. 22.
35. *Britain in the World* (2000), p. 27.
36. Miller (1995), p. 108.
37. See *Observer* newspaper, 27 February 2000: 'It's apocalypse now as world overheats.'
38. *Britain in the World* (2000), p. 27.
39. Held et al. (1999), p. 77.
40. Held et al. (1999), p. 445.
41. Held et al. (1999), p. 445.
42. Held et al. (1999), p. 446.
43. E. M. Ucarer (1997) 'The Coming of an Era of Human Uprootedness: A Global Challenge', in E. M. Ucarer and D. J. Puchala (eds), *Immigration into Western Societies: Problems and Policies*, p. 5. Also see S. Castles and M. J. Miller (1998), *The Age of Migration: International Population Movements in the Modern World*, p. 4; and see T. Hammar, G. Brochmann, K. Tamas and T. Faist (1997), *International Migration, Immobility and Development*, p. 1; they are concerned to explain why *so few* people migrate.
44. P. L. Martin (1997), 'The Impact of Immigration on Receiving Countries', in Ucarer and Puchala (eds), *Immigration into Western Societies: Problems and Policies*, p. 21.
45. Ucarer (1997), p. 7.
46. Ucarer (1997), p. 8.
47. Castles and Miller (1998), p. 4.
48. Ucarer (1997), p. 1.
49. Castles and Miller (1998), p. 1.
50. Castles and Miller (1998), p. 5.
51. Held et al. (1999), p. 305.
52. Held et al. (1999), pp. 281–95.
53. Held et al. (1999), p. 297.
54. Held et al. (1999), p. 299.

55. Held et al. (1999), p. 312.
56. Held et al. (1999), p. 312.
57. Held et al. (1999), p. 313.
58. Held et al. (1999), p. 313.
59. Held et al. (1999), p. 313.
60. Held et al. (1999), p. 313.
61. Held et al. (1999), p. 313.
62. P. H. Schuck (1998), *Citizens, Strangers and In-betweens: Essays on Immigration and Citizenship*, p. 354. Schuck is replying to P. Brimelow (1995), *Alien-nation: Common Sense About America's Immigration Disaster*, where Brimelow calls for an end to immigration.
63. E. R. Barkan (1996), *And Still They Come – Immigrants and American Society 1920 to the 1990s*, p. 187.
64. Barkan (1996), p. 187.
65. Barkan (1996), p. 188.
66. A. Kuijsten (1997), 'Immigration and Public Finance: The Case of the Netherlands', in Ucarer and Puchala (eds), *Immigration into Western Societies: Problems and Policies*.
67. J. Simon (1989), *The Economic Consequences of Immigration*.
68. Kuijsten (1997), p. 212.
69. Kuijsten (1997), p. 224.
70. Castles and Miller (1998), p. 20.
71. Castles and Miller (1998), p. 20.
72. Castles and Miller (1998), p. 21.
73. Castles and Miller (1998), p. 21.
74. Castles and Miller (1998), p. 22.
75. Castles and Miller (1998), p. 23.
76. Castles and Miller (1998), p. 24.
77. Castles and Miller (1998), p. 24, and Schuck (1998), p. xi.
78. R. Plender (1988), *International Migration Law*, p. 2.
79. Plender (1988), p. 70.
80. F. Fukuyama (1992), *The End of History and the Last Man*, p. 278.
81. R. A. Huttenback (1976), *Racism and Empire: White Settlers and Colonial Immigrants in the British Self-Governing Colonies 1830–1910*.
82. Huttenback (1976), p. 138.
83. Huttenback (1976), p. 141.
84. Huttenback (1976), p. 141.
85. Huttenback (1976), p. 141.
86. Huttenback (1976), p. 141.
87. Huttenback (1976), p. 317.
88. Huttenback (1976), p. 280.
89. Huttenback (1976), p. 323.
90. Huttenback (1976), pp. 323–4.
91. J. Jupp (1998), *Immigration*, p. 73.
92. Jupp (1998), p. 73.
93. Jupp (1998), p. 77.
94. Jupp (1998), p. 73.

95. T. Hammar (1990), *Democracy and the Nation-State: Aliens, Denizens and Citizens in a World of International Migration*. See also Castles and Miller (1998), p. 45.
96. J. Fisher (ed.) (1993), *International Immigration and Nationality Law*, pp. 1–3.
97. See A. Owers (1984), *Sheep and Goats: British Nationality Law and its Effects*, and V. Bevan (1986), *The Development of British Nationality Law*.
98. Bevan (1986), p. 112.
99. Ucarer (1997), p. 4.
100. J. L. Coleman and S. K. Harding (1995), 'Citizenship, the Demands of Justice, and the Moral Relevance of Political Borders', in W. F. Schwartz (ed.), *Justice in Immigration*, p. 34.
101. Ucarer (1997), p. 4.
102. Ucarer (1997), p. 4.
103. Ucarer (1997), p. 4.
104. Ucarer (1997), p. 4.
105. Barkan (1996), p. 14.
106. Barkan (1996), p. 116.
107. See A. H. Richmond (1994a), *Global Apartheid: Refugees, Racism, and the New World Order*, pp. 142–3.
108. Schuck (1998), p. 327.
109. Schuck (1998), p. 328.
110. Owers (1984), p. 6.
111. V. Bevan (1986), p. 129.
112. K. Paul (1997), *Whitewashing Britain: Race and Citizenship in the Postwar Era*, p. 189.
113. Ucarer (1997), pp. 4–5.
114. Ucarer (1997), p. 12, note 10.
115. Ucarer (1997), p. 5.
116. D. A. Martin (1997), 'Refugees and Migration', in C. C. Joyner (ed.), *The United Nations and International Law*, p. 155.
117. Martin (1997), p. 163.
118. Martin (1997), p. 167.
119. Martin (1997), p. 166.
120. Martin (1997), pp. 166–7.
121. Martin (1997), p. 168.
122. Martin (1997), p. 169.
123. Home Office (1998), *Fairer, Faster and Firmer: A Modern Approach to Immigration and Asylum*, p. 37.
124. Home Office (1998), p. 38.
125. Home Office (1998), p. 39.
126. Home Office (1998), p. 53.
127. Martin (1997), p. 172.
128. Martin (1997), p. 179.
129. Martin (1997), p. 179.

Chapter 3

FREEDOM OF
INTERNATIONAL MOVEMENT

———◦———

SECTION 1: INTRODUCTION

This chapter examines what I take to be the liberal 'orthodoxy' in both theory and practice on the question of freedom of international movement. The point is, of course, that if there is such a thing as freedom of international movement, we might suppose that it amounts to the freedom to cross national borders from one state into another. There are, therefore, two movements here: the first of emigration, the second of immigration; and any discussion of freedom of international movement has to at least acknowledge that it can take either of these two directions, and therefore gives rise to two moral rights: the moral right to emigrate and the moral right to immigrate. The concern of this book is with the moral right of immigration, as I take it that from a liberal point of view the moral right of emigration is unproblematic. In fact, as we shall see in this chapter, the extent to which I am entitled to make this assumption is questionable. There are reasons to suppose that the moral rights of immigration and emigration cannot be kept apart and dealt with separately and that one implies the other – how can one have the moral right to leave a state if one does not have the moral right to enter another, and vice versa?

My assumption is, however, defensible in that my arguments for a moral right to immigration do nothing to undermine the moral right of emigration[The problem for liberal philosophy is that, for the most part, its proponents argue for a constrained right of immigration without taking into account the implications this has for the moral right of emigration, which they take to be unconstrained.]This, then, is the liberal orthodoxy – that there is a moral asymmetry between emigration and immigration, such that there is a moral right of emigration which cannot be justifiably constrained by a liberal state (except under extreme conditions when liberal principles no longer apply) but there is no moral right to immigration; or if there is, it can be justifiably constrained by a liberal state.]Freedom of international movement, therefore, amounts only to a moral right of emigration, and not to a moral right of immigration. In this chapter I question the coherence of this orthodoxy.

The standard position in liberal theory concerning freedom of international movement, then, is that this gives rise only to the moral right of emigration; there is no moral right of immigration. For example, Alan Dowty's book, entitled *Closed Borders: The Contemporary Assault on Freedom of Movement*,[1] is concerned only with emigration: 'Whatever the arguments over the authority of the state to block emigration, there is little dispute over its right to limit *immigration*.'[2] This is also the position in international law. Article 13 of the United Nations Declaration of Human Rights states that: 'Everyone has the right to leave any country including his own'; while the Fourth Protocol of the European Convention states that: 'No-one shall be arbitrarily deprived of the right to enter his own country.'[3] The standard position can be reconstructed along the following lines:

> A sovereign state has discretionary power over movement across its borders except in two cases:
>   1. All agents have the right to exit; and
>   2. Its citizens have the right to enter.

To put it in its corollary form:

> There is complete freedom of international movement, except that no one has the right to enter a state of which they are not a citizen.

Which of these is the more useful expression of liberal asymmetry is debatable. The first emphasises the state's discretionary power to control movement across its border, but for two exceptions; the second emphasises international freedom of movement, except for one limitation. Whichever of these is the most coherent way of expressing the situation, freedom of movement for citizens of the state is symmetrical, in that they have rights of both arrival and departure; but it is asymmetrical for non-citizens, who only have rights of departure. It is worth noting here, then, that the asymmetry view has a level of complexity that is often overlooked. It is not simply that agent P has the moral right to do X but no moral right to do Y, but *also* that agent Q has the moral right to do both.

It is worth pointing out that the liberal asymmetry view has a relatively short history. David C. Hendrickson observes that:

> In the traditional understanding of international law, the right of the state to forbid entry had a parallel in its right to control exit. In the customary understanding, both were matters that lay entirely within the internal jurisdiction of individual states.[4]

A subject was taken to be bound to their sovereign from birth, and this reasoning justified various restrictions on the emigration of skilled labour from European states. Hendrickson cites the US Attorney General Caleb Cushing speaking in 1856:

> [T]he assumption of a natural right of emigration, without restriction in law, can be defended only by maintaining that each individual has all possible rights against the society and the society none with respect to the individual; that there is no social organization, but a mere anarchy of elements, each wholly independent of the other, and not otherwise *consociated* save than by their casual coexistence in the same territory.[5]

This view is also captured in one of the most comprehensive studies of immigration concerning the United States of that period, by Richard Mayo-Smith in 1890:

> [W]e must disabuse ourselves of the notion that freedom of migration rests upon any right of the individual. It is simply a privilege granted by the state, the product of circumstances, the result of expediency. The state, therefore, that conferred the liberty may also withdraw it. The state that feels a loss of strength by emigration may forbid its inhabitants leaving the country. The state that suffers injury from immigration may put restrictions on persons coming to its shores, – may keep them out altogether if it so choose. The individual has no rights at all in the premises.[6]

The liberal asymmetry view became the orthodoxy in theory and practice in the period after the second world war; but it is still recognised that the right of emigration can be restricted under extreme conditions. For example, says Hendrickson, it seems reasonable that the state should have 'a right to forbid exit to individuals who have not fulfilled a period of military service (if required by the laws of the state); who are genuinely in possession of state secrets; or who are criminals seeking to escape their just reward'.[7] Although liberal theorists and states may differ over their views upon what counts as the extreme conditions that justify constraint of emigration, I think we can justifiably take the liberal orthodoxy to be the position I have sketched.

In this chapter I examine arguments that attempt to justify this asymmetry between arrival and departure. One argument that can be dismissed immediately, however, is the positivist response that the asymmetry is justified *just because* certain people are citizens and therefore hold rights against the state, while others are non-citizens and therefore hold no rights against the state. An argument about *moral* rights cannot be settled by such a positivist move, and the liberal theorist who believes in the moral right of *emigration* should, of course, reject it. My conclusion will be that there are no plausible arguments for the asymmetry position. Further, I argue that there is at least one plausible argument *against* it: that one cannot consistently assert that there is a fundamental human right to emigration but no such right to immigration; the liberal asymmetry position is not merely ethically, but also conceptually, incoherent. If this is a convincing argument, it does not in itself establish the overall assertion of this book – that there are no coherent liberal arguments that can establish the state's right to control immigration. What it does establish, however, is that if it can be shown that the state *does* have the right to control immigration, it must follow that it also has the right to control emigration: the two stand and fall together. It is this implication of an *illiberal symmetry* that most liberal theorists, in their efforts to show that the liberal state can justifiably control immigration, seem to have overlooked.

SECTION 2: APPEALS TO CONSEQUENCES

In subsequent chapters we will see that most of the liberal arguments aimed at justifying the state's right to control immigration are based on an appeal to consequences: the supposedly disastrous consequences of opening borders to free movement. While the argument from consequences *could* establish the state's right to control immigration – and we will assess its success in subsequent chapters – what is seldom noticed is the implication this argument has for the moral right of emigration. What the argument from consequences precisely *cannot* establish is the liberal asymmetry view.

To argue that the asymmetry between emigration and immigration is justified because immigration imposes a cost upon receiving states while emigration does not is to take a crudely one-dimensional view of both immigration *and* emigration. It is to suppose that immigration always imposes a cost upon the receiving state, while emigration is cost-free. We saw in Chapter 2 that this is an oversimplified view of both these processes: immigration can bring great benefits for a state while emigration can carry great costs. And so this version of the consequences argument leads us, not to liberal asymmetry, but to an illiberal symmetry whereby the state must have discretionary power over *all* border crossings.

A second version of the consequences argument is less crude: it acknowledges that immigration/emigration cannot simply be given negative/positive scores, and that under differing circumstances either process can bring costs or benefits or neither. However, it claims that a *mass* immigration *would* impose great costs upon the receiving state under most imaginable circumstances; and it is this that justifies the state having control over arrivals. However, this argument simply misses the point. Just as a mass immigration into a state would most likely impose great costs, so would a mass *emigration*. If the state has the moral right to control arrivals because a hypothetical mass immigration would damage it severely, why does it not also follow that the state has a moral right to control departures because a hypothetical mass emigration would damage it severely? And so this argument, while it avoids the crudity of the first version, fails to avoid its conclusion – which is once more an illiberal symmetry of state control over both arrival and departure.

A third version of the argument attempts to be more commonsensical by dropping the threat of a *hypothetical* mass immigration. Rather, according to this argument, certain states face a very *real* threat of mass immigration if controls were dropped, and it is this very real threat, and the damage it would cause, that justifies the state's right to control arrivals. The argument is that if there were complete symmetry of freedom of movement, certain states would be 'flooded' by immigration, and therefore these states have the right to control it. This avoids the weakness of the previous argument, as these states would not face a similar threat of mass emigration if border controls were dropped, and so there is no justification here for state control over departures. However, even if such predictions had reasonable grounds, it is difficult to see how the argument could avoid leading us back to the illiberal symmetry of state control over all movement across borders. For the implication for emigration is that people have the right to leave these 'threatened' states only because, under present circumstances, emigration poses no threat to their interests. Some would regard this as an extremely fragile theoretical basis for a moral right of emigration – indeed, some might find it difficult to see any *moral* right here at all. The argument seems to have surrendered people's right to emigrate to state interests.

Of course, it could be replied that most moral rights are prima facie rather than absolute, and that therefore there is nothing incoherent in saying that people have a moral right to do X unless too many of them want to do it: under those circumstances the right is overridden.[8] Therefore there is nothing incoherent in saying that people have the moral right to emigrate from these states, in the absence of a moral right of immigration: if too many *did* want to emigrate, the right would be suspended but there is nothing necessarily illiberal about this. However, notice that this gets us back to a symmetry between the ethical status of emigration and immigration: if emigration is a moral right that can be overridden if too many people want to exercise it, why not allow that immigration is a similar moral right? And so if we take *this* argument seriously, its conclusion is that there *is* a moral right to immigration, which has exactly the same prima facie status as the moral right of emigration. The argument, therefore, cannot establish the liberal asymmetry position.

Appeals to consequences to justify immigration controls therefore cannot justify the liberal asymmetry position. They usually lead to the illiberal symmetry position where the state must have discretionary control over all border movement, or at least the power to suspend the 'moral' rights of free movement in either direction. What is surprising is how many liberal writers seek to justify immigration control by appeal to consequences seemingly without noticing this implication of their arguments – very rarely, as we shall see in subsequent chapters, do they feel any obligation to show *why* emigration and immigration are so morally different; and where they do, those arguments fail because they take the form I criticised above. There are, of course, other arguments, but, we shall see, they do no better.

SECTION 3: APPEALS TO RIGHTS

Appeal to consequences alone, as we have seen, results in illiberal symmetry, but certainly not to the liberal asymmetry position. Something other than consequences has to be appealed to. This could take the form of rights or duties, and the claims they give rise to. Alan Dowty, for example, in dismissing complete freedom of international movement, offers the following points:

> [D]eparture ends an individual's claims against a society, while entry sets such claims in motion. Control of entry is essential to the idea of sovereignty, for without it a society has no control over its basic character.[9]

Notice that the second part of Dowty's justification looks like an appeal to consequences, and certainly gets us to illiberal symmetry (if a state has the right to control immigration because it poses a threat to its basic character, then surely it should have the right to control emigration because it, too, poses a threat to its character.) Even though Brian Barry, in claiming that immigration 'will inevitably change' a society, asserts that 'emigration does not change a society in the same way',[10] it is clearly possible that emigration could change it – if not in exactly the same way then by posing parallel problems. To the rejoinder that it depends on the size and nature of the emigration, we can reply that exactly the same holds for immigration.

To avoid this illiberal symmetry, something other than consequences has to play the decisive role. Dowty's preliminary claim seems to be that the crucial difference between arrival and departure is that arrival activates a set of claims against the state while departure does not. But this is exactly the one-dimensional view of both immigration and emigration we have already rejected. Arrival activates both a set of claims by the individual against the state, and a set of claims by the state against the newly arrived individual; while departure certainly means that the individual ceases to be able to make claims against the state, equally the state can no longer make claims against the departed individual.[11] It is therefore perfectly possible that the arrival of a particular individual could constitute a net gain for the state, while their departure could constitute a net loss. And so while there is an obvious practical difference between immigration and emigration here, it is difficult to see how this justifies the moral difference between them needed to ground the liberal asymmetry position.

John Finnis defends the asymmetry view by appealing to the notion of duty:

> It is quite clear who has the duty correlative to the right to emigrate. It is quite unclear that . . . every other community

> everywhere has an equivalent duty to admit unlimited numbers
> of foreigners whatever the foreseeable consequences for the
> economic, political and cultural life of its citizens.[12]

Again, while Finnis starts with a point about duty, he ends with an
appeal to consequences. If we set that appeal aside – as I have argued
we must –(all we are left with is a difference between emigration and
immigration: the right to the former places a duty upon a specific
state, while a right to the latter places a duty upon all states.)But of
course, while this *is* indeed a difference between them, we need to
know how this might establish the liberal asymmetry of a moral right
to emigration but no moral right of immigration, and that is not made
clear here. Also, there is reason to think that Finnis is overstating even
this difference. If there is a moral right to immigration, then it is true
that the individual holds it against all states, but can enact it only
against *one* particular state at a time; and if there is a moral right to
emigration, one can enact it against only one particular state at a time,
while one still holds it against *all* states (one has the right to leave *any*
state). In that sense, both rights impose duties upon all states at the
level of theory, but in practice both would extract that duty from one
particular state at any given moment. There *is* still a difference here,
in that in advance of enacting the right of departure, we know which
particular state will have to undertake the duty – the state they depart
from; while in advance of an individual enacting the right of immigration, we do not know which particular state will have to undertake
the duty – which state they will subsequently enter (although we must
not overdramatise this absence of advance knowledge; it is not *that*
absent). But the latter kind of right is not unfamiliar in liberal theory,
and there is no obvious reason to claim that there cannot *be* a moral
right of immigration simply because it would have this form.

Michael Walzer is another writer who asserts the liberal asymmetry
view. He says that the 'right to control immigration does not include
or entail the right to control emigration'.[13] And: 'The fact that individuals can rightly leave their own country . . . doesn't generate a right
to enter (any other). Immigration and emigration are morally asymmetrical.'[14] This is because 'restraint of entry serves to defend . . . liberty
and welfare',[15] while restraint of exit involves 'coercion', and therefore,
presumably, the violation of liberty and welfare. However, it is difficult
to see how an argument for asymmetry might arise here. The liberty
and welfare *protected* by immigration controls is clearly that of citizens.
If we take into account the liberty and welfare of the non-citizens
who wish to enter, then those immigration controls involve coercion,

and therefore *harm* the liberty and welfare of this group. Walzer's argument seems to depend on the assumption that when it comes to the issues of immigration and emigration the state need only be concerned with the interests of its own citizens, but what could justify such a view? One way of making it plausible is to appeal, not to the *actual* liberty and welfare interests at stake, but to the existing *rights* to have those interests protected. The fact is that only citizens of the state hold rights against it; and so immigration controls do not violate anybody's rights because there are no rights here to violate.

But this is exactly the positivistic move I warned against in Section 1 of this chapter: an appeal to the *fact* of citizenship. The question here is whether non-citizens have a *moral* right of immigration into a state, in a similar way that citizens do, and this cannot be settled by appeal to the fact that citizens are granted this right by the state while non-citizens are not. If we avoid this by talking directly about welfare and liberty as such, or people's interests in them, it would seem that the welfare and liberty of non-citizens who wish to enter cannot be set aside without begging all too many questions. Therefore Walzer's appeal to welfare and liberty should, on the face of it, lead to a liberal symmetry view: borders should be open in both directions.

Brian Barry seeks to establish liberal asymmetry by appealing to the general nature of 'associations' and the sorts of rights we feel people have in relation to them. He asserts that: 'It is a general characteristic of associations that people are free to leave them but not free to join them.'[16] The first example he gives is of employment: people can leave a job, at least by giving reasonable notice, but they cannot just *take* a job. However, one feature of employment that Barry overlooks and which has unfortunate implications for its use as an analogy here is that people can, of course, be *forced* to leave a job, but liberal theorists would not support expulsion of citizens. The second example is of marriage, where once more people can leave the arrangement, but cannot simply enter without the consent of the other partner. But again the example has unfortunate features, in that many people would argue that it should not be *too* easy to leave a marriage; and even when people do, they should carry with them legally binding responsibilities to the other party or parties. The third example is of clubs – anybody can leave a club, but clubs have the right to choose their members. The problem with this example is that it is just not true that clubs can have any membership rules they like: in many liberal democratic states, membership rules can be legally challenged. I will criticise the club analogy in more detail in Chapter 4, as Walzer makes extensive use of it.

The problem with all of these examples – and why it is important to point out the ways in which they differ from states in their rules of association – is that there is something puzzling about the logic of the arguments that appeal to them. It is hard to see why the practices of asymmetry employed in any one of them *justifies* the practice of asymmetry employed by states when it comes to immigration and emigration. Any argument that justifies the asymmetry of membership in, for example, marriage, cannot *justify* the asymmetry of membership practised by states, precisely because marriages and states are not the same thing. The argument can only work as a *justification* if it can be shown that the reasons which justify the asymmetry in the case of marriage or employment or clubs also hold in the case of the state; but *this* form of the argument is not stated by Barry, and it is hard to find it stated anywhere where these analogies are appealed to. In the absence of such an argument, each case of asymmetry of membership has to be justified on its own merits – and so even if all other associ-ations genuinely did practise asymmetrical membership, such a practice by states in the case of emigration and immigration would have to be justified in its own terms, and not by appeal to those other associa-tions. Indeed, Barry does not take it that these examples in any way *demonstrate* the justification of asymmetry when it comes to the state; he merely takes them to show that 'almost all associations operate with an asymmetry between entrance and exit' and therefore there seems to be 'a presumption in favour of asymmetry'.[17] It could be replied that the asymmetry of entrance and exit when it comes to states has such serious implications and consequences, that a presumption in its favour should not be allowed to replace the need for a clear *argument* in its favour.

What also has to be remembered, and which makes all of the examples detailed by Barry unhelpful, is the complexity of the asym-metry in the case of freedom of international movement. In all the cases Barry cites, an agent P has the moral right of departure but not the moral right of arrival. In the case of international movement, the asymmetry has an added crucial layer, in that while agent P has the moral right of departure but not arrival, agent Q enjoys both moral rights.

To summarise the argument so far, there are three possible positions on freedom of international movement: illiberal symmetry, where the state has discretionary power over both immigration and emigration; liberal asymmetry, where the state has discretionary control over the immigration of non-citizens only; and liberal symmetry, where there is no control over cross-border movement in either direction. Arguments from consequences generally lead to illiberal symmetry, once it is recognised that both mass immigration and mass emigration can harm states. Arguments from rights only get us to liberal asymmetry by appeal to a positivistic account of rights – the appeal to the fact of citizenship; the *moral* rights to freedom of movement that were at stake at the beginning of the argument are surrendered. Arguments from liberty and welfare lead to liberal symmetry, once it is accepted that setting aside the liberty and welfare of prospective immigrants is morally arbitrary, and therefore unacceptable from a liberal viewpoint. No arguments have been found, then, that can get us to the liberal asymmetry view, despite the fact that this is the orthodoxy in both liberal theory and practice.

SECTION 4: ASYMMETRICAL ARGUMENTS

The problem with the arguments we have examined so far is that they are, by their nature, symmetrical – if they are sound arguments, they apply to both directions of travel, entry and exit. However, there are at least two arguments which are asymmetrical, in that they do apply only to one direction of travel: the first is an argument from property; the second is an argument from political consent. I will discuss the argument from property in detail in Section 5 of Chapter 7. Here I will only deal with the argument from consent. For now we should note that if the argument from private property works as an argument for immigration control, then it is certainly not vulnerable to the problem I have identified with the other arguments in this chapter, in that it is clearly asymmetrical between rights of entry and exit. However, it is not clear that it does work as an argument; and even if it does, it is one that would appeal only to a particular section of liberal theorists, which may explain its complete absence from left-liberal writing on this subject.

The consent argument, in contrast, is not a *direct* argument for liberal asymmetry. According to this approach, the legitimacy of the liberal state rests on the consent of its members, and one important signifier of consent is residence. However, residence can only be taken to signify consent if there is a right to leave. A legitimate liberal state therefore could not exercise control over emigration without losing its legitimacy. The argument helps to establish the liberal asymmetry position on international movement, in that even if we accept my view that all the arguments against freedom of immigration are also arguments against freedom of emigration, here we have a very powerful argument for freedom of emigration. If we take it that the consent approach is so powerful that it actually overrides this entire body of argument with respect to emigration, then we have the liberal asymmetry view.[18]

However, there are at least two problems with the consent approach: the first is that it is too weak; the second is that it is too strong. The weakness lies in the notorious and well-documented problems with the argument that residence can be taken to imply consent. I will not go over those arguments here.[19] The second problem arises if we accept that residence does imply consent, because now the argument becomes too strong. If residence is to signify consent, then the right to leave has to involve the right to enter another state. If we do not have the right to enter another state, then we remain a resident against our will, even though our own state is not detaining us. Our residence, therefore, cannot be taken to signify consent. The right to emigrate therefore implies the right to immigrate.

It could be replied that the consent argument is not *that* strong: all we need for residence to signify consent is the right to enter at least one other state, and so this does not establish complete freedom of cross-border movement. But this surely will not do. Let us imagine that agent P wishes to withdraw his or her consent from state X, and is free to enter only one other state, Y. Can his or her subsequent residence in Y be taken to signify his or her consent to the legitimacy of that state? Well, only if agent P is free to enter at least one other state; but as things stand, he or she is only free to re-enter state X, the legitimacy of which they have already rejected. We therefore surely cannot take it that residence in either state X or state Y signifies consent to their legitimacy. To make the argument more plausible, we need to introduce state Z, which agent P is also free to enter, but then the same problem arises. As long as P's choice of residence is constrained, it is difficult to see how his or her residence in any one state can signify the legitimacy of that state. Of course it may be replied that we do not have to move to complete freedom of international movement to make the consent argument credible, just a reasonable number of states with a reasonable range of constitutions to choose from. After all, the globe itself contains a limited number of states and a limited range of constitutions. But still, there is a nagging doubt here that if P's choice of residence in the states that do exist is constrained, his or her residence in any particular state which he or she is free to enter or exit can only signify a limited consent to the legitimacy of that state. For the consent argument to work at all, it might be suggested,

I must have a free choice of residence, and this means complete freedom of international movement.

Of course, from the perspective of an individual liberal state, the consent argument is, indirectly, an argument for asymmetry, in that it places an obligation on that state to allow free emigration, but it places no obligation on that particular state to allow free immigration. The point is, though, that for the consent argument as such to make sense, complete symmetry of free movement *is* required.

SECTION 5: THE COHERENCE OBJECTION

While we have, so far, failed to find a plausible argument for the liberal asymmetry view, there is at least one plausible argument against it – that it is conceptually incoherent. Ann Dummett, for example, comments that:

> Logically, it is an absurdity to assert a right of emigration without a complementary right of immigration unless there exist in fact . . . a number of states which permit free entry.[20]

To bring this possible incoherence into view, we need to make a distinction between two kinds of state boundaries: borders and frontiers. Borders are boundaries between territorial states, while a frontier is the boundary between a territory of a state and an area of 'unowned' space.[21] Our concern is with the freedom of cross *border* movement, the movement of agents from one state into another. As a matter of fact, very little, if any, migration in the contemporary world involves crossing frontiers.[22]

Once we make this distinction, the possible incoherence comes into view. Suppose that we have two states, X and Y, and agent P who wishes to cross the border from X into Y. There are three possible situations:

1. P is a citizen of X.
2. P is a citizen of Y.
3. P is a non-citizen of X or Y.

Let us suppose that liberal asymmetry is practised, so that there is an unrestricted right of emigration but no right to immigration. This means that there is only one case where P has an unconstrained right to cross the border from X and enter Y: that is situation (2), where P is a citizen of Y. In situations (1) and (3), although P has the 'right' to leave X, he or she has no right to enter Y. And so the only case where someone has the unrestricted right to cross the border from one state into another is in fact where one is a *returning* citizen of the latter state.

The supposed incoherence, then, concerns the plausibility of the claim in the other two cases, that P has the moral right to emigrate from X where he or she has no moral right of immigration into Y. The only way to avoid the incoherence is to formulate the moral right of emigration so that it does not depend upon or imply the moral right of immigration, such that the freedom of international movement no longer entails the right to *cross* a border. This can be done if we understand the right to emigrate as simply imposing a duty upon one's state not to interfere; it does not entail, therefore, success in leaving the state. One way to make the point is to assert that the rights at stake here are negative, amounting only to the right of non-interference. To claim that the right to emigrate entails the right to cross the border into another state is to transform it from a negative into a positive right, and this is to go too far for liberal philosophy. If we remain within the bounds of negative rights, then, the liberal asymmetry view is perfectly coherent.

But this response will not do. The problem is *not* a clash between negative and positive interpretations of the right to leave – rather, the puzzle arises because of a gap between two *negative* liberty rights. The right to emigrate can be seen as imposing only duties of non-interference upon one's own state, although of course it does not impose those duties upon the neighbouring states who retain their right to prevent your entry. The right of freedom of international movement imposes duties of non-interference upon one's own state *and* other states one wishes to enter. It is the gap between these two *negative* rights that constitutes the puzzle for those who believe in both. If the right of emigration is interpreted only as the right not to be interfered with by one's own state, then it does not entail the right to leave the state – because others can prevent you from doing that at the border. The right to leave the state, even in its most negative form, therefore *requires* the right to enter another state – the right to *cross* the border.[23] Therefore if the moral right of emigration does amount to or entail the right to leave one's state, the charge of incoherence is successful. There can be no such right without a corresponding right to enter another state. The only way to avoid this conclusion is, then, not simply to assert that the right of emigration is a negative liberty, but to assert that it does *not* amount to or entail an (equally negative) right to leave one's state. We can ask whether this interpretation of the moral right of emigration is an acceptable representation of freedom of international movement from a liberal point of view. The preservation of liberal asymmetry seems to involve, not only setting aside the moral right to immigration, but the reduction of the moral right of emigration to an unacceptably impoverished level.

There is one final response. That is to concede that the moral right of emigration is made up of the two negative rights I described above: the right not to be prevented from leaving one's own state and the right not to be prevented from entering another state. However, if at least one other state is willing to receive such emigrants, the moral right of emigration is met, but this falls far short of the international freedom to cross borders which I have described here. We encountered the 'at least one other state' response when we considered the argument from consent, and saw that, by itself, it is much too thin to ground a moral right of emigration. A fuller response is to claim that if a reasonable number of states are willing to receive these emigrants, then the moral right of emigration is fully met. After all, there is a finite number of states occupying the globe.

But still, surely this places the moral right to leave one's state in too precarious a position. There are three problems. First, the appeal to the finiteness of the number of states is beside the point. While the finiteness of the globe does constitute a boundary to freedom of movement, it is very different to a *political* boundary which restricts movement within any given zone. Second, the right of emigration now depends on agreements entered into with other states to receive one's emigrants, and the fact remains that if it is a genuinely moral right, it cannot be wished away by states that do not wish to enter into such an agreement. This would mean that there could be a state that failed to enter into any such agreements through no fault of its own, and as a consequence we would have to say that its citizens' moral right to emigrate is being violated. The interesting question is by whom?

The third problem is perhaps clearer and more decisive. If a group of states do enter into such an agreement, the question will always arise whether their citizens have the right to emigrate from the group as such. To claim that the right to leave a state does not amount to the right to leave a confederation or zone of states is, at least, peculiar, if not dangerous. It would allow that a confederation of states could prevent its citizens from emigrating, and yet claim that it has not violated their right to leave, because they retain the right to move around within the confederation. Therefore the 'at least one state', and even the 'reasonable number of states', response misses the point. If the

United Nations is correct that *everyone* has the human right to leave his or her country, then it would seem that the only adequate protection of that right is complete freedom of cross-border movement.

SECTION 6: CONCLUSION

The claim of this chapter is not that liberal democratic states cannot morally justify exclusive membership by appeal to the arguments we have examined. That claim will be examined in the rest of this book. Rather, the claim has been that there are grounds to believe that the arguments that are supposed to justify the state's control over immigration would also justify its control over emigration. What the arguments *cannot* justify, therefore, is the liberal asymmetry view. The challenge for the liberal theorist at this stage is to show why immigration and emigration are so morally different that the latter is immune from the force of the arguments against the moral right of immigration; but those writers we examine in subsequent chapters, in constructing what they take to be convincing arguments for state control over immigration, simply overlook or set aside their implications for emigration. What has to be remembered is that the liberal asymmetry here is more complex than it may appear – it is not simply that one person has the moral right to depart but not arrive, but also that another person has the moral right to do both. What can justify this difference between them?

It is *this* difference – between the moral status of the 'insider' and the 'outsider' – that constitutes the major moral puzzle that emerges when we examine the question of immigration; and it is this puzzle that we examine in the rest of the book.

NOTES

1. A. Dowty (1987), *Closed Borders: The Contemporary Assault on Freedom of Movement*.
2. Dowty (1987), p. 14.
3. See A. Dummett (1992), 'The Transnational Migration of People seen from within a Natural Law Tradition', in B. Barry and R. E. Goodin (eds), *Free Movement: Ethical Issues in the Transnational Migration of People and of Money*, p. 173.
4. D. C. Hendrickson (1992), 'Migration in Law and Ethics: A Realist Perspective', in Barry and Goodin (eds), *Free Movement*, p. 223.
5. Hendrickson (1992), p. 224.
6. R. Mayo-Smith (1890), *Emigration and Immigration: A Study in Social Science*, pp. 290–1.

7. Hendrickson (1992), p. 225.
8. Brian Barry makes precisely this point. See B. Barry (1992), 'The Quest for Consistency: A Sceptical View', in Barry and Goodin (eds), *Free Movement*, p. 280.
9. Dowty (1987), p. 14.
10. Barry (1992), p. 286.
11. This is, of course, still a radically oversimplistic view of the reality of nationality law, which seems to assume that citizenship itself is activated or de-activated upon arrival and departure. However, the complexities of nationality law are not helpful here, and this particular oversimplification can actually help us to see the problems with the argument more clearly.
12. J. Finnis (1992), 'Commentary on Dummett and Weithman', in Barry and Goodin (eds), *Free Movement*, p. 207.
13. M. Walzer (1983), *Spheres of Justice: A Defence of Pluralism and Equality*, p. 39.
14. Walzer (1983), pp. 39–40.
15. Walzer (1983), p. 39. Walzer's overall argument for immigration controls is, as we shall see in Chapter 6, thoroughly consequentialist. His extraordinarily brief and, in my view, inadequate attempt to evade the illiberal symmetry implied by his approach is deeply illuminating.
16. Barry (1992), p. 284.
17. Barry (1992), p. 284.
18. I am grateful to Professor Stephen R. L. Clark for suggesting this argument to me.
19. See A. J. Simmons (1979), *Moral Principles and Political Obligations*.
20. Dummett (1992), p. 173.
21. This is an oversimplification of the distinction, but I hope it is permissible to make my point. For a more detailed account see J. R. V. Prescott (1987), *Political Frontiers and Boundaries*.
22. Remember that space is only the 'final frontier' in a fictional context.
23. Unless one is content to let one's departing citizens enter some kind of limbo between states, and so become stateless.

Chapter 4

MEMBERS AND STRANGERS:
WALZER ON IMMIGRATION

SECTION 1: INTRODUCTION

Liberal political theory addresses the problems of the distribution of freedom and welfare within bounded political communities, but rarely addresses the question of how membership of these boundaries is to be fixed. There seems to be an assumption that the question of membership can be set aside, but the fact remains that it can only be set aside on the added assumption that it is answerable in ways that are compatible with the central principles of liberal political theory – in other words, on condition that the policing of the external boundary of the community is in harmony with the moral and political principles that are applied within that boundary; there is what I have termed a liberal coherence between internal and external principles. However, once this issue is raised, it becomes clear how difficult this external question of membership is: can we draw a boundary that constitutes insiders and outsiders in a way that embodies the principles of equal respect and concern for humanity as such – not only insiders – that many regard as the central commitments of liberal theory?

While the majority of liberal theorists overlook this question, one exception is Michael Walzer, who made it the subject of a chapter in *Spheres of Justice: A Defence of Pluralism and Equality*.[1] It is, of course, arguable whether Walzer is a liberal theorist at all, and many would characterise him rather as a communitarian. However, the broad range of his value commitments place him, I believe, firmly within the liberal family – although of course his emphasis on the nature of community and the consequences this has for his theory make it a peculiar form of liberalism. This blend of liberalism and communitarianism could either be seen as communitarianism-on-liberal-foundations or as liberalism-on-communitarian-foundations,[2] and in Walzer's case it is best seen, I suspect, as the latter.

Walzer's communitarianism shapes his response to the membership question. He argues that political communities need a shared identity, and that the only way to ensure this is by choosing members; therefore political communities have the right to determine their membership with policies of admission and exclusion. These policies are constrained in two ways: first, by the community's understanding of itself; and, second, by the principle of mutual aid for 'necessitous strangers'. But beyond this, the political community has the right to operate principles of admission and exclusion of its own choosing. Walzer defends his position by arguing that a political community is in important ways like a club, and to the extent that clubs have the right to constitute their membership, so too should political communities.

There are problems with Walzer's treatment of this issue. The first concerns his use of various models of membership such as the club and the family: he derives both too much and too little from these particular models, and there are others available which give very different answers to these questions. The second is the extent to which this communitarian approach allows an external criticism of communities' self-conceptions and their membership practices. The third is the extent to which Walzer's approach is compatible with the principle of the moral equality of persons. The next section outlines Walzer's thesis on membership, and these problems are explored in the rest of the chapter.

SECTION 2: MEMBERS AND STRANGERS

Walzer describes a political community as a world of common meanings: language, history and culture produce a 'collective consciousness'.[3] National character is a myth, but 'the sharing of sensibilities and intuitions among the members of a historical community is a fact of life'.[4] While historical and political communities may not coincide, in a political community the moral settlement of issues must still appeal to common meanings that are available to all citizens. One of these common meanings must be membership itself; membership is what the members of a political community understand it to be. This means that as members of the political community we must choose criteria for membership 'in accordance with our own understanding of what membership means in our community and of what sort of a community we want to have'.[5]

One possible principle of membership is the principle of mutual aid:[6] duties owed to persons generally, in the absence of any cooperative arrangements. According to this principle, positive assistance is required if 'it is needed or urgently needed by one of the parties', and 'if the risks and costs of giving it are relatively low for the other party'.[7] Mutual aid is a possible external principle of membership, and is independent of the view of membership taken by the community; it is owed to strangers regardless of that view. However, Walzer concludes that: 'The force of the principle is uncertain.'[8]

The only two ways of avoiding the question of membership are either a system of global libertarianism in which all are independent economic units, a world of strangers; or a system of global socialism, where there is a single collective system, a world of members. However, 'neither of these arrangements is likely to be realized in the foreseeable future';[9] and more importantly, there are good arguments against either arrangement which show that there is a need for immigration controls. Such policies will be shaped by arguments about (1) the economic and political conditions of the host country; (2) the character and 'destiny' of that country; and (3) the character of political communities in general. The subject of discussion for Walzer is (3), because it is our understanding of political communities as such that determines whether we think they have the right to determine their membership by their own criteria: therefore what Walzer is exploring is the general character of a political community. However, as we only have 'dim perceptions' of what a political community is,[10] Walzer proposes to examine it by appealing to clearer perceptions of smaller units, specifically neighbourhoods, clubs and families. These three, then, become models of membership which can, or cannot, be applied to the political community itself.

The first model Walzer discusses is that of the neighbourhood, which he takes to be a 'random association':[11] an association without an organised or legally enforcable admissions policy.[12] People choose neighbourhoods, and are not chosen, except to the extent that economic factors constrain such choices. Walzer agrees with Henry Sidgwick that such a model is unsuitable for the state, as there would be no 'patriotic sentiment' and therefore a lack of cohesion.[13] While Walzer rejects the neighbourhood as a model for membership, he thinks clubs and families do provide more convincing models. To the extent to which he considers that political communities have the right to determine their membership, he takes it that the nation-state is like a club, in that no one has the right of entry: 'The members decide freely on their future associates, and the decisions they make are authoritative and final.'[14] We may feel there are moral obligations to admit in some cases: for example a group of 'national or ethnic "relatives"'; and in this sense states are like families: 'it is a feature of families that their members are morally connected to people they have not chosen, who live outside the household'.[15] This means the household can be a refuge in times of trouble, and states behave in the same way: 'They don't only preside over a piece of territory and a random collection of inhabitants; they are also the political expression of a common life and (most often) a national "family" that is never entirely enclosed within their legal boundaries.'[16] And so Walzer concludes that nation-states have the right to determine their membership. They are not like neighbourhoods, but are like clubs and families in certain respects: that is, no one has a right of entry, and where we do feel a moral obligation to admit others it will be people who belong to our national 'family'.

There are two problems Walzer acknowledges he must deal with before his account is complete: first, 'alien' groups already within the national boundary; and, second, the problem of 'necessitous strangers'. On the first issue, Walzer declares that the nation-state has no right to expel 'alien' groups already within its territory. Such groups have a 'territorial or locational right'. Walzer comments:

> Initially, at least, the sphere of membership is given: the men and women who determine what membership means, and who shape the admissions policies of the political community, are simply the men and women who are already there. New states and governments must make their peace with the old inhabitants of the land they rule.[17]

The second problem is more complex. To what extent are nation-states obliged to take in necessitous strangers under the principle of mutual aid? For Walzer, the question is how the principle of mutual aid applies to political communities. To some extent, this will depend on 'territorial extent and the population density.'[18] Here, Walzer comments on the white Australia immigration policy. Given the amount of space, the right of white Australians to exclude 'necessitous men and women' could not be defended.[19]

Thomas Hobbes makes the point that where a country is not sufficiently inhabited, people have the right to move in as long as they do not harm the original inhabitants.[20] If those original inhabitants try to prevent them getting what they need to survive, for the sake of 'things superfluous', they can be read as breaking the fifth law of nature, of mutual accommodation, and so are responsible for the state of war that must follow.[21] Walzer points out that Hobbes takes 'things superfluous' to be anything not needed for survival, but this is too narrow. The conception of what must be protected has to be 'shaped to the needs of particular historical communities', and so would include 'ways of life'.[22] In the case of white Australia, ways of life in any significant sense were not at stake, and so the exclusion of necessitous strangers was not justified.

But still, to what extent do we have an obligation to let in 'immigrants from poorer countries?'[23] Henry Sidgwick says that immigration of this kind must be restricted once it interferes with the local standard of living, especially that of the poor;[24] but Walzer suggests that restrictions can be introduced before that stage, by giving aid to necessitous strangers where they happen to be: 'the community might well decide to cut off immigration even before that, if it were willing to export (some of) its superfluous wealth'.[25] This means, then, that a state can refuse admission to migrants whose economic position has become untenable, and instead can justifiably send some kind of economic relief or aid to where they happen to be (but only if, one assumes, where they happen to be is not the cause of their difficulty in the first place – for example in a war zone, or in an area devastated by an ongoing natural disaster).

Economic migrants, then, including those who are 'necessitous', can be justifiably excluded under Walzer's scheme. What of refugees? Walzer defines refugees as people who need membership itself rather than wealth or territory.[26] Once more, obligations to refugees are limited, in this case to any refugees we helped to create, and to those with whom we share some kind of affinity, perhaps a political one. 'Perhaps every victim of authoritarianism and bigotry is the moral comrade of a liberal citizen.'[27] Walzer thinks we do not have to make these distinctions at present because numbers are small (or were at the time he was writing); but if faced with increased numbers we would be forced to choose between victims, and 'we look, rightfully, for some more direct connection with our own way of life'.[28] If there is no affinity at all, 'there can't be a requirement to choose them over other people equally in need'.[29] In the end:

> [C]ommunities must have boundaries; and however these are determined with regard to territory and resources, they depend with regard to population on a sense of mutual relatedness and mutuality. Refugees must appeal to that sense. One wishes them success; but in particular cases, with reference to a particular state, they may well have no right to be successful.[30]

And: 'political communities . . . have a right to protect their members' shared sense of what they are about'.[31] And we can deduce from this that they have the right to protect their shared sense of themselves not only from strangers, but also from necessitous strangers and 'strange' refugees.

The final category Walzer discusses is the asylum seeker, the political refugee who has succeeded in entering the territory; the question here is whether the state has the right to expel them? Walzer thinks not, but in a qualified sense: 'at the extreme, the claim of asylum is virtually undeniable. I assume that there are in fact limits on our collective liability, but I don't know how to specify them.'[32] There have to be some limits because 'actually to take in large numbers of refugees is often morally necessary; but the right to restrain the flow remains a fact of communal self-determination. The principle of mutual aid can only modify and not transform admissions policies rooted in a particular community's understanding of itself.'[33]

In the end, political communities have the right to shape their population, and this right frames not only the issue of general immigration, but also issues of 'necessitous' economic and political migration. The principle of mutual aid does constrain this right, but the right also seems to limit the principle. Walzer concludes that:

> Admission and exclusion are at the core of communal independence. They suggest the deepest meaning of self-determination. Without them, there could not be *communities of character*, historically ongoing associations of men and women with some special commitment to one another and some special sense of their common life.[34]

SECTION 3: THE MODELS OF MEMBERSHIP

One possible objection to Walzer's position can be disposed of immediately, and concerns his claim that members have the right to determine the rules of membership. It might be objected that members of an association are bound by the rules that applied to their *own* membership; they are at least under an *ethical* constraint to recognise that the principles that determined their own membership should also determine future membership. Therefore if they became members through random and arbitrary factors, then they have no right to impose *rules* upon future applicants. One reply to this objection is that we can distinguish between the *formative* members of an association and the *subsequent* members: the formative membership may have been constituted by random and arbitrary factors, but this does not mean they cannot *subsequently* impose some sort of systematic rules for membership from that point on. The justification for having two different standards of membership practices here is that the two situations are, of course, radically different: the actual formation of the association is a very different situation to that of ensuring its continued existence. But this reply is not helpful, because the situation we are examining in relation to states and their membership practices is rarely, if ever, like this: *all* members are subsequent members rather than formative members, and therefore the objection still holds – that current members are constrained in their choice of membership rules by the rules that determined their own membership; they have no moral right to impose different criteria of membership on future applicants.

However, it could be replied that a state is never fixed, and therefore *all* membership is formative. In that case there is no reason to suppose that current members are constrained by the rules that were applied to their admission. Indeed, there are good moral reasons, from a liberal point of view, to hold that current members should *not* be constrained in this particular way, because it may well be that they consider the rules that determined *their* membership to have been unfair and immoral. It could be the case that their membership was determined on racist grounds, for example: they were admitted because they were white. It would be complete nonsense, from a liberal point of view, to claim that they do not have the power to revise those membership rules, indeed to scrap them altogether and start again. To that extent, it seems that Walzer is correct and that current members *should* have the power to determine the rules of membership. However, notice that all we have done is establish that they are not ethically constrained by *past* practices: specifically the rules that applied to them. It does not follow from this that they are not ethically constrained *at all* in their choice of rules. We shall see in this section that there are good reasons to suppose that they should *not* be free to choose whatever membership rules they wish.

Walzer's thesis can be summarised like this: (1) political communities need a conception of themselves if they are to be successful; (2) this self-conception needs to be protected through immigration and naturalisation controls. The problem I will investigate here is the use Walzer makes of his 'models of membership': the neighbourhood, the club and the family. Walzer reads both too much and too little into these models, and in fact none of them helps him to establish either of the two claims that make up his thesis. I will discuss the family model first.

1. The Family Model

It is important to remember that families are a mixture of genetic, legal and conventional connections. It is not that there are three kinds of family, depending upon whether they are genetically connected (the 'natural' family), legally connected (e.g. formed through adoption), or conventionally connected (e.g. a group that lives as a family in the absence of genetic or legal connections). Rather, the vast majority of families are, to an important extent, a mixture of all three. Under 'western' practices one is legally connected to one's partner through marriage, or conventionally connected where there is no legal act of union; genetically connected to one's children, biological parents and siblings, and so on; and conventionally connected to one's partner's family and to a wide range of family members (e.g. my mother's sister's husband/partner has no genetic connection with me, but is normally an important family member). This means that families are often a mixture of choice and determination, in that one may choose one's partner or have them chosen for one,[35] but find oneself in a set of conventional relationships with one's family that no one has chosen; and of course one lacks choice when it comes to genetic connections. Crucially, however, overlaying all of this, including the family's genetic connections, is another convention which gives these connections their form and significance – which makes them into *relationships* rather than mere connections. This means that although the genetic *connection* cannot be broken by choice, the *relationship* that gives it significance can be; or, in some situations, it may never carry that significance in the first place: there may never have been *any* relationship built around that particular genetic connection. 'Natural' families can break up; adoptive families can be created.

When it comes to the use of the idea of the 'family' in political theory, for example in relation to the idea of the nation, we should therefore be cautious about which of these aspects of the family is being emphasised and which overlooked. The fact is that in this context the family is more often 'read' as a natural entity rather than a constructed one, and this can encourage an approach to identity and nationalism which modern political philosophy may find unacceptable – for example, in the form of 'ethnic' nationalisms which appeal to discredited and racist notions of shared blood. Walzer, of course, would maintain a considerable distance between his own position and such notions, but he does still seem to read the family as primarily 'natural' when he refers to national and ethnic relations,[36] and emphasises the connections with such people that are not chosen. Once we take into account the degree to which families *are* chosen and constructed, it is no longer a useful analogy, as we need to know what it is that gives a particular connection with some group living outside the state its ethical significance – the fact of connection by itself may not be enough.

Of course Walzer may reply that there is still a degree to which families are 'natural' or at least unchosen, and that is the sense in which he is using them as an analogy here. But then it emerges that there is something odd about this reasoning. Walzer wishes to show that political communities can be like families, to the extent that on occasion they involve relations with 'outsiders' that are unchosen but nevertheless significant, in that they give rise to ethical obligations. But political communities are only like families in that respect if one already believes they involve this kind of relationship. If one rejects this kind of relationship, then political communities are simply not like families in this respect. The reasoning cannot be: (1) political communities are like families; (2) families involve ethical relationships with others that are not chosen; and (3) therefore political communities involve ethical relationships with others that are not chosen. This would only follow if the first premise were (1) political communities are like families *in all respects*; but Walzer is not putting forward such a dubious argument. Rather, the reasoning must be something like this: (1) families involve ethical relations with 'outsiders' that are not chosen; (2) political communities involve ethical relations with 'outsiders' that are not chosen; and therefore (3) they are alike in this respect. This is not so much an argument as an observation, and it is obvious now that we cannot *deduce* anything about the nature of political communities from the nature of families.

The final question must be, then, how we feel about Walzer's assertions about obligations to refugees, in the light of this observation about the nature of families. The implication of Walzer's claim here is that if we are faced with refugees from two different areas, and can only help one of these groups, we are entitled to look to some connection that may exist in order to prioritise one of these groups. If it turns out that there is such a connection, we are morally justified in helping that group at the expense of the other. Let us suppose that the United States is faced with two refugee groups: the first fleeing a conflict in Malaysia, the other fleeing a conflict in the United Kingdom. Under Walzer's formulation, the United States is justified in prioritising the latter group over the former, because there is clearly some 'family' connection between a significant number of the population of the United States, and the population of the United Kingdom (the connection can be historical rather than simply genetic). This move emphasises the communitarian side of Walzer's approach, because it is clearly non-liberal – from a purely liberal perspective these connections count as arbitrary from a moral point of view.

John A. Scanlan and O. T. Kent have deep misgivings about this strategy.[37] They argue that once a state is committed to a policy that is ethnically and ideologically neutral, it is hard to see that an increase in numbers can justify a shift from that neutrality to a policy where it can choose on ideological or ethnic grounds. Scanlan and Kent distinguish between the *scope* and the *magnitude* of a principle or law: the scope determines who falls under the application of the principle – in this case all refugees who apply to the United States; and the magnitude determines how much must be done to meet the obligations under the principle. These are 'logically independent variables' and therefore a change in one does not necessarily entail a change in the other.[38] For example, if there were a food shortage in the United States, there would be a policy that all hungry citizens have the right to food aid regardless of ethnicity or ideology; no subsequent increase in the numbers of the hungry could justify limiting the scope of that principle by appeal to ethnic and ideological features. Therefore if we have a refugee policy that is ethnically and ideologically neutral, one cannot, in the face of increased pressure of numbers, solve the problems that arise by introducing ethnic and ideological features.

To use another, more basic example, suppose I come across two needy people and can only assist one, and I decide to help the one most closely connected to me; the point is that there is nothing that can *ethically* justify that decision from a liberal point of view. Some background conditions may help me here: first, that there is some agreement or convention that recognises that the primary obligation to assist the other needy person falls upon some agency other than myself; and second that I have reasonable grounds to suppose that in this case those agencies will in fact come to their assistance. Given those background conditions, I can justifiably assist 'my' person. But in the absence of either of them, there is nothing that can justify my decision to assist that person. Walzer seems to assume that our 'mutual relatedness' by itself justifies my choice, but the danger is that this reduces to a psychological explanation of that choice and not an ethical justification of it. It could be complained that I am criticising Walzer's position from a purely liberal standpoint, and leaving out the importance of the communitarian aspect of his theory. Once we introduce the ethical significance of the community, then that choice can make moral sense. But I cannot see that, in the absence of either of the conditions I describe above, the choice can be described as ethical even from a communitarian-liberal perspective; if it is genuinely the case that I can only help one and the other must perish, then that choice can be described as desperate, tragic, understandable even, but never ethical. We will have entered a condition which is so extreme that moral judgement is suspended. In practice, whether liberal democratic states ever do genuinely face such a tragic choice when it comes to the admission of refugees is highly debatable. To be fair on Walzer, we should take it that he is imagining only a situation which is *genuinely* tragic, but even here I cannot accept that what he shows is that a choice based on 'family' connection is ethically justifiable.

2. The Club Model

Walzer extracts most from the club model of membership, in that with a club: 'The members decide freely on their future associates, and the decisions they make are authoritative and final.'[39] The first problem is the extent to which this is true: in many situations the membership of clubs can be subjected to judicial, as well as moral, review; and so it does not seem to be the case that we believe clubs can have any membership rules the members want. One could argue that applications for membership should depend upon the goals and purposes of the club – to refuse entry to an applicant on any other grounds would look arbitrary and open to challenge. Therefore the only relevant ground for refusing membership is that the applicant will prevent the club from achieving its purposes. There are two sets of purposes here: (1) the purposes of the club as such; (2) the purposes of the individual members of the club which are relevant to its constitution – the club is designed so that people can achieve these particular purposes. It needs to be shown that the applicant will prevent the club from fulfilling its overall purpose, whatever it is, and/or that they will prevent individual members achieving their relevant purposes. It might be argued that another constraint on membership is that a club can legitimately limit its numbers. However, a limit on numbers has to be justified, and once more the only justification would seem to be that to admit more than that number would undermine the purposes of the club – and so the numbers argument is a version of the overall argument about purposes.

This argument about membership can only be applied to states if they have purposes and their members have legitimate individual purposes. It can then be argued that a state can refuse to admit people if they can be shown to threaten the overall purpose of the state, or prevent individual members achieving their legitimate goals. For this to make sense we would have to (1) identify the overall purposes of the state; (2) define the legitimate individual purposes of its members; and (3) show how admitting a particular applicant could undermine either or both of these. If the argument takes this form two obvious limits suggest themselves: first, where a specific individual can be identified as posing a threat to the order of the state or to individuals – in liberal states one assumes these would only be extreme cases and so they would be rare; and second, the numbers argument – that to admit more than a certain number would threaten the community in these ways.

But for Walzer, there is another consideration – the political community's self-conception. The community has the right to protect its members' conception of themselves and the community as a whole, and they therefore have the right to exclude anybody who they consider would disrupt that self-conception. This still falls under the general argument for exclusion if we accept that a self-conception is necessary for a political community in order to achieve its purposes. However, it is not obvious that we should accept this claim. We should note that the club model of membership does not help on this specific question as it is not clear that all clubs need the sort of shared self-conception Walzer describes in order for it and its members to achieve their goals. And so while the club model seems most useful for Walzer, it cannot help him to establish his most important claim.

Walzer seems to assume a single model of membership for clubs, when they may exhibit a variety of membership practices. There seem to be four possible models of membership for any association: first, where membership is determined solely by the members; second, where membership is determined solely by the applicant; third, where membership is negotiated by members and applicants; and fourth, where membership is determined by factors beyond the control of either party. For Walzer, clubs are of the first type, neighbourhoods the second, and families the fourth; he does not seem to consider the third. As we have seen, families are not necessarily pure examples of the fourth type, and equally it seems possible that clubs could be any of the first three types, or impure mixtures of them. Of course, it could be replied that at least *some* clubs are of the type Walzer describes, but then why suppose that the political community is like *this* kind of club in particular, unless we have already decided that political communities just do have the right to control membership?

This brings us to the same concern over the logic of the argument as with the use of the family model. Again the argument cannot be that (1) political communities are like clubs; (2) clubs have the right to determine their membership; therefore (3) political communities have the right to determine their membership. For this to follow, the first premise would, once more, have to be (1) political communities are like clubs in *all* respects, and this is just false. Therefore Walzer cannot *derive* the right of political communities to determine their membership from the fact that clubs (but not all of them) have this right. All he can do is offer the observation that they are similar in this respect; but this involves accepting the truth of the claim that political communities have this right. In other words, no one can be persuaded that political communities must have this right from the fact that some clubs have it, unless the question is begged. Of course, it may be that Walzer is not offering this form of inference in his use of the club or family models – but the point is then worth making that we misread him if we see the use of the models in this way; and a further point follows, that it is very unclear what work the models have left to do once this role is taken away from them.[40]

Walzer's thesis, then, has two claims: (1) that a political community needs a shared self-conception if it is to achieve its purposes; and (2) that this self-understanding has to be protected by having control over membership in the form of immigration and naturalisation restrictions. While the club model does provide a reason for controlling membership – in order to protect the goals and purposes of the club – it does not show that a shared understanding is a ground for exclusion. First, clubs do not necessarily need a shared understanding in order to achieve their purposes; and second, even if they did, it has not been shown that controlling membership is necessary in order to protect that self-understanding; it may be robust enough to survive without such controls, and it may even depend on there being no such controls. And so the club model provides us with no reason to accept either of Walzer's claims. However if, for the sake of argument, we accept the first claim, that a self-understanding *is* essential for a political community to achieve its purposes, we can ask whether there is any reason to accept the second claim, that membership control is needed to protect that self-understanding. We shall see how unconvincing this second claim is when we look closer at the neighbourhood model.

3. The Neighbourhood Model

Although the neighbourhood is unsuitable as a model of membership (it is an anti-model), it is here that we get the most explicit statement of Walzer's arguments for immigration control. He says:

1. Neighbourhoods can be open only if countries are at least potentially closed. Only if the state makes a selection among would-be members and guarantees the loyalty, security, and welfare of the individuals it selects, can local communities take shape as 'indifferent' associations, determined solely by personal preference and market capacity.[41]
2. The distinctiveness of cultures and groups depends upon closure and, without it, cannot be conceived as a stable feature of human life. If this distinctiveness is a value, as most people . . . seem to believe, then closure must be permitted somewhere.[42]
3. The restraint of entry serves to defend the liberty and welfare, the politics and culture of a group of people committed to one another and their common life.[43]

Therefore there must be a level of political organisation that has the right to have an admissions policy, the 'right to control immigration'.[44]
   There are three arguments for immigration control here:

1. The freedom of movement argument. The argument has two stages: (a) greater freedom of movement is preferable; and (b) open borders at the state level will in fact lead to lesser freedom of movement, because local areas will then introduce restrictions.
2. The distinctiveness of culture argument. Again the argument has two stages: (a) distinctiveness of groups and cultures is

desirable; and (b) such distinctiveness depends on immigration controls.

3. The welfare argument, which once again has two stages: (a) the provision of welfare depends upon having a fixed membership of those entitled to be taxed to provide welfare and those entitled to claim it; and (b) such a membership can only be provided through having immigration controls.

Now, Walzer's description of a neighbourhood as an 'indifferent association' strikes me as impoverished. As I sit and write this chapter in Stamford Hill in London, the Hassidic Jewish community that makes up a significant proportion of the population in this neighbourhood is celebrating the festival of Purim, and the streets are full of noise and colour. And yet the neighbourhood, while not a random association, is open: there are no border controls or membership restrictions for the neighbourhood as such, taken as a territory. The same story can be told within any cosmopolitan city throughout the globe, and it is a story which seems to cast doubt on Walzer's second argument, that the 'distinctiveness of cultures and groups depends upon closure'. Iris Marion Young points out that in the city we often find social differentiation without exclusion: 'In the ideal of city life freedom leads to group differentiation, to the formation of affinity groups, but this social and spatial differentiation of groups is without exclusion.'[45] She says: 'groups do not stand in relations of inclusion and exclusion, but overlap and intermingle without becoming homogeneous'. And: 'In the normative ideal of city life, borders are open and undecidable.'[46]

Now of course, Young is talking of the ideal city, and we should also note that the Hassidic community I gave as an example is not open but has strict membership controls and methods of excluding outsiders through which they maintain their identity as a group. However, the point is not so much about this particular religious group, but about the neighbourhood itself, a territory which has no such controls and yet has a distinct character – and Walzer's argument about the distinctiveness of culture in the end has to justify the sorts of territorial controls states exercise at borders. One could reply that it is not so much the neighbourhood that has this character as the different groups that happen to reside there, but this would be true of any territorial space, whether it be a neighbourhood or a political state; and the point remains that this neighbourhood, by virtue of having these groups residing within it, does have a distinct character and it does not need border controls to do it – most importantly, there is no control over who enters the neighbourhood. Again, it might be replied that any such character a neighbourhood happens to have is fragile and passing, in that the groups that give it this character can always leave and go elsewhere; the fact that the neighbourhood has no control over its 'membership' means this is always a possibility. But this is surely the same for the territorial state and brings us back to the points made in the previous chapter – that if one is concerned to maintain the identity of a state, just as important as control over entry is control over exit. If a particular group contributes significantly to the character of a state, then it is crucial to the maintenance of that character that this group is prevented from leaving. And yet, as we have seen, Walzer and those who follow him do not seriously contemplate this control.

All three of Walzer's arguments look unconvincing if we consider another possible model of membership, which I will call the regional model. Most modern states have levels of local organisation and association at the level of regions or provinces, which themselves are broken up into distinct areas. At all of these levels local authorities have powers and responsibilities within their boundaries. Such a body can have responsibility for the provision of services such as policing, waste disposal, education and the provision of leisure facilities; and can also have responsibility for taxation to raise funds to pay for these services. And yet the boundaries of such regions, and so on, operate like Walzer's neighbourhood: they remain open in the sense that the regional authority has no control over who enters its territory or becomes a resident. Walzer discusses the ideas of Marxist theorist Otto Bauer, who makes the point that an authority can have control over its members in two senses: (1) in the sense that it can make demands of them, for example in the form of taxation; and (2) in the sense that it can determine who is and is not a member. Bauer proposes a scheme in which territorial states have control in the first sense but not in the second; they have the right to tax, and so on, those who are within their territory, but no right over who *is* within the territory.[47] Walzer considers this unsuitable for modern political communities; Bauer was writing in the time of the multi-national European empires, and now modern nations look for control over a territory: 'Nations look for countries because in some deep sense they already have countries: the link between people and land is a crucial feature of national identity.'[48] Also, issues of welfare, education and so on need to be solved within a particular territorial location.

However, Bauer's approach fits the regional model when it comes to the provision of welfare and education, for example, and the rights of taxation. Such authorities precisely have control over their members in that they have the right to make demands of those who reside in their territory, and have no control over them in that they have no power to determine who can be in that territory. There seems to be no evidence that this handicaps them in fulfilling their purposes. If we move beyond the concern for welfare provision, and consider Walzer's notions of 'identity' and 'place' to be important, then again the regional model undermines his argument. There are plenty of examples of regions or provinces that enjoy a strong sense of identity and place and distinctiveness: people can feel strong attachments to regions or provinces or federated states, despite the fact that these bodies have no control over membership.

And so Walzer's arguments from welfare and from identity are both contradicted by this model of membership: it seems to show that border controls are not needed in order to provide welfare services or to have a distinct identity. Of course, Walzer may reply that his first argument, about freedom of movement, is decisive here: that these regional boundaries can only be open because there is closure at the national level. But, in the end, it is difficult to see what evidence can be produced for or against this as an argument.

SECTION 4: UNREASONABLE IDENTITIES

We have seen that Walzer's thesis consists of two claims: (1) a political community needs a self-conception if it is going to succeed in fulfilling its purposes; and (2) that self-conception needs to be protected by immigration and naturalisation laws. In the previous section I argued that neither of these claims is obviously true, and provided some grounds for doubting them. But there is a third claim to Walzer's thesis which is absolutely fundamental to it which we have not fully confronted: that it is for a political community to decide upon its own self-conception and its decision is final. Although many left liberals would find such a position unacceptable, it is central to Walzer's perspective, as the source of the self-understanding and the moral principles that govern a community can only be that community itself. His way of doing political philosophy is to 'interpret to one's fellow citizens the world of meanings that we share'.[49] David Miller characterises Walzer's theory as 'radically pluralistic in nature. There are no universal laws of justice. Instead, we must see justice as the creation of a particular political community at a particular time, and the account we give must be given from within such a community.'[50]

However, to say that any conception will do is not quite accurate, as Walzer does qualify the claim that the authority of the members of the community is final:

> One can argue about particular admissions standards by appealing, for example, to the condition and character of the host country and to the shared understandings of those who are already members. Such arguments have to be judged morally and politically as well as factually.[51]

He gives two examples of what he considers to be either an unreasonable self-conception or an unreasonable application of a self-conception (this distinction is important and I will apply it below: it allows that a self-conception can, in itself, be reasonable but can be applied in unreasonable ways).

The first example picks out those in the United States in, for example, the 1920s, who argued for restricted immigration to defend a 'homogeneous white and Protestant country'.[52] Walzer argues that such a claim was both inaccurate in that it ignored the extent to which the United States was already a highly heterogeneous community, and unjust in that it set aside the original intention to create such a society: 'the moral realities of that society ought to have guided the legislators of the 1920s'.[53] So this is an example of an unreasonable national identity. However, we should note that the qualification of what can count as a self-conception is itself qualified; for, appealing to the club analogy, Walzer says that earlier decisions, if different, would have meant that subsequent immigration controls on these grounds would have been neither inaccurate nor unjust.

The second example is of the white Australia immigration policy. As we saw in Section 2, Walzer criticises that policy because of the amount of space that was available:

> The right of white Australians to the great empty spaces of the subcontinent rested on nothing more than the claim they had staked, and enforced against the aboriginal population, before anyone else. That does not seem a right that one would readily defend in the face of necessitous men and women, clamoring for entry.[54]

Although Walzer argues that what needs to be defended is not just economic prosperity and territory, but also 'ways of life' or 'life plans',[55] he concludes that no significant ways of life were at stake in the case of the white Australia policy. It is important to note that Walzer's

critique of the policy is set in the context of his discussion of 'necessitous strangers' and refugees: the policy cannot be defended when it
comes to these applicants for membership. But the policy was designed
to exclude strangers as such, where 'strangeness' was measured in terms
of racial characteristics – and so, oddly, Walzer has nothing to say here
about the justice of the policy in excluding non-necessitous strangers
on these racial grounds. For this reason, I think that what we have here
is an example of unreasonable membership controls, but not necessarily
of an unreasonable self-conception.

And so Walzer does provide some grounds for critically assessing
self-conceptions and their application. A multi-cultural community
cannot impose a mono-cultural identity and immigration controls
based on that false identity; but a mono-cultural community can
impose immigration restrictions to defend itself from invasions of
plurality, where it judges those invasions will change its self-conception,
and as long as those defences are not applied too harshly to 'necessitous
strangers'. These grounds may strike some as rather shallow.

But if we look closer, we will notice that the scope for criticism
is even shallower than we might suppose. In the case of the white
Australia policy, Walzer says that while ways of life must be taken into
account as well as territorial and economic considerations, there were
no significant ways of life at stake in this case. He argues:

> [L]et us suppose that the great majority of Australians could
> maintain their present way of life, subject only to marginal shifts,
> given a successful invasion of the sort I have imagined.[56]

He does concede that some individuals could come to 'need' vast
expanses of empty territory for their way of life, but 'such needs cannot
be given moral priority over the claims of necessitous strangers. Space
on that scale is a luxury'.[57] Strangely, having argued that territorial and
economic considerations are not the only ones, and that ways of life
have to be taken into account, Walzer seems to give a reading of ways
of life primarily in terms of territorial considerations, assessing them
only in terms of the space available to lead them. It could surely be
argued that a way of life is threatened by admittance of 'strange'
refugees even though there are no territorial or economic factors at
stake: one's way of life is violated by the mere presence of such
strangers, irrrespective of how much space they occupy. Members can
no longer 'imagine' their nation and therefore themselves in the same
way, and so have lost their sense of who 'they' are. Having introduced
ways of life as an important factor when it comes to the inclusion or

exclusion of necessitous strangers, Walzer seems to have left himself with few or no grounds to reject any particular way of life as unreasonable. He therefore seems to have no grounds to criticise the white Australia policy, even when it comes to the exclusion of necessitous strangers.

His critique of the 'white America' proposal is equally problematic. As we have seen, he seems to allow that if the United States was, more or less, a white Anglo-Saxon Protestant nation, the community could legitimately adopt this as a national identity and defend it through its immigration policies. However, given the plural nature of the United States, such an identity could not be imposed. There are two problems here. First, it would seem legitimate from this viewpoint for a nation to call a halt to its plurality, as was not merely proposed but also practised by the United States towards the end of the nineteenth century, especially concerning Chinese immigration.[58] Second, why shouldn't a political community *revise* its self-conception? The United States could have decided that it would consider itself to be a white Anglo-Saxon Protestant nation for purposes of future immigration policy, and those already within the borders who do not fit that identity could be re-defined as internal 'aliens'. Note that Walzer allows for the existence of internal aliens when he considers the rights of the original inhabitants of a territory. As we saw in Section 2, such inhabitants have a locational right and cannot be expelled:

> New states and governments must make their peace with the old inhabitants of the land they rule. And countries are likely to take shape as closed territories dominated, perhaps, by particular nations (clubs or families), but always including aliens of one sort or another – whose expulsion would be unjust.[59]

Walzer argues that any such internal aliens must be allowed full citizenship rights, but they seem to remain alien in that they are not included in the 'dominant' national identity. The fact that the dominant (majority) group is not obliged to negotiate a *national* identity that includes *everybody* who has a legitimate right to be within the territorial boundary is worrying. My concern here is that, given the absence of such an obligation to 'original' inhabitants, there seems to be no good reason why a political community, if dominated by a particular group, should not decide to revise a pluralist self-conception into a more exclusive one. Those re-defined as aliens cannot be deprived of their citizenship rights and cannot be expelled, but others like them will no longer be admitted. In fact one does not need to go as far as creating a new category of internal aliens to add to the already existing category of 'original' inhabitants: the community could simply decide that it has achieved a certain balance of cultural groups, and so decide to halt any further immigration from that particular group. This could allow that the white America policy could have been imposed, and still could be, without any inaccuracy or injustice. After all, if we appeal to the analogy of a club, it is always open for the current membership of the club to revise the membership rules – and so they are under no obligation or constraint even if past members exercised a plural policy. Of course, such a decision has to be open to democratic review, but if a particular group dominates in terms of numbers, then it would seem unreasonable to frustrate its democratic will on this question.

This is to take into account the extent to which 'strangeness' is a construction imposed upon others, rather than something naturally given. Who counts as 'strange' can therefore be reviewed and revised. Kitty Calavita describes the case of Spain, where people from the former colonies such as Peru were regarded as unproblematic until Spain became embodied in the European Union: once Spain became part of the EU's overall immigration policy, those people from Spain's colonial past became subject to severe immigration control, as privileged entry was granted to members of EU states.[60] Within Walzer's framework, there seems to be no grounds for objecting to such a revision, as long as those already within the territory are not expelled or deprived of their citizenship rights. But even if this was the case, it seems likely that those already on the inside will be subjected to increased social and legal harassment because of their connection with or similarity to those now defined as outsiders. And so once more Walzer seems to have no grounds to criticise even the 'white America' policy which he considers to be unjust. We have to wonder whether his approach has *any* scope to criticise unreasonable self-conceptions, or unreasonable applications of a self-conception.

SECTION 5: MORAL EQUALITY

One basis for criticising unreasonable self-conceptions or unreasonably restrictive membership rules is that they violate the principle of the moral equality of persons, which, we saw in Chapter 1, is central to modern political philosophy. Any political philosophy seriously committed to this principle must have deep concerns over the moral arbitrariness of membership rules. Of course, this concern has its place in a liberal viewpoint which holds the principle of moral equality as universally valid, and Walzer does not occupy this position. But this does not mean he can evade the difficulties the principle raises for immigration practices, because it may well be that 'our' political community holds a philosophy which is itself liberal and democratic, and therefore holds the principle of equality at its core. Whether we are 'universalist' or 'local' liberals, we hold the same principle: the only difference is that in the former case the principle can be critically applied globally, while in the latter case we can only apply the principle to our own institutions, and to those of any other political community that also claims to be a liberal democracy. Joseph H. Carens makes the point that liberals must be guided by the principles of their own tradition even if they do not seek to impose those principles globally, only locally, and one such fundamental principle is that of moral equality:

> No moral argument will seem acceptable to *us*, if it directly challenges the assumption of the equal moral worth of all individuals. If restrictions on immigration are to be justified, they have to be based on arguments that respect that principle.[61]

The point is that if we shift from a universal liberalism to a local liberalism, this does not justify a shift from a principle of the moral equality of *persons* to a principle of the moral equality of *citizens*. The only defensible shift is from applying the principle of moral equality to all institutions, and applying it only to liberal institutions – after all, only liberal institutions need to respect liberal principles. But the fact remains that the principle those liberal institutions need to respect commits them to the moral equality of humanity, not merely of citizens of a liberal polity. Therefore immigration, if it is to be a *liberal* institution, has to respect that principle: and so we return to the central question of whether it is possible for an immigration policy to respect the moral equality of humanity. The move to a liberalism based on communitarian foundations cannot, if it is to be a form of liberalism, abandon that principle – neither, of course, can a communitarianism based on liberal foundations.

This is, of course, to shift the level of argument from Walzer's level 3, the character of political communities as such, to level 2, the character of a particular political community, which in this case happens to be the liberal democratic polity. Walzer may reply that if 'our' self-conception is of a liberal democratic polity, then his approach shows, perfectly consistently, that we have to put in place immigration and naturalisation policies that reflect that self-conception – they have to be liberal practices. But this is to remain at level 3, and it tells us nothing about how to solve 'our' problem – of how those membership practices can be made compatible with liberal democratic principles.

SECTION 6: CONCLUSION

In this chapter we have seen that Walzer's treatment of the membership question is distinctive, in that within his framework any answers to it must depend upon a particular community's understanding of itself, and upon its central political and moral principles and commitments. This seems to make it difficult, if not impossible, to mount any external criticism of particular membership practices. However, within this particularistic framework we can still engage in internal criticism of 'our' community, and of any other community which claims to share our fundamental principles and commitments. So if we live in a community which describes itself as liberal and democratic, this gives us a set of principles and commitments we can apply to that community's institutions and practices, and also to any other community that claims to be a member of the 'family' of liberal democratic states. And so Walzer's approach does not limit our scope for critical examination of immigration practices when it comes to states that describe themselves as liberal democracies.

We have seen that Walzer makes three central claims: (1) that political communities need a shared understanding – states need a national identity; (2) that this shared understanding must be protected through membership practices – states have the right to impose immigration restrictions based on that understanding; and (3) that, within certain limits, members of the community have the final say on their shared understanding and therefore on the content of the membership rules. I questioned all three claims. (1) It is not obvious that communities need a shared understanding in order to function, and therefore not obvious that states require a national identity. (2) Even if they do, it is not obvious that this shared understanding needs to be protected through membership rules – it may be robust enough not to need protection. (3) The right of a community to arrive at whatever self-understanding its members choose is problematic – we need to ask whether that self-understanding reflects the way *all* members of that community see themselves and others, and also whether that understanding excludes others on grounds we would consider to be unacceptable.

However, in a sense very little has been settled. Walzer states his claims and none of his arguments, in my view, establish them; but this does not mean the claims themselves cannot be established by other arguments or more detailed arguments than Walzer provides. The central question, then, remains to be resolved. Can convincing arguments for membership controls be constructed within a communitarian-liberal framework? To explore this we need to go back over Walzer's claims and examine them in more detail. He supplies three arguments for immigration control: (1) the freedom of movement argument: that open borders at the state level will lead to restrictions of movement at the local level, and therefore less freedom of movement overall; (2) the welfare argument: that the provision of welfare needs a fixed membership available to be taxed and qualify for welfare, and this membership can only by fixed by immigration controls; and (3) the distinctiveness of culture argument: that distinctiveness of groups and cultures can only be maintained through immigration controls. I have questioned all three arguments, but more detailed versions could still be convincing. In the next chapter I pursue the communitarian emphasis on the distinctiveness of culture, and will consider the other arguments in subsequent chapters. The focus of the next chapter will therefore be what can be made of the idea of national identity within the liberal tradition, and to what extent it can be used to justify immigration controls. I examine the arguments of two writers in particular, David Miller and Yael Tamir. Miller's arguments come more clearly from a communitarian perspective, while Tamir describes her position as *liberal* nationalism. We should, therefore, be in a position to assess the role that the idea of national identity can play across the spectrum of liberal political philosophy.

NOTES

1. M. Walzer (1983), *Spheres of Justice: A Defence of Pluralism and Equality*.
2. D. Miller (1995), *On Nationality*, p. 193. Miller is using the latter to describe his own approach.
3. The notion of a collective consciousness is, of course, developed in the work of Emile Durkheim, especially in Durkheim (1947), *The Division of Labour in Society* trans. with introduction by G. Simpson. There it means something like 'the body of beliefs and sentiments common to the average of the members of a society' – R. Aron (1970), *Main Currents in Sociological Thought 2*, p. 24. Walzer makes no references to Durkheim here.
4. Walzer (1983), p. 28.
5. Walzer (1983), p. 32.
6. Walzer (1983), p. 33.

7. Walzer (1983), p. 33.
8. Walzer (1983), p. 33.
9. Walzer (1983), p. 34.
10. Walzer (1983), p. 35.
11. Walzer (1983), p. 37.
12. Walzer (1983), p. 36.
13. H. Sidgwick (1881), *Elements of Politics*, pp. 295–6.
14. Walzer (1983), p. 41.
15. Walzer (1983), p. 41.
16. Walzer (1983), p. 42.
17. Walzer (1983), p. 43.
18. Walzer (1983), p. 45.
19. Walzer (1983), p. 46.
20. T. Hobbes (1968), *Leviathan*, p. 387.
21. Hobbes (1968), pp. 209–10.
22. Walzer (1983), p. 47.
23. Walzer (1983), p. 47.
24. Sidgwick (1881), pp. 296–7.
25. Walzer (1983), p. 48.
26. Walzer (1983), p. 48.
27. Walzer (1983), p. 49.
28. Walzer (1983), p. 49.
29. Walzer (1983), p. 50.
30. Walzer (1983), p. 50.
31. Walzer (1983), p. 50.
32. Walzer (1983), p. 51.
33. Walzer (1983), p. 51.
34. Walzer (1983), p. 62.
35. Having one's partner chosen for one has always been an important part of the 'western' convention of marriage, often overlooked because of a dubious contrast with essentialist characterisations of 'eastern' conventions.
36. Walzer (1983), p. 41.
37. J. A. Scanlan and O. T. Kent (1988), 'The Force of Moral Arguments for a Just Immigration Policy in a Hobbesian Universe: The Contemporary American Example', in M. Gibney (ed.), *Open Borders? Closed Societies? The Ethical and Political Issues*.
38. Scanlan and Kent (1988), pp. 87–8.
39. Walzer (1983), p. 41.
40. As I pointed out in the previous chapter, the only way to *derive* a conclusion about the membership practices of states from the membership practices of clubs is to show that the family of features that make it necessary for clubs to have this kind of membership practice are also present for states. But Walzer does not put forward such a detailed argument.
41. Walzer (1983), pp. 38–9.
42. Walzer (1983), p. 39.
43. Walzer (1983), p. 39.

44. Walzer (1983), p. 39.
45. Iris Marion Young (1990), *Justice and the Politics of Difference*, p. 238.
46. Young (1990), p. 239.
47. See T. Bottomore and P. Goode (eds) (1978), *Austro-Marxism*, pp. 102–25.
48. Walzer (1983), p. 44.
49. Walzer (1983), p. xiv.
50. D. Miller and M. Walzer (eds) (1995), *Pluralism, Justice, and Equality*, p. 2.
51. Walzer (1983), p. 40.
52. Walzer (1983), p. 40.
53. Walzer (1983), p. 40.
54. Walzer (1983), p. 46.
55. Walzer (1983), p. 47.
56. Walzer (1983), p. 47.
57. Walzer (1983), p. 47.
58. For a defence of the exclusion of the Chinese written at the time from a 'liberal' perspective, see R. Mayo-Smith (1890), *Emigration and Immigration: A Study in Social Science*. Mayo-Smith argues that the United States has the right to limit immigration where this will damage its 'civilization', and that this can extend as far as excluding 'a whole race on the ground that their civilization is not desirable . . .' (p. 297). The Chinese, for Mayo-Smith, were such a 'race' due to what he describes as their inability to assimilate. For a vigorous contemporary rebuttal of that view see M. R. Coolidge (1909), *Chinese Immigration*, who argues that Chinese exclusion was simply an act of racism: 'It does, indeed, take two to assimilate; and non-assimilation is the least convincing and most inconsistent of all the arguments against Chinese immigration, in the mouths of those who have not wished them to assimilate nor given them opportunity to do so, and who do not, even now, recognize that many of them have become intelligent and patriotic Americans' (p. 458).
59. Walzer (1983), p. 43.
60. K. Calavita (1998), 'Immigration, Law, and Marginalization in a Global Economy: Notes from Spain', *Law and Society Review*, vol. 32, no. 3, pp. 529–66.
61. J. H. Carens (1995), 'Aliens and Citizens: The Case for Open Borders', in W. Kymlicka (ed.), *The Rights of Minority Cultures*, p. 346.

Chapter 5

EMBRACING THE 'NATION'

SECTION 1: INTRODUCTION

In the previous chapter we explored Michael Walzer's attempts to justify restricted membership by appeal to the idea of 'community'. There are two ways in which the idea can be used. Both of them, however, rely on showing that the community is constituted by relations of reciprocity, and which are therefore ethical; and that, in addition, these relations carry such moral weight that they override any ethical obligations owed to moral agents as such. We can say, then, that the principle of community outweighs the principle of humanity. We can see that these kinds of arguments rest on the claim that the principle of community outweighs the principle of humanity, and this claim, as it stands, is one most people would find puzzling, and certainly at odds with many of their central moral intuitions. It fails to deal with the *generality* of the sorts of relationship people find themselves in, and indeed the generality of the communities of which they are members. We are not in a position to say that every kind of community-based relationship will ethically outweigh any kind of universal relationship: it depends on the relationships in question. Equally, if relationships based in different communities clash, it is not obvious which should take priority.

And so the challenge for those who wish to continue along the lines set out by Walzer in *Spheres of Justice* is to show that there *is* a form of community that *can* consistently outweigh the principle of humanity, and one particular way of answering this challenge is to claim that the *nation* constitutes such a community. We now have a much more specific and plausible claim, that the principle of nationality outweighs the principle of humanity – our obligations to co-nationals come first. And this justifies immigration controls, where it can be shown that admission would harm the interests of co-nationals, even if exclusion harms the interests of non-nationals – and this includes the harm of changing the sense of national identity through which members identify themselves and others. We therefore move to something that can be described as 'liberal nationalism'.

The idea of the 'nation' has, until very recently, played little role in modern political philosophy, especially within liberal theory.[1] Resistance to it can be understood against its apparent violation of two of the central principles of liberalism, both of which express its claim to universalism: the principle of the moral equality of persons – that all human agents are entitled to equal respect and concern; and the principle of rationality – that all public political institutions and practices must be capable of justification to all rational agents. The idea of the nation seems to conflict with these principles, in that it implies special moral duties towards co-nationals which do not apply to 'outsiders', a form of moral partiality; and it is taken to be an idea that defies rational justification – at the very least, one group's self-conception as a nation cannot be rationally justified to outsiders.

However, political philosophers have begun to acknowledge that to make no reference at all to such a major force in human affairs is to detach their work from reality to an unacceptable extent. The question then is how to respond to the nation? There seem to be three possible responses. The first is to be heroic and to reject the idea of the nation in totality, and to continue as before. The second is toleration, to acknowledge that nations remain a major force in political activity despite their amoralism and irrationalism, and try to construct a political philosophy that can at least co-exist with them. The third and most radical response is accommodation – to find a way of making sense of the nation such that it becomes acceptable to the sensibilities of modern political philosophy, even within the context of liberal theory. This involves demonstrating that the nation can be a genuinely ethical community, and that one's nationality can be a rationally defensible component of one's cultural identity – the charges of amoralism and irrationalism can be rejected.

The two writers I examine in this and the next chapter, David Miller and Yael Tamir,[2] both pursue the third option of accommodation, and seek to develop theories that can be described as liberal nationalism.[3] For example, Tamir explicitly argues that liberalism should 'accommodate' the 'worthy elements' to be found within nationalism.[4] However, both writers approach nationalism from different theoretical directions, with Miller coming from communitarian origins, and Tamir from liberalism. Whether there is, in the end, any great theoretical distance between them is debatable, as Miller's project can be understood as 'liberalism-on-communitarian-foundations',[5] while Tamir, in her attempt to 'translate' nationalist discourse into terms understandable within liberal theory, 'relies on the current terms of communitarian discourse, which is akin to the nationalist one in its content'.[6] However, I do think that their points of departure and therefore background ideas are significantly different, and so believe that each deserves separate attention. Close examination of Miller's arguments exposes specifically communitarian difficulties in dealing with the question of membership; while in the case of Tamir, we discover problems specific to liberal theory.

This chapter cannot deal with the idea of 'nation' in its entirety, nor even with its implications for liberal political philosophy. The project must remain focused on the question of immigration. The point of introducing the idea of nationality is to diffuse the power of the principle of the moral equality of persons, and so enable us to solve the problem of membership. Liberal nationalists therefore argue that the gaping holes that open up within liberal theory around this question can only be filled by appeal to the idea of the nation. Tamir goes so far as to claim that: 'Except for some cosmopolitans and radical anarchists, nowadays most liberals are liberal nationalists.'[7] By incorporating ideas from nationalism, liberal theory has been 'able to circumvent such thorny issues as membership and immigration, as well as the more general question of how groups are structured'.[8]

Having said that the primary focus must remain upon arguments concerning membership and immigration in particular, it will be impossible to avoid taking a more expansive view of the ideas of the 'nation' and 'national identity' described by Miller and Tamir and others, and so of the philosophical coherence of the idea of the 'nation' itself. For this argument to work at all, we need a coherent idea of the nation which can show that it has moral value, and this moral value has to be compatible with the liberal tradition. Then it has to be shown that this ideal can be appealed to in formulating a set of immigration controls that can be accommodated within liberal theory. I will raise puzzles about both these moves. In the first place, it is hard to see how the principle of nationality escapes the problem of generality which undermines the principle of community. It has to be shown that the nation is an ethical community, but we shall see that at least one attempt to show this – that of Miller – does so simply by appealing to the principle of community itself: the nation is an ethical community simply because it *is* a community, and communities are, by definition, ethical, because they embody relations of reciprocity. This cannot be good enough, because we come back to the implausible claim that *any* community outweighs the principle of humanity. It has to be shown that nations are a special kind of community.

Part of my concern here is that the principle of humanity is simply set aside by appeal to a kind of moral relativism, which can be described as moral communitarianism. According to this approach, all moral principles arise from communities, and therefore there cannot be a moral principle of humanity because humanity does not constitute anything recognisable as a community – and even if it does, it is such a watered-down version of a community that any moral principle it generates must itself be watered down, and so easily outweighed by those principles generated by the much more cohesive and 'thick' communities at more local levels. One problem with this approach – apart from concerns about the coherence of ethical relativism – is that the nation itself is a watered-down version of community compared with more local levels, and so the principle it generates ought to be outweighed by those more local principles. It may be that the consistent communitarian is happy with this implication, but then it may be that nationalists are inconsistent communitarians.

Another major concern is that to suppose nations are ethical communities simply because they embody relations of reciprocity is to allow that *any* association that embodies those relations is itself an ethical community. In this sense, the phrase 'ethical community' is tautological, in that communities are ethical by definition – without these relations of reciprocity, we have no community. These relations of reciprocity, again by definition, involve rights and duties, expectations and obligations, which are recognisably *moral* expectations and obligations. And so, again, simply by showing that nations are communities, we have shown that they are ethical. The problem here is that this leaves us with no resources to make normative judgements about these associations and the basis upon which people form them. Although liberal nationalists would all reject the value of associations based upon racist or sexist or homophobic beliefs, for example, it becomes difficult to see *how* they can criticise them. We seem to want, quite reasonably in my view, to move beyond saying that nations are ethical communities in what seems to be a purely descriptive, tautological sense, to a level which allows us to make the judgement whether a particular nation is ethical or unethical. I explore both these concerns in relation to Miller's theory. So there are grave difficulties in fulfilling the first part of the liberal nationalist project: to show that 'nations' are the sort of association that can carry moral value from the liberal perspective. Putting this aside, the second stage of the project is to show how liberal nationalism can solve the problem of membership: how it enables us to formulate a set of immigration practices that do not contradict core liberal values. Here, the problem is to arrive at a national identity for liberal nationalist states which can inform a set of immigration practices. I explore this particular issue in relation to Tamir's theory. My concern is that a liberal nationalist identity collapses either into an unacceptably 'thick' ethnic identity or an impractically 'thin' civic identity. We either get an identity which *can* be used to exclude outsiders but which cannot be accommodated with liberal theory, or an identity which *can* be accommodated with liberal theory but which cannot be used to exclude outsiders.

SECTION 2: MORAL COMMUNITARIANISM

Miller's project is to show that nations are genuinely ethical communities, and so can play a legitimate role in normative theory. But to do this, he argues that we must adopt a framework for moral thinking which he describes as ethical particularism. He contrasts this with ethical universalism, which he describes as claiming that 'only general facts about other individuals can serve to determine my duties towards them'.[9] 'Relational' facts can only enter into our moral reasoning at a lower level, where they have to be justified by our general principles: they can never be basic reasons for action. The fundamental basis for moral reasoning is therefore a set of facts about humanity in general, and particular relations with others only take on moral significance against the background of this general framework. We can assume that as these local, relational, moral principles are derived from the general principle of humanity, the general principle takes priority over them. We can already see how difficult it will be to justify a principle of nationality in such a context.

Ethical particularism begins from the opposite direction – relational facts are basic:

> [A]gents are already encumbered with a variety of ties and commitments to particular other agents, or to groups or collectivities, and they begin their ethical reasoning from those commitments.[10]

Ethical universalism 'relies upon an implausible picture of moral agency',[11] with a picture of moral reasoning which is too abstract and artificial. On the other hand, ethical particularism 'appears as the capitulation of reason before sentiment, prejudice, convention, and other such rationally dubious factors';[12] it could lead to uncritical acceptance of tradition, and to incoherence as the complexity of relational facts pulls us in contradictory directions.

Miller argues that there are two ways we can try to accommodate the principle of nationality within the universalist perspective, but neither of them succeeds. The first is to see nations as voluntary creations, and to argue that it is 'valuable from a universal view for people to have the moral power to bind themselves into special relationships with ethical content'.[13] This method fails with respect to nations precisely because they are not voluntary in the right sense, and they are on too large a scale for this model to be applied to them. The second method sees nations as useful fictions: national relations are simply conventions that happen to be useful in delivering what our universal moral principles demand. And so if the principle of humanity demands that all people should enjoy a certain level of welfare, the nation-state is the most useful convention for ensuring that this happens within their locality. But, says Miller, this is simply not true – nation-states, with their vastly unequal powers and resources – are obviously not the most rational or ethical way of ensuring the universal delivery of such values.

Miller concludes that 'attempts to justify the principle of nationality from the perspective of ethical universalism are doomed to failure'.[14] From the universalist perspective:

> Nationality should be looked upon as a *sentiment* that may have certain uses in the short term . . . but which, in the long term, should be transcended in the name of humanity.[15]

The only choice is 'to adopt a more heroic version of universalism, which attaches no intrinsic significance to national boundaries, or else to embrace ethical particularism'.[16] Miller takes the latter option.

Before looking at how Miller claims to show that nations are ethical communities, I wish to explore some of the implications of taking an ethical particularist approach at this level. From the particularist perspective, we have seen that we begin our moral reasoning from relational facts about ourselves and others: our rights and duties, expectations and obligations, arise from these relationships. Therefore these relationships generate moral principles. Now, it seems to me that moral principles that arise in this way have two important properties. First, they are autonomous, in that they do not depend upon any higher moral principles for their authority. This gives the agents within these relationships a significant degree of self-determination: rights and obligations cannot be imposed upon them from the 'outside'; in a sense, from a moral point of view there *is* no 'outside', no external perspective from which one could criticise what the internal agents take to be their moral rights and responsibilities. This quality is crucial for what Miller goes on to say about nations as ethical communities: an important feature of our understanding of nations is that they are, or ought to be, autonomous and therefore self-determining; there can be no legitimate authority that can impose duties upon them. The second feature of particularist moral principles is that they have boundaries of exclusion: those who are not in the relationship are excluded from the rights and responsibilities that arise from it; moral duties and expectations cannot extend beyond the relationship. And so these moral principles, generated from within relationships, have two kinds of boundaries of exclusion. We can call the first kind a boundary of *legitimation*, in that only those within the relationship are called upon to legitimate it: it does not have to be justified to any external agencies. We can call the second kind a boundary of *distribution*, in that it distributes the rights and obligations to members of the relationship. We should notice for now that, from this particularistic point of view, the two boundaries of legitimation and distribution coincide: only members of the relationship can legitimate the moral principle it generates, and only they can be included within its distribution of rights and responsibilities. From a moral point of view, there is no 'external world'.

Now, we might think that this constitutes a clear contrast between particularism and universalism, in that particularist principles, because of the way they are generated, have boundaries of exclusion, whereas universalist principles do not. And this shows that particularism is a more plausible approach, as universalism entails us distributing all goods without limit, therefore draining our moral commitments of any content. However, the claim that moral principles have to be bounded has never been controversial, and even the most universalist of moral theorists have seen the scope of their principles as limited to a particular group. For example, the boundary might be drawn between those that have the capacity to be moral agents and those who do not, or those with the capacity for rationality and those without. Universalist moral principles therefore have borders and those borders are contested. The difference between universalist and particularist principles cannot, then, be that the latter have boundaries while the former are somehow borderless.

Universal moral principles have both kinds of boundaries I have described: of legitimation and distribution. One can be excluded from a moral principle in two ways: first from its legitimation and second from its distribution. In many ways the former kind of exclusion is more serious than the latter. If we are included in the process of legitimation we can reach an agreement about who is to be excluded from the distribution of a good, even where *we* are among the excluded – we can agree to our exclusion because we can see it as rationally and morally justifiable; there are good reasons for our exclusion. For example, an able-bodied person is able to see that there are good reasons for excluding them from the distribution of a particular resource aimed to benefit physically disabled people. Both are included in the process of legitimation, even though the able-bodied are excluded from the distribution. This shows that the two boundaries do not need to fall in the same place, and where one is excluded from a distribution what is important is that one has been included in the legitimation process. Indeed, what matters most from the universalist perspective is not that moral principles include all humanity in their distribution of goods – this *would* make a nonsense of the majority of moral issues – but that any moral principle has to be capable of being accepted as rationally and ethically legitimate by any moral agent.

What distinguishes particularism and universalism here is not, therefore, that the former generates moral principles with boundaries while the latter generates limitless principles. Rather, it is that for particularism the two boundaries of legitimation and distribution *always* coincide, while for universalism they do not coincide, or at least only in two exceptional cases. The first would be where the good being distributed is of no value to those excluded from its distribution – there is therefore no *need* to justify their exclusion. The second would be where those excluded are not capable of understanding the legitimation process – they are in some sense not moral or rational agents; it is therefore not *possible* to include them within the boundary of legitimation.[17] However, these two cases where the boundaries of legitimation and distribution converge are exceptions,[18] and what remains important for the universalist is that the boundary of legitimation includes, except for these rare cases, all moral agents, and is therefore much wider than most boundaries of distribution.

What is distinctive about particularist moral principles, then, is that their boundaries of legitimation and distribution converge. The distribution of rights and duties is confined to the ethical relationship that generates the principle, and only those agents within that relationship have any say in determining the content of the principle. This raises a worrying puzzle for the particularist, in that it seems that there is never an obligation to justify a distribution to those excluded from it, because they, by definition, fall outside of the boundary of legitimation. There is no external perspective from this point of view, and therefore no possibility of external justification. How are we to make sense of this convergence and its implications? If we look at nationalist principles of distribution, we see the clearest example where boundaries of distribution and legitimation coincide: the distribution of goods comes to a halt at the national border, and there is no need to justify that distribution to those excluded from it, because they are outside the border. We saw that from the universalist perspective there are two cases where the boundaries can coincide: where the excluded are incapable of benefiting from the good being distributed, or that they are incapable of comprehending the process of legitimation; but does the nationalist distribution fall into either one of these categories?

If we take the first possibility, it may be that there are some goods that are distributed within a nation where this argument works, but they are going to be too rare to justify the principle of nationality as such. Anyway, the most crucial kinds of goods, such as welfare, are clearly not like this – and indeed it seems plausible to suppose that the principle of nationality only has any work to do when it covers goods that *can* be enjoyed by outsiders. If we take the second possibility, then it has to be argued that outsiders cannot comprehend our processes of legitimation, and therefore it is not *possible* to include them within that process. There are two problems with this response. First, we have seen that even if someone cannot comprehend the process of legitimation, it does not follow that they can legitimately be excluded from the distribution of the good for *that* reason (e.g. children). Second, it is a very strong claim to make about outsiders, and it amounts to what I have called 'moral communitarianism': a form of moral relativism which claims that certain kinds of groups, moral communities, can generate moral principles that are purely internal and autonomous, independent of any universal perspective; and, crucially, they can only be fully comprehended by members of the moral community. This seems to be an implausibly strong claim to make about communities in general, and seems to transform them into curiously closed places in which, from a moral and cultural perspective, there can be no 'external world'. In such a place, we cannot recognise 'outsiders' as moral and rational agents like ourselves: in other words, we cannot recognise such others as individuals, as individuals are understood in liberal political philosophy. From a moral perspective, they remain utterly strange to us, and completely incapable of understanding how we have come to our moral and political principles. The only other possibility for Miller's particularist nationalist is simply to assert that the boundaries of distribution and legitimation just do coincide, or at least they do in the case of nationalist principles: when it comes to outsiders, it is just none of their business how a good is distributed within such a community. But at the level of theory such assertions just won't do: we need to know why it is none of their business, especially when the good they are being excluded from is one that could benefit them. The assertion as it stands is simply incomprehensible unless placed in the context of moral communitarianism.

To review what has been a complex argument, it is crucial from the particularist viewpoint, especially if we are going to use particularism to move to an ethical nationalism, that the boundaries of distribution and legitimation coincide: the distribution of goods can come to a stop at the national border, and exclusion does not have to be justified to those excluded. What is incomprehensible from the universalist viewpoint is the ethical justification of excluding people from the distribution of a good that will benefit them, unless they have consented to it or somehow acknowledged its legitimacy. Miller's particularist solves this puzzle by removing the need for that justification. The concern I have raised is that they can only do this by assuming its impossibility, and this is to move to a type of moral relativism.

I am not going to argue here that Miller is a communitarian as that term is understood in modern political theory, nor that communitarianism *necessarily* entails the kind of moral relativism I have described. I have been trying to draw out some of the implications of his version of ethical particularism, and the picture of 'moral communitarianism' I have constructed around it may be overdramatised. However, having said this, there is at least some circumstantial evidence in my favour. Miller's writings *can* be seen as coming out of a communitarian tradition.

He does observe that 'liberalism v. nationalism may be a specific instance of what is frequently now regarded as a more general contest between liberals and communitarians'.[19] On the latter issue, there is some suspicion among commentators that communitarianism does entail some form of moral relativism. Shlomo Avineri and Avner de-Shalit observe 'it has been argued that some of the consequences of the metaethical premises of communitarianism may tend towards moral relativism';[20] and Allen Buchanan notes that communitarianism is in danger of 'lapsing into an extreme ethical relativism'.[21]

Whether or not Miller would embrace moral communitarianism, it would carry a cost for his thesis. We can assess this cost if we follow Jeff McMahan when he makes the distinction between particularist nationalism and universalist nationalism.[22] For him, particularist nationalism holds that: '[A] morality... is a communal project whose range of application is properly restricted to the community in which it evolved.'[23] The implication is that we 'should neither condemn nor endorse the nationalism of others'.[24] When it comes to moral principles:

> [W]hatever the local morality determines to be the appropriate degree of partiality within the community is authoritative for the members of the community. There is no neutral, external standpoint from which the local morality's determinations can be challenged or overruled.[25]

Universalist nationalism holds that 'all people are morally entitled to value their own nation, to seek to ensure its self-determining character, and to show partiality to its members'.[26] This partiality still depends on relational facts, but according to this position there must be something objectively valuable about the relationship in order for the partiality to be justified; otherwise 'racist and other pernicious forms of partiality could be readily defended'.[27] Miller would, of course, want to close off such a possibility; but the question is, given his ethical particularism, whether he has any resources to enable him to do so. In the next section we shall see that the way he establishes that nations are ethical communities faces a similar challenge.

SECTION 3: THE NATION AS ETHICAL COMMUNITY

Miller goes on to establish that nations are genuinely ethical communities in the context of ethical particularism, and without the need for external justification: the boundary of national partiality is not justified to those excluded from it. He begins his argument with 'the assumption that memberships and attachments in general have ethical significance'.[28] This means that:

> Because I identify with my family, my college, or my local community, I properly acknowledge obligations to members of these groups that are distinct from the obligations I owe to people generally. Seeing myself as a member, I feel a loyalty to the group, and this expresses itself, among other things, in my giving special weight to the interests of fellow-members.[29]

Identification by itself is, of course, not sufficient – for a genuine community to be in place, the felt loyalties and obligations have to be reciprocal.[30] Miller uses his college as an example of a community, arguing that the obligations he has as a member depend on its 'general ethos'.[31] So as a member of the college, giving academic advice to students will be near the core of that ethos. Miller does acknowledge that his 'collegial obligations extend to general human interests',[32] but even here membership comes into play. If two students need help to go to hospital and he can only take one, Miller decides he 'ought to give priority to the one who belongs to my college, taking the other only if his need is considerably more urgent'.[33]

The argument so far has proceeded on the assumption of the moral value of membership, and Miller applies this assumption at the level of nationality. The only problem with this application, for Miller, is the abstract nature of the nation: it is easier to determine rights and duties in face-to-face communities, but nations are not like this. The gap, for Miller, is filled by the 'public culture': that is, 'a set of ideas about the character of the community which . . . helps to fix responsibilities'.[34] The rights and duties of the nation depend on its particular public culture, and therefore 'we cannot derive the obligations of nationality simply from reflection on what it means for a group to constitute a nation in the first place'.[35] Instead, 'these obligations in their particular content are an artefact of the public culture of that nation'.[36]

In the end, we can ask if Miller has provided any argument that nations are ethical communities. He sets out to do so by placing nationality within the context of ethical particularism; however, this is a theoretical framework in which Miller believes the argument for nationality can make sense, but it is not itself the argument. As we have seen, Miller starts with 'the assumption that memberships and attachments in general have ethical significance', and that is where he ends up: nations are made into ethically significant communities by the assumption that membership as such is ethically significant. To the extent that there is an argument here, it runs something like this: nations are ethical communities because nations are, by definition, communities, and communities are, by definition, ethical; communities are ethical because they involve relations of reciprocity and loyalty, and such relations are by their nature ethical. The concern is, as Simon Caney puts it, that this argument is 'insufficiently discerning'.[37]

The discernment we are seeking is, I suggest, between groups or communities that have moral significance or value and those that do not, and, as Caney observes, Miller has left us with no resources to tell the difference. Miller's point, of course, is that *any* group or community gives rise to reciprocal obligations simply by *being* a community, and these obligations themselves just *are* ethical responsibilities that fall upon members: they have ethical relations with each other. But we may still want to ask how seriously these internal relations have to be taken by making some external judgement about the moral value of the group as a whole. When it comes to a racist organisation, we might concede that its members *feel* loyalty and therefore *experience* moral obligations towards each other to the exclusion of others; but we would also want to say, from an external perspective, that this group has no moral value or ethical status, and therefore there is no reason why we should accept their felt moral obligations to each other as any justification for what they do, or have any respect for such internal relations of obligation.

What is disturbing about Miller's approach is that it seems to provide no resources for this kind of external moral judgement. Jeff McMahan observes that 'the fact that a relation elicits partiality is no guarantee that it is a legitimate basis for partiality'.[38] To assess that legitimacy, we have to be in a position to judge the 'objective moral significance of the relations that obtain'.[39] In Miller's scheme, that position does not seem to exist. If we return to Miller's two injured students, he bases his choice on which one to assist on the grounds that one is a member of his college. We have already seen problems with this choice in Chapter 4. There, I argued that such a choice could only be *morally* defended if two background conditions are true: first, that there is some explicit agreement between colleges that they have the primary obligation to assist their members in such situations; and second, that I have reasonable grounds to believe that they will actually assist in this case. If either of these background conditions is missing, then my decision is not ethically defensible, and to appeal to some kind of connectedness begins to look rather more like a psychological explanation. In Miller's scheme, the loyalty he feels to his student which justifies his choice is not open to external assessment: only fellow members can appreciate the ethical content of his action. The concern is how he can defend this kind of exclusion and at the same time condemn someone who bases exclusion on race.

Miller *does* explicitly condemn racist exclusion, but the point is that it is not clear how he can. He argues that it is a mistake to claim that the shared characteristics that are taken to constitute a nation are 'based on biological descent, that our fellow-nationals must be our "kith and kin"', and that this is a view that 'leads directly to racism'.[40] But this is merely to observe that an exclusion based on biological descent is wrong because it is racist; it is not to say what is wrong with a racist exclusion. What is the difference between restricting one's primary moral concerns to those one perceives or imagines as members of one's race, and restricting one's primary moral concerns to those one perceives or imagines as members of one's nation? Miller's answer is that because the first preference is based on perceived shared biology while the second is based on perceived shared culture, this means the first is a racist exclusion and the second is not.

But even if we set aside the question of cultural racism,[41] this is not enough to settle the moral difference between the two exclusions: we need to know what makes a racist exclusion morally unacceptable before we can be sure that the cultural exclusion does not commit the same ethical mistakes. We could argue that the racist exclusion is morally wrong because it divides ethical concern on the basis of an arbitrary factor, but there are two problems with this move. First, it would only help if we could argue that shared public culture is not arbitrary in the same way, and it is not obvious how to do this. Second, what features are morally arbitrary surely depend on the group's judgement – how can we be in a position to say they have made a mistake? Daniel Weinstock may be correct when he observes that:

> [A] particularist can only prevent nationalist sentiment from giving rise to the kinds of policies he wants to disavow by recourse to purely *ad hoc* grounds, or by tacitly presupposing universalist, non-culture specific concepts and modes of moral reasoning.[42]

And so the overriding concern here is that Miller simply *makes* national membership based on a shared public culture morally significant, and in doing so re-opens the door for those who want to make membership based on shared race morally significant. We therefore have no guarantee that the immigration policies based upon this approach can be accommodated within a liberal perspective.

SECTION 4: MILLER ON IMMIGRATION

Miller does address the immigration issue directly. He does so by contrasting a liberal nationalist approach to immigration to that demanded by conservative nationalism. For Miller, the central feature of conservative nationalism is its demand for 'piety' from its members – that is, the acceptance of authority as legitimate despite the lack of any consent to that authority. The nation needs to be like a family in the sense that parental authority is acknowledged without any question that it needs consent to be legitimate. What is essential to this notion of piety is that one cannot demand rational justification for authority; instead, one must accept that an institution has authority embodied within itself. That authority, then, displays itself, rather than having to be rationally demonstrated.[43] This approach leads to a 'discouraging if not prohibitive attitude towards would-be immigrants who do not already share the national culture'.[44] The danger is that the national identity itself embodies loyalty to traditional institutions and practices, and newcomers simply cannot be held to embody such a loyalty. Their lack of piety for those institutions will therefore be destabilising.[45] For Miller, this conservative approach is incoherent, in that the modern conservative is well aware that national identity is an ever changing fiction, and that the traditions it is supposed to hold dear are themselves recent inventions.[46]

His version of liberal nationalism avoids such problems, as the liberal nationalist realises that national identity is always in a process of change. What matters is that this process should be open and not biased towards any particular identity:

> This idea of nationality is liberal in the sense that the freedoms and rights defended by liberals are valued here as the means whereby individuals can develop and express their ethnic and other group identities, while at the same time taking part in an ongoing collective debate about what it means to be a member of this nation.[47]

This gives us a very different perspective on immigration: 'Why should immigrants pose a threat to national identity once it is recognized that that identity is always in flux, and is moulded by the various sub-cultures that exist within the national society?'[48] But there are still two problems that immigration can pose for the liberal nationalist as *nationalist* (rather than liberal). The first is that the rate of migration could be so high that the public culture which defines the liberal national identity cannot adjust without conflict. The second is that the immigrant group might be such that it could itself stake a claim to nationhood. Both these problems can be solved by 'setting upper bounds to immigration, not a policy of preserving existing national identities by refusing to admit those who do not already share them'.[49]

Here Miller is offering what is on the face of it a liberal immigration policy, in that its concern is with numbers. But in fact the liberal argument about numbers goes something like this: we cannot admit over a certain number because we shall reach a point at which the goods to be distributed among members will break down – here cultural difference is not an issue, or if it is, it remains marginal. But for Miller, cultural difference is central. Both the cases he cites involve identifying a group as being so culturally different that they will cause problems for the receiving state if they are admitted over a certain rate. This means that the gap between the conservative and liberal nationalist may not be as great as Miller suggests. He characterises the conservative position as blocking immigration from groups that do not share the national culture, while his own position calls for *controlled* immigration from certain groups. While there have been cases where immigration from specific groups *has* been blocked entirely, the more common strategy for the modern conservative has been that which Miller suggests: control over the rate of groups considered to be problematic.[50] At the level of theory, there seems to be no distance between the liberal nationalist and the conservative here: they are both applying the same formula, that is control over the rate of immigration from culturally 'problematic' groups. Of course, one trusts there would be a considerable distance in practice, with the liberal nationalist offering a far more open interpretation of what counts as culturally problematic and a fair rate of immigration, but liberals may have been hoping for a gap in theory as well as in practice between themselves and the conservatives.

It could be replied that there *is* a gap in theory, in that the conservative nationalist will not countenance any change in cultural traditions, while Miller makes it clear that for the liberal nationalist little is sacred – all that matters is that change takes place in a way and at a pace that does not give rise to conflict. However, we have to remember that from a more 'purely' liberal point of view it is individuals who apply for membership, not groups, and here a group is being judged as culturally troubling. The irony of Miller's proposal is that while no group as such is banned from entry, individual members of those groups *are* excluded, because they do not make it into the quota – and they are, in the end, excluded not because of any judgement about their individual suitability, but purely because of their membership of the group, something over which they have no control. So even while we can allow that there is some distance between Miller's position and conservative nationalism on immigration, the approach he offers is, on the face of it, non-liberal if not potentially illiberal.

There is a third limit on immigration for Miller: prospective members must be willing to accept current political practices – they must be willing to be *liberal* citizens. The liberal nationalist state can demand of immigrants that they show 'a willingness to accept current political structures and to engage in dialogue with the host community so that a new common identity can be forged'.[51] They must be willing to enter the liberal conversation about national identity. On the face of it, this seems only to demand a commitment to a liberal constitution; but for the liberal nationalist this is not enough. Miller gives a hint of what might be demanded of prospective members when he presents, in a footnote, the view of H. Van Gunsteren:

> The prospective citizen must be capable and willing to be a member of this particular historical community, its past and future, its forms of life and institutions within which its members think and act. In a community that values autonomy and judgement, this is obviously not a requirement of pure conformity. But it is a requirement of knowledge of the language and the culture and of acknowledgment of those institutions that foster the reproduction of citizens who are capable of autonomous and responsible judgement.[52]

This goes beyond the commitment to a constitution; it also demands commitment to a history, to forms of life, to language and culture, and this presents the prospective member with a possibly difficult hurdle. In the next chapter we shall see that Yael Tamir, approaching from a liberal rather than communitarian direction, arrives at the same conclusion.

Miller's communitarian approach, however, gives rise to a particular concern here. Prospective members have to show 'a willingness to accept current political structures', or make an 'acknowledgement' of these institutions: in other words, they have to acknowledge the authority of these institutions. For groups that are non-liberal in the sense of simply being unfamiliar with liberal institutions or practices, we have to ask what such an acknowledgement can amount to? This is especially problematic for the moral communitarian, for whom any new member is entering an unfamiliar landscape, and who cannot possibly be expected to *understand* that community's political institutions. This means that all we can demand of such 'strangers' is something that looks suspiciously like conservative piety, rather than rational consent. They are, to paraphrase Miller's conservative nationalist, 'to acknowledge the authority of institutions . . . which form the substance of national life'.[53] There is still, of course, a considerable practical distance between the conservative and liberal nationalist here: the conservative nationalist would not admit such 'strangers' at all, while the liberal nationalist would admit them under a quota system; the conservative nationalist demands piety from all members, in that rational consent is inappropriate, while the liberal nationalist is committed to rational consent – it is merely that it doesn't seem possible in this particular case; and the conservative nationalist demands piety for traditional institutions, while the liberal nationalist demands it for liberal institutions. But once more, whatever the distance in practice, the theoretical distance between liberal and conservative may seem disconcertingly small.

What the liberal would want to show, of course, is that these institutions are rationally and ethically legitimate, and it is the process of legitimation that distinguishes them from the conservative, for whom traditional institutions simply embody their legitimacy. So for the liberal there ought to be some sort of trade-off between the state and the prospective member: the prospective member has to demonstrate a commitment to legitimate political institutions, while the state has to demonstrate that its political institutions are legitimate. For Miller's liberal nationalist, there will be a certain class of immigrant for whom there can be no such trade-off – they must simply take it that these institutions are legitimate; and for the moral communitarian, *all* immigrants are in this position. There has to be a concern, then, that Miller's version of liberal nationalism leads to what some may regard as conservative constraints upon immigration.

In the introduction to this chapter I said the major reasons why the 'nation' has played such a small role in modern political philosophy have been its apparent irrationalism and amoralism. Miller's project of accommodation has to be judged on whether it has overcome those charges, and I have drawn attention to a number of problems which could lead us to doubt that he has succeeded. The first is that his version of ethical particularism leads to 'moral communitarianism', a kind of ethical relativism. The consequence of this relativism is that a community's moral principles and their boundaries of exclusion cannot be justified to those who are excluded, even though they may be harmed by their exclusion. It is hard to see how the charge of irrationalism can be avoided. Following from this, we arrive at a purely internal perspective of whether a group and its internal relationships are morally valuable; a group is an ethical community if it considers itself to be so. There is no position from which to judge which sorts of groups are morally valuable. Miller does not so much argue that nations are ethical communities as assume that they are: a nation is an ethical community just because it is a community. This means that while Miller asserts that what makes a nation is a perceived or imagined shared public *culture*, he is not in a position to reject those who assert that what makes them a nation is a perceived or imagined shared *race*. Nations are ethical communities, and they are all equally ethical however much Miller outlines the content of a morally acceptable national identity. The charge of amoralism still seems to carry a great deal of weight. This means it is hard to see how the idea of the 'nation' can help liberal theory to solve the puzzle of membership. On the specific question of immigration, Miller first leaves us with no resources to identify illiberal immigration controls, and second provides us with an approach which itself has a tendency to collapse towards its nationalist element, towards conservatism. In the next chapter we shall see that Tamir's version of liberal nationalism has a similar tendency to collapse, but in unpredictable directions.

NOTES

1. That this is no longer the case is demonstrated by the now long list of texts on political philosophy and nationalism that lament the fact that political philosophy has neglected the idea of the 'nation'. For now I will cite only two, Margaret Canovan's excellent *Nationhood and Political Theory* (1996); and Ronald Beiner's edited collection of recent work, *Theorizing Nationalism* (1999). Other works will be referred to in this chapter, and/or contained in the bibliography.
2. D. Miller (1995), *On Nationality*, and Y. Tamir (1993), *Liberal Nationalism*.
3. Miller never directly applies the term to his own position: Miller (1995), p. 192; however, I justify this description of his position later in this chapter.
4. Tamir (1993), p. 5.
5. Miller (1995), p. 193.
6. Tamir (1993), p. 14.

7. Tamir (1993), p. 139.
8. Tamir (1993), p. 139.
9. Miller (1995), p. 50.
10. Miller (1995), p. 50.
11. Miller (1995), p. 57.
12. Miller (1995), p. 56.
13. Miller (1995), p. 53.
14. Miller (1995), p. 64.
15. Miller (1995), p. 64.
16. Miller (1995), pp. 64–5.
17. This in itself is, of course, not a *ground* for excluding them from the distribution; it simply removes the duty to justify their exclusion from them. It is perfectly coherent to include beings within the distribution of a moral principle even though they are incapable of being included within its legitimation, e.g. children and non-human animals.
18. To go back to the good aimed to benefit physically disabled people in particular, the point is that even if this particular good was not one able-bodied people *could* benefit from, they could still benefit from the resources invested in its production. This is therefore not an example of the first kind of convergence.
19. Miller (1995), p. 193.
20. S. Avineri and A. de-Shalit (eds) (1992), *Communitarianism and Individualism*, p. 4.
21. A. Buchanan (1998), 'Community and Communitarianism', in E. Craig (ed.), *Routledge Encyclopedia of Philosophy*, p. 465. And also see E. Frazer (1998), 'Communitarianism', in A. Lent (ed.), *New Political Thought: An Introduction*.
22. J. McMahan (1997), 'The Limits of National Partiality', in R. McKim and J. McMahan (eds), *The Morality of Nationalism*.
23. McMahan (1997), p. 108.
24. McMahan (1997), p. 108.
25. McMahan (1997), p. 110.
26. McMahan (1997), p. 108.
27. McMahan (1997), p. 113.
28. Miller (1995), p. 65.
29. Miller (1995), p. 65.
30. Miller (1995), p. 65.
31. Miller (1995), p. 66.
32. Miller (1995), p. 66.
33. Miller (1995), p. 66.
34. Miller (1995), p. 68.
35. Miller (1995), p. 69.
36. Miller (1995), p. 69.
37. S. Caney (1999), 'Nationality, Distributive Justice and the Use of Force', in *Journal of Applied Philosophy*, 16, pp. 123–38, p. 127.
38. McMahan (1997), p. 125.
39. McMahan (1997), p. 114.

40. Miller (1995), p. 25.
41. See D. T. Goldberg (1993), *Racist Culture*, pp. 70–4, and his (1997), *Racial Subjects: Writing on Race in America*, ch. 10.
42. D. M. Weinstock (1996), 'Is there a Moral Case for Nationalism?', *Journal of Applied Philosophy*, 13, pp. 87–100, p. 91.
43. Miller (1995), p. 124.
44. Miller (1995), p. 126.
45. Miller (1995), p. 126.
46. Miller (1995), p. 127.
47. Miller (1995), p. 153.
48. Miller (1995), p. 128.
49. Miller (1995), p. 129.
50. For example the United Kingdom has had conservative immigration policies but has never attempted to block immigration of certain kinds of cultural groups altogether; see S. Castles and M. J. Miller (1998), *The Age of Migration: International Population Movements in the Modern World*, p. 213.
51. Miller (1995), pp. 129–30.
52. H. Van Gunsteren (1987–8), 'Admission to Citizenship', *Ethics*, 98, p. 736; Miller (1995), p. 130, note 15.
53. Miller (1995), p. 124.

Chapter 6

NATIONAL VALUES

—·vvʌʌʌʌⱭⱭⱭⱭⱭvvvv·—

SECTION 1: INTRODUCTION

Whatever the virtues and vices of liberal nationalism in general, our task is to consider it in relation to the question of immigration control. To what extent can restrictions on membership be morally justified by appealing to the 'nation'? If it is to play any role at all in this respect, liberal nationalism's main challenge is to enable us to formulate an idea of national identity which can provide the test for membership. There are two questions to consider here. First, what grounds are there for supposing that an individual's *national* identity ought, for them, to outweigh other forms of identification? Why *should* anybody value their national identity so much that it outweighs the relations they may have at a more local or more global level? So far, we have considered Miller's claim that the nation is an ethical community, but we have noted that this, by itself, does not get us far, for here the idea of 'ethical' is not doing the work we need it to do: Miller hasn't yet shown that the nation is a morally worthwhile form of community. The second question concerns the content and role a national identity can play in liberal politics. How can the content of a national identity be defined in a way that is compatible with liberal principles? I explore the first of these questions in the next section of this chapter, and address the second question in the rest of the chapter.

SECTION 2: CULTURAL NATIONALISM

The first question is why an individual should, from a liberal point of view, value their national identity over other forms of identification, and so prioritise their national relationships over other relationships they have at a more local and global level. There are two possible responses here. The first demands that political philosophy should swallow a dose of realism, and accept that people just *do* value their national identities, and so just do prioritise their national relationships: it is pointless to do political philosophy in a way that does not take this into account. Therefore liberal political philosophy must take the form of liberal nationalism. We can reply, as one always can to realist responses, that this simply misses the point. Whatever people do in practice, the question remains whether they ought to do it: what we are interested in is whether individuals are justified in prioritising national relations. And so there is a second, more philosophical, response, which is to look for an argument which shows that the nation is a particularly valuable form of community, and therefore that national relationships can justifiably be prioritised. The challenge here is to avoid the type of objection that can be raised against communitarian nationalism – that its argument for the priority of the nation is based upon an appeal to the value of community as such, and yet there are evidently more valuable communities than the nation; any reason the communitarian nationalist can find for valuing the nation can be found more coherently and consistently in relation to other more local, or global, forms of community. Nationalists are therefore inconsistent communitarians. Yael Tamir, as we noted, approaches liberal nationalism from the more liberal direction, as opposed to Miller who approaches from the communitarian direction, and so we might hope she avoids this accusation. Indeed, we have grounds for optimism when we note that she argues not from the value of community, but from the value of culture.

Tamir argues that liberal philosophy must recognise the importance of culture in people's lives. While liberal theory emphasises the importance of choice, it often overlooks the fact that individual choice is importantly influenced by cultural frameworks in at least two dimensions. First, the options that are available within a particular community are usually cultural in form: one chooses from a particular cultural range of options. Second, one's set of values is itself going to be influenced by that cultural framework, and therefore the options one chooses will be partially determined by those cultural values. The cultural framework therefore shapes the range of options to choose from, and shapes the range of choices an individual is likely to make. This is no bad thing from a liberal point of view – otherwise it would be difficult to see how one could be a chooser at all in any meaningful sense. The free person is embedded within a cultural community and the range of options from which they choose must be part of the structure of that community in order to be meaningful. Freedom is, therefore, not the absence of a cultural context which constrains choice, but the presence of a particular kind of cultural context which gives choice meaning. Tamir therefore claims that liberal theory must recognise a right to culture – that individuals have the right to 'live within the culture of their choice, to decide on their social affiliations, to re-create the culture of the community they belong to, and to redefine its borders'.[1] She states: 'A right to culture . . . entails the right to a public sphere in which individuals can share a language, memorise their past, cherish their heroes, live a fulfilling national life.'[2] We can see, then, that for Tamir the 'nation' and 'culture' are connected: in fact the nation is to be defined in terms of culture: 'culture, in its widest sense, is what holds a nation together and preserves it as separate from others'.[3] Therefore there must be, for every nation, a 'public sphere where the national culture is expressed'.[4] A national culture is a 'set of specific features that enable members of a nation to distinguish between themselves and others'.[5] Therefore we must see 'nations as cultural communities demarcated by the imaginative power of their members'.[6] We can see that an important element of a national culture is that it is distinctive – it enables those who belong to it to distinguish themselves from others; and this distinctiveness, it seems, is the crucial aspect of a *national* culture. This difference is what enables people to draw a boundary between themselves and others – to *identify* themselves; a national identity therefore rests on cultural difference.

Whatever the virtues of this way of understanding national identity – and we shall see below that it is probably the only way of understanding it – we do not yet know why a national culture should carry the ethical significance placed upon it by liberal nationalism; why should it justify us in prioritising national relationships? So far we have established the value of a cultural framework for the liberal individual, but we have not yet established that the most valuable framework will be the national one. And this, unfortunately, highlights a central weakness in the cultural nationalist argument, that having established the value of culture, it simply assumes that the nation provides the most valuable cultural context. For example, Tamir states:

The ability of individuals to lead a satisfying life and to attain the respect of others is contingent on, although not assured by, their ability to view themselves as active members of a worthy community. A safe, dignified, and flourishing *national* existence thus significantly contributes to their well being.[7]

The danger for the liberal nationalist is that in order to show why a national culture is especially valuable, they have to rely on an over-generalised and romantic conception of the national community, or on examples that are too particular. Tamir does both. First, she claims that the nation provides 'a set of beliefs, interests, and behaviours, as well as a coherent, transparent, and intelligible environment in which individuals can become self-determining'.[8] While we are, of course, arguing at the level of theory here, we can still legitimately ask for any examples of a national identity that is coherent, transparent, intelligible and liberating in the way she describes, because there is a considerable body of evidence to suggest that national identities are simply not the sort of thing that *can* be coherent, transparent, intelligible and liberating. Second, she uses examples from Israeli national identity which are, I feel, overparticular:

> One of the distinctive features of membership in a constitutive community is that members view their self-esteem and well-being as affected by the successes and failures of their individual fellow members and of the group as a whole. Consider, for example, the pride and excitement Israeli-Jews felt when the writer S.Y.Agnon became the first and only Israeli ever to win a Nobel prize, the elation on the streets of Tel-Aviv when the Israeli basketball team defeated the Soviet team in the 1970s, and the country's delight when the Israeli representative became Miss Universe.[9]

For any of these, we can pose telling counter examples. First, I am not in a position to judge that the Israeli 'nation' was delighted at 'their' victory in the Miss Universe contest, but in many similar cases it is not implausible to suggest that there might be national indifference rather than delight, and that any delight that did get expressed was a media construction. Second, it is perfectly possible to take delight in another nation's victory over one's own, for all sorts of good reasons, and it would be dangerously reactionary to suggest that one was doing anything ethically dubious in such cases. Third, one may react not with indifference or delight when a co-national prospers, but with dismay, because one may not accept them as a genuine representative of one's nation. For example, the Israeli 'nation' was not delighted when Dana

International triumphed in the 1998 Eurovision Song Contest – rather, a significant section of that community was outraged, having difficulty in seeing her as a legitimate representative of their nation because of her transexuality. We can see, then, that Tamir is overstating the importance of national connection, in that she takes it as obvious that any individual will or ought to be (and in a sense this disjunction is centrally important to the argument) delighted at a co-national's success. And at the same time, and more importantly, she underestimates the complexity of national identity: whether or not an individual is a genuine representative of the 'nation' can be highly controversial, and can give rise to deeply reactionary responses. We should note that she herself refers to the excitement of Israeli-Jews in one of her examples, rather than Israelis as such. To go back to the crucial disjunction, it is not obvious that people just do identify with co-nationals in these cases – very often they just don't. And if the liberal nationalist argument is that we *ought* to identify with co-nationals in this way, this has dangerous and reactionary implications. There may be all sorts of good reasons why other aspects of identity, more local *or* more global, should take priority in particular cases.

There is a vast body of theory on national identity which shows why the treatment it gets in liberal nationalist writing is oversimplistic.[10] All I can do here is stress once more the dangerous territory liberal nationalists have entered. If their claim is that people just do prioritise co-nationals over others, they are vulnerable to counter examples and the charge that they are missing the ethical point. If their claim, however, is that people *ought* to prioritise co-nationals over others, they are vulnerable to dangerously reactionary readings of such a claim. Of course, the central claim we are exploring is that the nation is a particularly valuable form of association, and it is this value that justifies individuals in prioritising national relationships. But the problem is that, despite searching for that value, we have not yet found it, or at least not any value that can carry the considerable moral weight liberal nationalism is placing upon it. There is an essential weakness at the heart of the appeal to culture, which Alan Patten highlights.[11] According to Patten, the argument for cultural nationalism has four stages:

1. Individual autonomy is a fundamental value within liberal theory.
2. A liberal state must establish the conditions for this autonomy.
3. A meaningful range of options requires a cultural framework.

Therefore:

4. The liberal state ought to promote a national culture.

However, Patten notes that we can only move to the conclusion on the assumption that '"national" cultures are important to their members' autonomy'.[12] Without this assumption, all we have is an argument for the importance of cultural frameworks for individual choice, but not one which demonstrates the importance of a *national* culture. The picture the liberal nationalist presents us with is once more an over-simplified one, in which an individual's choices are only meaningful for them if they are made within a range of options represented by their national culture; or at least the *most* meaningful options are national ones. A far more realistic picture is one in which individuals can find choices that are deeply meaningful for them in a range of cultural frameworks, national or otherwise: choices can be multi-cultural, or culturally hybrid, and still remain meaningful. We have very little reason to suppose that a national culture offers individuals their most meaningful life choices. Of course, liberal nationalists may be able to appeal to particular cases where their view holds true; but first, in any such case there are going to be complexities and dangers in how it is read, and so it can always be questioned whether any particular case *is* a true example; and second, any such cases are surely going to be much too rare to ground a general theory of nationality.

The charge remains that the liberal nationalist argument oversimpli-fies the nature of a national culture: the way in which it is undergoing constant reinvention, relying on fictions and forgettings, the way in which it is the product of manipulation and exclusion. Instead, we get a picture of a national culture that has historical depth and authenticity, and, most importantly, has been shaped by individual choice. Putting aside these problems, the most we can say for the argument from individual choice is that it shows that the liberal state should promote a rich and diverse cultural background.

In the end, the cultural nationalist faces a problem similar to that of the communitarian nationalist. From the communitarian perspective the nationalist is inconsistent because there are more coherent, cohesive and authentic communities available than the nation, and so the appeal to the value of community cannot justify the nationalist position. The appeal to culture fails on similar grounds: we have no reason to suppose that a national culture will be overridingly valuable, in the face of the evidence of the impossibility and arbitrariness of fixing a culture as representative of the nation. It seems, then, that a cultural understanding of the nation cannot bear the weight placed upon it by the liberal nationalist; it cannot fix the nation as the central focus for political, social, economic or even cultural association.

To an important extent, Tamir would agree with this conclusion, as the nation-*state* as such has no place in her version of liberal nationalism. She does not believe in the possibility of the 'homogeneous and viable nation-state'.[13] Instead, she favours some form of 'regionalism':

> [T]he move from the centralized nation-state, anxious to present itself as representing a homogeneous nation, to regional or international organizations that are explicitly multinational will ease the pressure on minorities and help to ensure their rights and interests within the larger frameworks.[14]

This leads some to question whether Tamir is any sort of nationalist. According to Ronald Beiner, 'in Tamir's statement of the liberal-nationalist case, the nationalist side of the equation is so watered down that the nationalism in her political theory is barely detectable'.[15] He concludes:

> It seems to me quite misleading to call this a version of nationalism; a more accurate description of her position is: liberalism, with an attention to the ways in which people care about national identity and wish to see it expressed in some fashion.[16]

This is, I think, an important response, for the whole weight of the argument is to show why the nation as such has value, and therefore why one is justified in valuing one's co-nationals over others. And this, one assumes, means valuing them over others with respect to politics, economics and social policy as well as culture. If the only respect in which we value fellow members of our nation over others is with respect to their taste in culture, one is left wondering whether the idea of the nation has much important work to do in political theory. Tamir's vision is of

> a world in which traditional nation-states wither away, surrendering their power to make economic, strategic, and ecological decisions to regional organisations and their power to structure cultural policies to local national communities.[17]

There is, therefore, this division of labour between regional authorities which deal with economic, strategic and ecological questions, and national communities which deal with cultural policy. But this distinction, which seems to be absolutely fundamental to Tamir's whole project, is simply unsustainable. In an important sense, it actually *underestimates* the importance of culture, in that it supposes that economic, strategic and ecological issues are somehow culture-free.

But whatever one thinks of Tamir's nationalist credentials, the overriding problem has been to find a reason to morally value the 'nation' that has some credibility within the framework of liberal political theory. At the beginning of this section I outlined two replies. The first was the realist response, that people just do value their nation and do prioritise national relations over others, and so political philosophy had better take account of this. The second was the philosophical response, to find an argument to show that people are morally justified in prioritising national relations. However, we have seen reasons to doubt that the philosophical response gets us much further than the realist response. In the end, when we pose the question: why should a national culture be held to be morally valuable?, we get a reply that looks suspiciously like the realist response – that people just do value their national culture as a resource; and this may not be the sort of answer we were looking for. It may still be replied that while this is not the sort of answer we were looking for, it is still the only answer available; but this is far from clear. We are presented with a picture of a national identity which is coherent, transparent, intelligible, inclusive, unifying, liberating, and which presents its individual members with the most fulfilling, meaningful options for their life choices. For the liberal nationalist to claim that political philosophy, by taking such a conception of national identity into account, is taking a more *realistic* picture of the political landscape strikes me as extremely bizarre. And yet we shall see that this duality – between liberal nationalism's demand for realism in political philosophy and its idealised, abstracted conception of nationalism and national identity – is a theme that runs through its core.

SECTION 3: LIBERAL NATIONALITY – DAVID MILLER

In the rest of this chapter I will explore this duality in relation to attempts to establish a liberal national identity. If liberal nationalism is to provide a justification of membership controls, it needs to provide a national identity that can be used to distinguish between insiders and outsiders. In this section I examine David Miller's version of a liberal national identity, and in the next section return to Yael Tamir's account. Central to David Miller's project is the claim that a national identity can be both rationally and ethically defensible: 'it may properly be part of someone's identity that they belong to this or that national grouping'.[18] For Miller, nationality differs from other forms of identity in five ways: (1) nationalities are constituted by belief – people have to believe that they share a nationality in order for it to exist at all; (2) there has to be historical continuity, such that present members feel loyalty and obligations to past and future generations; (3) nationality is an active identity, in that nations are 'communities that do things';[19] (4) a national identity 'connects a group of people to a geographical place', in terms of a homeland;[20] and (5) a national identity 'requires that the people who share it should have something in common', rather than seeing themselves as a group thrown together by circumstances – they must believe that they 'belong together by virtue of the characteristics they share'.[21]

It is the nature of this 'something in common' which is crucial and problematic. For Miller, rather than biology or any physical characteristic, what people share is a 'common public culture' which is 'compatible with their belonging to a diversity of ethnic groups'.[22] The national identity will emerge from this common public culture. What I hope to show is that Miller offers a highly normative conception of a national identity, which in effect rules out its application in practice. There are three elements to this normative conception: (1) a public/private distinction; (2) a position on the legitimate role of invention; and (3) a view of authenticity. However, we should note that Miller has already supplied a preliminary normative test of an acceptable national identity – that it should not be based on supposed shared biology, and therefore should not be racist.[23]

1. The Public/Private Distinction

Miller asserts that the common public culture needed for a national identity to emerge need not be 'monolithic and all-embracing'.[24] Rather, we should see it as a 'set of understandings about how a group of people is to conduct its life together'.[25] How far this public culture extends can vary; it includes political principles, but Miller allows that it can have other elements such as language and religion. However, it should not intrude into private cultures: for example, food, dress and music 'are not normally part of the public culture that defines nationality'.[26]

There is, therefore, a boundary between the public culture of the nation and private cultures, and national identity is formed and applied within the space of public culture. If we interpret 'citizenship' broadly, we could understand the public culture as the way we relate to each other as citizens, as long as we note how fluid the public/private boundary can be. The good citizen is therefore not necessarily one who merely adheres to political principles, but could also be someone who exhibits certain cultural characteristics, such as language and religion. Miller rejects what he describes as 'constitutional patriotism' as insufficient to ground a political community.[27]

The crucial point here is that the boundary is contested, and while Miller observes that things like food, dress and music are not 'normally' part of the public culture that defines a national identity, there is nothing here to rule out their inclusion in principle, especially if language and religion qualify: indeed, we know from experience that food, dress and music have played a very central role in constituting national identities. The point is that here Miller is in fact asserting his second normative test: that national identities can be judged on the extent to which they intrude into what ought to be regarded as private space – and that Miller's preferred private/public boundary is a more-or-less liberal conception. He says:

> [N]ational identities are not all-embracing, and . . . the common public culture that they require may have room for many private cultures to flourish within the borders of the nation.[28]

While, on the surface, this can be read as a descriptive account of national identities, I think it more plausible to see it as importantly prescriptive of a morally acceptable national identity.

2. Myth and History

It is in his discussion of myth and history that Miller confronts the issue of the rationality of national identities. Given the fact that much of the creation of a national identity involves 'veil-drawing' over what actually took place,[29] and that 'national identities typically contain a considerable element of myth',[30] it surely follows that they cannot be rationally defended.

> If one applies to them normal canons of rationality, they are revealed to be fraudulent. It seems to follow that there can be no justification for giving national loyalties any role in our ethical and political thinking.[31]

Miller's case is that this rejection is too quick: 'it may not be rational to discard beliefs, even if they are, strictly speaking, false, when they can be shown to contribute significantly to the support of valuable social relations'.[32] If we are talking in terms of national myths, then the fact is these play a valuable role. They 'provide reassurance that the national community of which one now forms a part is solidly based in history, that it embodies a real continuity between generations';[33] and 'they perform a moralizing role, by holding before us the virtues of our ancestors and encouraging us to live up to them'.[34] And so, if nations are ethical communities, then 'it seems very likely that their ethical character will be strengthened by the acceptance of such myths'.[35]

It is important to be clear here that what is rationally justified by this argument is someone's *holding* a belief, not the content of the belief itself. Miller's point is that it would be irrational to discard a belief where it has instrumental value, even though we are aware that it is false. There are two possible perspectives from which the belief can be rationally justified in this (limited) way: an external and an internal perspective. From an external perspective, it may be rational from B's point of view for A to hold belief X, which B knows to be false, given the value of the belief to A or B (we do not need to assume that B is self-interested – it may be in A's interests to continue to believe X). From an internal perspective, we would have to argue that it is rational from A's point of view to hold belief X, because of its use value, when they know that X is false. While the external perspective is perfectly understandable, the internal perspective is more puzzling, because it seems to involve a contradiction. If one knows a belief is false, one cannot then believe it, in that belief is a commitment to the truth of what is believed. Therefore A does not believe X in that he or she knows it to be false, but at the same time he or she does believe X because of its use value. And so this kind of self-deception looks puzzling. We have to remember, of course, that when it comes to national identity we are not talking about individuals but the community as a whole, but it is not clear that this helps to solve the puzzle. At the community level, what matters is that *all* members know that certain beliefs that constitute the national identity are false, but that they continue to believe them. If any individual members hold these beliefs to be true, they must be enlightened. If this is not done, then we have a divided community in which a certain section is being deceived by those who know the belief to be false. While this latter scenario is much easier to make sense of, it will not do for Miller because he explicitly rejects any such manipulation of any section of the population – all members must be aware of the falsity of the beliefs in question.

We can have two reactions to the contradiction we have identified.

The first is that to be concerned about it is to be overly analytic, and this may not be an appropriate approach – perhaps a more psychological or existential account can make better sense here; for example, we could see it as a form of Sartrean bad faith, or Freudian repression. However, while it is strikingly illuminating to see nationalism as bad faith, the fact remains that Sartre's notion is held to be deeply flawed precisely because it involves the same contradiction; and Freud's account of repression is equally unhelpful because it involves splitting the consciousness in two, such that we have A being deceived by B, rather than A being deceived by A.[36] A second problem is that, for Miller's argument to keep its grip on the claim that national identity is rational, A must be fully conscious of what he or she is doing, and so in a sense not deceived at all. As we have seen, it is perfectly clear that it can be rational for B to deceive A into continuing to hold a false belief; but what we have to show is that it is rational for A to 'deceive' A.

The second response to the contradiction involved in this self-deception is to re-describe the situation. A knows that a proposition is false (he or she does not believe it), but he or she does believe that it has a use value, and therefore they continue to act as though it were true. There is no contradiction here, and no self-deception.[37] However, for this to make sense, we have to consider what value such a false belief can have which justifies us in acting as though it were true. Two obvious answers suggest themselves. First, it may be that acting in this way is in itself valuable, and the false belief motivates us to act in this way. But this brings back puzzlement when we ask how a false belief can motivate someone to act in a particular way, when he or she is fully aware of its falsity. The second, and perhaps better, answer is that the belief makes the national identity valuable for us – it leads us to value our nation and ourselves; it helps us to feel good about the national project. But still, there is a nagging puzzlement. If we know that these beliefs are strictly speaking false, then we must be in a position to know the facts of the matter, what really happened. Therefore in continuing to act as though these false beliefs were true, at the same time we act as if some set of events never happened. We can assume that these events, the more accurate account of our national history, must be unpalatable, in order for us to go to the extent of fabricating an alternative narrative we know is false. What can justify this odd kind of self-deception? It can only be that the national project is held to be so valuable that any unpalatable facts must be 'forgotten' and new fictions created to replace them. But we can ask two questions here. First, is the national project so valuable that we need a fictional past – why not face up to the truth? Second, this remains a strange account of a *rational* national identity – that we are fully aware of the historical facts, and at the same time act as though they were false and some other account were true. What is odd here is that we are not acting in this way in order to deceive anybody but ourselves: and the question returns, why should we need to do that?

And so, even if we avoid the problem of contradiction involved in this self-deception, we face other puzzles. To what extent can a proposition the community is fully aware is false motivate its members to act in a particular way? How are members to balance two different accounts of their nation, one of which they know to be true and the other to be false, and then act as though the false one was true? Miller illustrates his point with what he takes to be a representative example of a false belief playing a valuable role in a national identity. That example is Dunkirk, the evacuation of British troops from mainland Europe in 1940, after their defeat by German forces.[38] Now, Miller reads the Dunkirk 'myth' in a particular way:

> It was taken to show, on the one hand, the instinctive solidarity of the British people in the face of a national crisis; on the other hand, it revealed something distinctive about their character: their ability to improvise a solution to a problem without being ordered to do so by some[one] higher-up.[39]

But this is not the general reading of the Dunkirk myth usually found in the narrative of British national identity – rather, Dunkirk was represented as a great victory in the face of apparent defeat.[40] The example of Dunkirk is actually unhelpful to Miller's argument here, in that it was created by an act of mass deception by the British government and media;[41] it is an example of A being deceived by B, rather than A's self-deception. And the likelihood is that appeals to Dunkirk by British politicians and others still rely on that deception, in that Dunkirk is still regarded in 'popular' history as a victory rather than the defeat it really was; the negative account of Dunkirk is not one that is widely known, and if it were it may be that its 'mythical' power would dissolve.

However, we should note that Miller moves on from considering strictly speaking false beliefs, and claims instead that national myths more often fill in empty spaces. 'Normally the imagined history fills in blanks where no direct evidence is (or even could be) available.'[42] This disposes of the puzzles, in that now there is no unpalatable account of the national history that members need to 'forget'; rather, there is simply the need to fill an empty space in the narrative of the nation. For Miller, the real distinction is not between true and false histories, but between 'national identities that emerge through open processes of debate and discussion to which everyone is potentially a contributor, and identities that are authoritatively imposed by repression and indoctrination'.[43] In the former case:

> [T]he collective sense of national identity may be expected to change over time, and, although at any moment some of its components may be mythical in the sense I have indicated, they are very unlikely indeed to invoke the outright denial of historical fact.[44]

In the end, for Miller, 'the historical accuracy of national stories seems to matter less in its own right than for the effect it has in the nation's present self-understanding'.[45]

Here, then, Miller has shifted from a concern about the content of a national identity, to a concern about the process that gave rise to it, and is arguing that the process is more important than the content. However, before we go on to examine this process, the fact is that Miller has provided us with the third normative test of national identity: there is an acceptable level of historical myth; as long as it does not amount to denial of historical facts, some level of myth-spinning is permissible. Putting aside the problem of judging what level of spin is acceptable, we should note that the practice of filling empty spaces in the national narrative rather than trying to cover up certain distasteful truths does not give us free reign to paint positive pictures of ourselves. The fact is that someone's history always involves someone else. Therefore what becomes distorted is not merely 'our' role in history, but also 'their' role, in that the former is sanitised while the latter is most usually demonised. If such demonisation of the other is ruled unacceptable in our national mythologies, then the normative requirements for an acceptable national identity become even more stringent.

3. Authenticity

As we have seen, for Miller it is not so much the content of the national identity that matters, as the process through which it is formed:

> To the extent that the process involves inputs from all sections of the community, with groups openly competing to imprint the

common identity with their own particular image, we may justifiably regard the identity that emerges as an authentic one.[46]

It is true that no national identity is pristine, 'but there is still a large
difference between those that have evolved more or less spontaneously,
and those that are mainly the result of political imposition'.[47]

It is here that Miller's nationalism takes an explicitly liberal form. The
national identity is not authoritative and is open to critical assessment
– it can change over time:

> Ideally, the process of change should consist in a collective conver-
> sation in which many voices can join. No voice has a privileged
> status: those who seek to defend traditional interpretations enter
> the conversation on an equal footing with those who want to
> propose changes.[48]

For this conversation to take place, liberal freedoms are needed:[49]

> Without freedom of conscience and expression, one cannot
> explore different interpretations of national identity, something
> that takes place not only in political forums, but in the various
> associations that make up civil society.[50]

This conception of nationality is liberal in the sense that:

> [T]he freedoms and rights defended by liberals are valued here as
> the means whereby individuals can develop and express their
> ethnic and other group identities, while at the same time taking
> part in an ongoing collective debate about what it means to be a
> member of this nation.[51]

It seems, then, that the authenticity of the national identity will depend
on the extent to which it is the result of what we might characterise as
free and equal contestation between groups. Clearly, Miller is providing
us here with the fourth normative test for judging the acceptability
of a nationality: it must be authentic, and for that to be achieved, the
public culture through which it emerges has to be liberal. The most
obvious problem here is that this test sets too high a standard. We
have to be in a position to judge that the contestation that gave rise
to a particular national identity was free and equal, with little or no
manipulation by powerful elites. It would be interesting to know
whether we are in a position to make such a judgement for any
particular national identity, and what would be revealed if we were.

The second problem is that we have to remember that in constituting
a 'we', an association at the same time constitutes a 'they', and this

happens without democratic consultation with those constituted as 'other'. It is important for Miller that the common public culture is a site of free and equal contestation between groups, but there is a radical sense in which this cannot happen, in that those constituted as outsiders have either had their input into the process ignored or overpowered, or have had no democratic input at all. Miller seems to present a picture of the process of constituting a national identity that is one-sided, simply a matter of inclusion: a group of people examine themselves to see what they value in common, and it is this body of values that constitute them as a nation. But this simply cannot be true, because what is emphasised over and over again in discussions of nationalism, liberal or otherwise, is that what is vital to the process is the ability to distinguish one's nationality from others. To return to Tamir, a national culture is a 'set of specific features that enable members of a nation to distinguish between themselves and others';[52] and as J. A. Armstrong comments: 'groups tend to define themselves not by reference to their own characteristics but by exclusion, that is, by comparison to "strangers"'.[53] Therefore the process of creating a national identity has two elements: constructing a set of values that all members of the nation can be taken to share, and, crucially, which non-members can be taken not to share. As I commented above, one problem with this is the extent to which, just as members of the nation create a fictional narrative of their own history, they necessarily create a fictional account of the history of others. But the problem here is that, in setting aside this aspect of the formation of national identities, Miller seems to have overlooked that it is importantly a process of *exclusion*. We could assume that those excluded have had a fair opportunity in the contest for inclusion in the national identity, but such an assumption remains alarmingly groundless.

To conclude this section, Miller's project is to show that nationality can play a legitimate role in liberal political philosophy. However, I have been concerned to show that it is implausible to see his project as purely descriptive, telling us what national identities are like in practice and how they actually work; rather, it is strongly prescriptive, telling us what a national identity *must* be like if it is to be acceptable within a liberal framework. He has therefore offered us a number of normative tests for a national identity: it must not be racist; it must have an acceptable balance between public and private culture; there is an acceptable role for historical fiction and myth-spinning; and it must arise through a free and equal process of public contestation – it must be authentic.

There are three difficulties here. First, if Miller's conception of nationality is to be of practical use, we need a clearer specification of these criteria so that we can apply them to actual national identities. Second, even if we succeed in filling out the details, there may be no actual national identities that meet the normative requirements; Miller's standards for acceptability may be too exacting. The most we can say is that in principle a national identity can be constructed that would be acceptable to liberal theory, but in practice no actual national identities are acceptable – and this means Miller's project cannot help us with any of the real problems that nations and nationalities give rise to. A more severe response would be to say that it is no surprise that actual national identities fail to meet Miller's normative criteria, because those criteria are essentially liberal, and in practice national identities are illiberal phenomena. Overall, the problem is that the liberal nationalist is proposing that liberal political philosophy needs to be more realistic by taking nations and national identities into account; and yet the idea of the nation and national identity they propose is itself idealised and abstracted from reality.

There is a third, deeper problem that we also encountered in the previous chapter. We have seen that Miller starts out specifying the acceptable content of a nationality, and ends up specifying the acceptable process through which a nationality is constituted. The content criteria are that it should be non-racist, non-intrusive and fictional within limits; the process criteria are that it must be arrived at through free and equal contestation through liberal institutions. We can ask which is most important, the content or the process? If it is the process, we have to allow the possibility that it could give rise to a nationality of a completely different content. It could be replied that any national identity that arose through the process Miller describes would have the sort of content he prescribes; but is there any reason to suppose this? If a community arrives at a self-conception which its members believe to be authentic and valuable to its social formation, how can outsiders be in a position to judge its content?

SECTION 4: LIBERAL NATIONALITY – YAEL TAMIR

If national identity is going to play any role in immigration control, then it has to play a role in distinguishing between people who are 'like us' in the relevant respects, and those who fail to be 'like us'. The question then is, of course, like us in what respects? We have seen that for the liberal nationalist it appears that the content of national identity is filled not by ethnicity, but by a specific kind of culture – a public political culture. In a liberal polity this will be a culture of liberal politics. But importantly it includes those cultural features of *this* liberal polity. In other words, there will not be a 'universal' national identity shared by all members of all liberal polities, but rather each individual liberal polity will have its own distinct national identity.

This becomes clear if we return to Yael Tamir's account. She believes that some restrictions on membership are justified, given that 'individuals have a right to preserve the uniqueness of their communal life'.[54] For a liberal polity this means preserving its liberal political culture. Tamir draws on Bruce Ackerman,[55] who argues that a liberal state is an arena of public dialogue. Anybody capable of participating in the liberal dialogue is eligible as a member. On the face of it, this seems to present the possibility of a universal political identity for all members of liberal states. But Ackerman goes on to say that in order to be capable of participating, their utterances have to be 'translatable': they have to be comprehensible to other members. Tamir reads this as implying that 'beyond an ability to understand the terms of participation, and beyond the willingness to take part in a liberal discourse, membership in a liberal state demands an ability to share in the ruling culture; it demands that members share certain cultural features that facilitate a deeper type of understanding'.[56] For Tamir, 'in order to engage in a fruitful dialogue, citizens of a liberal state must agree not only on the principles of their discourse, but must also share some sort of cultural and social background'.[57] We saw in the previous section that Miller holds a similar view: the common public culture goes beyond political principles, and includes cultural characteristics.

Tamir makes it clear that this means there are two levels to a liberal national identity:

1. General civic competence – the readiness and the ability to communicate, argue, and discuss matters with fellow citizens, and to form judgments on the basis of this dialogue.
2. A shared culture and identity – the competence to act as a member of *this* particular society.[58]

Therefore on immigration, she concludes that: 'Prospective citizens must be able and willing to be members of this particular historical community, its past, its future, its forms of life and institutions.'[59] And: 'A state that views itself as a community is justified in offering citizenship only to those committed to respect its communal values, collective history, and shared aspirations for a prosperous future.'[60]

We can see, then, that liberal nationalist identity has two elements: (1) general civic competence; and (2) specific cultural competence. Prospective members have to be able to participate in both elements. If we return to the question: how is membership to be policed?, then the difficulties begin to emerge. If we focus on the first element – general civic competence – then we can ask how potential immigrants are to be tested for this. A liberal polity with its commitment to individualism would not, of course, define, any *group* as generally incapable of possessing this competence, and therefore judgements would have to be made in each individual case. One possibility is to test individual applicants for membership on the border; but still, the question remains – how? Those familiar with the use of IQ testing on potential immigrants to the United States of America after the 1924 Immigration Restriction Act will not merely be puzzled, but alarmed, about the possible fairness of any such test.[61] A second problem, beyond fairness, is the effectiveness of such testing. How are we supposed to detect that applicants are telling the truth? If our aim is to preserve our liberal political culture by excluding, for example, fascists, why do we think they would parade their fascism open to view? In a liberal state one can easily conceal one's political commitments when one needs to; the intrusive methods needed to force people to 'confess' their politics are not an option for the liberal, and one assumes that such 'McCarthyism' remains totally unacceptable on the border.[62] The most the liberal polity could demand may be a declaration of intent to abide by the liberal constitution, but this falls short of the liberal nationalist position on two grounds. First, it seems relevant only in the context of the sort of thin 'constitutional patriotism' the liberal nationalist would reject. Second, Tamir makes it clear that what we need to ascertain before admission is not merely intent, but competence, and therefore some sort of test is required; to allow people to simply declare that they are competent will surely not do.

The issue is that the differences that need to be detected for this political identity to be effective – political beliefs and commitments – are, in a liberal state, in principle invisible, and so at this level the liberal nationalist has provided an identity that is impossible to detect without the violation of fundamental liberal principles. To enforce it would get us straight to the liberal dilemma on immigration: that liberal principles operate within the polity, but non-liberal ones – and in this case clearly illiberal ones – operate at the border. Of course, the second level of national identity then comes into play: the readiness and willingness to participate in *this* particular polity's customs and practices. Of course, for this to solve the problem, the criteria that fall under this second level must be legitimately visible, as opposed to other features that are visible but which cannot be legitimately used to form a political identity, such as skin colour: the latter kind of feature must remain, politically speaking, in principle invisible. One obvious candidate for the former kind of feature may be the ability to speak the state's official language, which is taken to be essential if one is to participate in political dialogue. The liberal nationalist may reject the use of the kinds of visible difference they would identify as 'ethnic', but other visible but non-ethnic differences can be relied upon here.

In fact, once we move beyond language, it becomes difficult to fix upon any more visible but non-ethnic differences that could be legitimately used to police membership in a liberal polity.[63] Tamir talks of a commitment to respect communal values, collective history and institutions, but both problems that apply to the first level of identity apply here. First, how can we fairly test prospective members for familiarity with such things? Second, even where we can, we have no way of telling that prospective members are telling the truth: the illiberal will have no difficulty in pretending to meet these criteria. A third, and fundamental, problem arises: that these features are no guide at all to a commitment to liberal politics and practice – for example the ability to speak the official state language. So at both levels the liberal nationalist has provided a political identity that is, in principle, invisible and so impossible to detect, except by illiberal methods.

Tamir almost concedes as much when she raises the problem of what to do with someone who is already a member, for example by birth, but who does not share the commitment to liberal politics.[64] Deportation is not a liberal option. For Tamir: 'Those born and educated within the state, who were trained to see it as their own, are therefore preferred as future members.'[65] The liberal polity therefore prefers the resident fascist to the liberal applicant.[66] In the end, the suspicion is that those who would be excluded are not so much illiberals, such as fascists, but those who are simply unfamiliar with liberal politics and practice. From the perspective of those doing the preferring, this amounts to a preference to those who are familiar to us over the unfamiliar, and the fascist is at least familiar to as well as familiar with liberal politics and practice. This rejection of the unfamiliar, rather than those explicitly opposed to liberal politics and practice, is, of course, much more difficult to define and rationally and ethically defend from a liberal point of view.

SECTION 5: VISIBLE DIFFERENCES

This brings us to the most complex difficulty for liberal nationalism. For its version of national identity to work, it must somehow be detectable, and must therefore appeal to some kinds of visible differences. Reliance on only the first element of its national identity gives us a political identity which is too thin: what we might call 'liberal constitutionalism', simply the commitment to a liberal political constitution. However, the liberal nationalist would also reject political identities that are too thick: what has been called 'ethnic nationalism'. Liah Greenfeld makes the distinction between civic and ethnic nationalism in her historical study *Nationalism: Five Roads to Modernity*.[67] Civic nationalism is 'identical with citizenship',[68] while ethnic nationalism 'is believed to be inherent', such that 'it has nothing to do with individual will, but constitutes a genetic characteristic'.[69] If this distinction is to be helpful here it has to be revised, in that while proponents of an ethnic nationalism may often regard their ethnicity as a matter of fixed biology, theorists would reject such a view and regard ethnicity as a matter of culture.[70] If we regard liberal politics and practice as a form of public political culture, and ethnicity also as a set of cultural practices, then both civic and ethnic nationalism are types of cultural nationalism. Another ground for questioning the civic/ ethnic nationalism distinction is that any *national* identity will have ethnic elements. David Miller is clear that ethnicity is a matter of culture, and therefore that ethnicity and nationality cannot be clearly separated:

> Both nations and ethnic groups are bodies of people bound together by common cultural characteristics and mutual recognition; moreover there is no sharp dividing line between them.[71]

What we have, then, are not two different types of nationalism, ethnic or civic, but different degrees of cultural nationalism, from 'thin' to 'thick'.

Liberal nationalism is therefore negotiating a space between the too-thin version of liberal constitutionalism – which is hardly a nationalism at all – and the too-thick version of ethnic nationalism. Daniel Weinstock warns that this negotiation is fraught with danger, and that:

[T]he sense of historical and traditional continuity upon which both Miller and Tamir want to insist as a condition for the existence of a nation is one that 'non-native' members of the nation cannot possibly be asked to share. Insisting upon this condition in the face of this impossibility risks collapsing the notion of civic nationalism into ethnic nationalism, and relaxing it involves the risk of ridding the notion of any recognisably 'nationalist' content whatsoever.[72]

However, this is not to say this space is impossible to negotiate – but how is liberal nationalism to prevent itself from becoming too thick? One obvious strategy is to refuse to include ethnic features, but this is only feasible if we assume a biologically essentialist view of ethnicity; once we allow that ethnicity is constituted by a body of cultural beliefs and practices it becomes difficult to draw any clear boundary here. A second, more plausible, strategy is to appeal to a public/private – rather than a cultural/biological – divide.

We saw in Section 3 that this strategy is adopted by David Miller: a nationality is a common *public* culture, and while its boundaries can vary to include elements like language and religion, it does not normally include, for example, food, dress and music. From this point of view, what is wrong with ethnic nationalism – putting aside its confusion about the nature of ethnicity – is that it intrudes too far into the private sphere. Or rather, it brings into the public realm, and so makes visible, aspects of life that liberals traditionally consider to be a private matter, and therefore in principle invisible. It therefore exerts control over membership by appeal to factors that people have the right not to have taken into account. Political identity, and therefore the national identity which is used to police membership, must appeal only to those features that legitimately belong in the public sphere. The problem with this strategy is, of course, that the public/private boundary is contested. It is not that liberal constitutionalism and ethnic nationalism do not have a public/private boundary – rather, they put it in radically different places. The challenge for liberal nationalists, if they are to avoid Weinstock's charge, is to find some way to anchor the public/private distinction where they wish it to be.

The issue, then, is what constitutes political identity, that identity one must possess if one is to be a legitimate member of a particular polity. Liberal nationalism's objection to what we have termed liberal constitutionalism is that its political identity is too thin: it will be shared by all members of all states that have a recognisably liberal constitution. The implication of this for membership is that a citizen of a particular liberal state will also be considered a citizen of any other liberal state, and will therefore have freedom of movement between such states. What is needed, therefore, is a *national* identity, which embeds the liberal citizen within a *particular* liberal state. However, the liberal nationalist objection to ethnic nationalism is not so clear, and this is where Weinstock's concerns become apparent. The objection can only be that ethnic nationalism brings into the public sphere considerations that properly belong in the private realm, but that would precisely be the liberal constitutionalist's objection to liberal nationalism. It is not possible for the liberal nationalist to object that the ethnic nationalist brings in features that are 'ethnic' and therefore inadmissible, because there is no clear distinction to be made here. Again Miller is clear that we cannot simply decide that all issues of ethnicity are to be regarded as a 'private cultural phenomenon', because 'nationalist identities invariably contain some ethnic ingredients'[73] – and that includes liberal nationalist identities. The only defence for liberal nationalism must be that the features it identifies are legitimately public while the features identified by the ethnic nationalist are not.

The only way to make this defence is to argue that the features identified by liberal nationalism are essential for the welfare of the polity in question, while the features identified by the ethnic nationalist are not; but it is not at all clear how such a defence can be mounted, except on a case-by-case basis. And even then it is not clear who is to adjudicate. For example, Miller argues that the state needs to protect its common public culture: its national culture. The elements of a national culture 'very often have an essentially public dimension: they concern features of a society whose existence is dependent upon political action'[74] – for example, architecture, landscape, television and film. 'If these are going to express and reproduce a common culture, they will have to be made subject to collective control.'[75] Therefore we are justified in using the power of the state 'to protect aspects that are judged to be important'.[76] The role of the state is 'to provide an environment in which the culture can develop spontaneously rather than being eroded by economically self-interested actions on the part of particular individuals', rather than to 'impose some preformed definition of national culture'.[77] Therefore the state can justifiably be non-neutral when it comes to the national culture: 'where some cultural feature – a landscape, a musical tradition, a language – has become a component part of national identity, it is justifiable to discriminate in its favour if the need arises'.[78]

First, we should note that while Miller says the role of the state is to allow culture to develop spontaneously by protecting it from being determined by economic interests, the examples he gives are to do with preservation rather than innovation – landscape, architecture, a musical tradition. Second, and more important with respect to this discussion, we can see how the public/private boundary here lacks any anchor: on page 26 of Miller's text music is not 'normally part of the public culture that defines nationality', but by page 195 a musical tradition could 'become a component part of national identity'. The public realm can therefore expand to include, in principle, *any* cultural feature depending upon the circumstances. Although Miller does not connect what he says here to the issue of immigration, we can see that the political identity required by liberal nationalism can take on an ever more expansive content, which seems to show that Weinstock's warning was well made.

SECTION 6: CONCLUSION

Tamir's claim that liberal theory's appropriation of nationalism has circumvented 'such thorny issues as membership and immigration'[79] no longer looks clear cut. I have argued that if a polity is to police membership it needs to establish a political identity that all prospective members must meet. For liberal nationalism, a commitment only to liberal constitutional politics and practice is too thin, and would lead to a political identity which would be too widely shared. However, ethnic nationalism is too thick, and would lead to a political identity which excludes others on unacceptable grounds. Liberal nationalism seeks to establish a national identity which will be shared by members and prospective members of a *particular* polity. However, we have seen that in order to establish this, a liberal nationalist identity will have two elements: first, the commitment to liberal constitutional politics and practice; and second, a commitment to the historical and cultural practices of this particular liberal polity. I have argued that this leads liberal nationalism into a dilemma. Either its interpretation of both these elements is too thin, in which case the political identity it establishes remains invisible, and therefore of no use when it comes to policing membership – it relies on the detection of beliefs and commitments, features that a liberal state cannot legitimately demand people to reveal. Or, in its search for visible differences, it opens the space for national identities that appeal to features that are unacceptable from a liberal point of view, nationalist or otherwise. In the latter case, it can only defend itself by anchoring its conception of the public/ private distinction in a particular location; but as soon as we open the public space for any cultural feature that is taken to be essential to the identity of a particular polity, it is difficult to see how liberal nationalism can hold a line.

One last defence may be to argue that what matters is not which features are *taken* to be essential to the identity of the polity, but which features *genuinely* are, and so a line can be drawn. But this goes against the 'nationalist' element of liberal nationalism, in that what a nation considers to be essential to its identity is authoritative. Miller makes this clear when he says that the guiding ideal is 'that of a people reproducing their national identity and settling matters that are collectively important to them through democratic deliberation'.[80] This means 'we cannot tell in advance which particular features of a society's way of life will come to assume importance as markers of national identity'.[81] Therefore what a nation decides it should have authority over is not open to external critique:

> [A] collective belief that something is essential to national identity comes very close to making it so. Once you combine the principle of national self-determination with the proposition that what counts for the purposes of national identity is what the nation in question takes to be essential to that identity, it follows that nothing in principle lies beyond the scope of sovereignty.[82]

The process of self-determination can therefore lead, in principle, to any content.

This gives rise to the concern that liberal nationalism, in opening the space for the idea of the nation within political philosophy, and in seeking to give it the guise of rationality and ethical respectability, also opens that space to conservative and reactionary politics, however much we may deplore them. The liberal nationalists we have considered have clear left-liberal credentials, but beyond asserting these and inserting them into their account of an 'acceptable' nationalism, they provide us with few, if any, resources to resist forms of nationalism and national identity that remain deeply unpalatable to the liberal taste. This is especially problematic when the national identity they offer in order to bring liberal philosophy closer to political realities is itself so abstract and idealised and distant from those realities. Certainly, Tamir's claim that nationalism has enabled liberal theory to circumvent the problems of membership and immigration seems to have little basis.

NOTES

1. Y. Tamir (1993), *Liberal Nationalism*, p. 8.
2. Tamir (1993), p. 8.
3. Tamir (1993), p. 8.
4. Tamir (1993), p. 8.
5. Tamir (1993), p. 67.
6. Tamir (1993), p. 68.
7. Tamir (1993), p. 73; my emphasis.
8. Tamir (1993), p. 84.
9. Tamir (1993), p. 96.
10. On the British experience, see P. Gilroy (1987), *There Ain't No Black in the Union Jack*; D. Hiro (1992), *Black British White British: A History of Race Relations in Britain*; J. Rutherford (ed.) (1990), *Identity: Community, Culture, Difference*; R. Cohen (1994), *Frontiers of Identity: The British and the Others*.
11. A. Patten (1999), 'The Autonomy Argument for Liberal Nationalism', in *Nations and Nationalism*, vol. 5 no. 1, pp. 1–17.
12. Patten (1999), p. 6.
13. Tamir (1993), p. 3.
14. Tamir (1993), p. xiv.
15. R. Beiner (1999), 'Introduction: Nationalism's Challenge to Political Philosophy', in R. Beiner (ed.), *Theorizing Nationalism*, p. 8.
16. Beiner (1999), p. 9.
17. Tamir (1993), p. 151.
18. D. Miller (1995), *On Nationality*, p. 10.
19. Miller (1995), p. 24.
20. Miller (1995), p. 24.
21. Miller (1995), p. 25.
22. Miller (1995), p. 25.
23. Miller (1995), p. 25.
24. Miller (1995), p. 26.
25. Miller (1995), p. 26.
26. Miller (1995), p. 26.
27. Miller (1995), pp. 188–9.
28. Miller (1995), p. 26.
29. Miller (1995), pp. 33–4.
30. Miller (1995), p. 35.
31. Miller (1995), p. 35.
32. Miller (1995), p. 36.
33. Miller (1995), p. 36.
34. Miller (1995), p. 36.
35. Miller (1995), p. 36.
36. See R. Grossmann (1984), *Phenomenology and Existentialism: An Introduction*, pp. 221–5.
37. While there may be a surface resemblance to the instrumentalist approach to scientific theories, this is deceptive, because according to that approach

theoretical propositions in science have no truth value either way, while the sort of proposition involved in nationalism is false, and so *does* have a truth value. See W. H. Newton-Smith (1981), *The Rationality of Science*, pp. 28–34.

38. Miller (1995), pp. 36–7.
39. Miller (1995), p. 36.
40. To paraphrase Harold Wilson's use of the Dunkirk myth, cited by Miller (1995), p. 37, note 41.
41. See N. Harman (1980), *Dunkirk: The Necessary Myth*. For the alternative reading of Dunkirk, see K. Williams (1992), 'Something more Important than Truth: Ethical Issues in War Reporting', in A. Belsey and R. Chadwick (eds), *Ethical Issues in Journalism and the Media*.
42. Miller (1995), p. 37.
43. Miller (1995), p. 39.
44. Miller (1995), p. 39.
45. Miller (1995), pp. 39–40.
46. Miller (1995), p. 40.
47. Miller (1995), p. 40.
48. Miller (1995), p. 127.
49. Miller (1995), pp. 127–8.
50. Miller (1995), p. 128.
51. Miller (1995), p. 153.
52. Tamir (1993), p. 67.
53. J. A. Armstrong (1982), *Nations before Nationalism*, p. 5.
54. Tamir (1993), p. 127.
55. B. A. Ackerman (1980), *Social Justice in the Liberal State*, p. 88.
56. Tamir (1993), p. 128.
57. Tamir (1993), p. 128.
58. Tamir (1993), p. 129.
59. Tamir (1993), p. 129.
60. Tamir (1993), p. 129.
61. See S. J. Gould (1984), *The Mismeasure of Man*, pp. 224–33.
62. Justice Robert H. Jackson declared: 'If there is any fixed star in our constitutional constellation, it is that no official, high or petty, can prescribe what shall be orthodox in politics, nationalism, religion or other matters of opinion, or force citizens to confess by word or act their faith therein.' In S. E. Morison, H. S. Commager and W. E. Leuchtenburg (1983), *A Concise History of the American Republic*, p. 685. See pp. 684–95 on McCarthyism.
63. This is not to concede that fixing an official state language is easy or even legitimate.
64. Tamir (1993), p. 129.
65. Tamir (1993), p. 130.
66. One could, of course, reject deportation by appeal to basic liberal rights, but Tamir rejects it in terms of preference.
67. L. Greenfeld (1992), *Nationalism: Five Roads to Modernity*, pp. 8–13.
68. Greenfeld (1992), p. 11.

69. Greenfeld (1992), p. 11.
70. See for example F. Barth (ed.) (1969), *Ethnic Groups and Boundaries: The Social Organization of Culture Differences*; S. Sokolovskii and V. Tishkov (1996), 'Ethnicity', in A. Barnard and J. Spencer (eds), *Encyclopedia of Social and Cultural Anthropology*; W. Sollors (ed.) (1989), *The Invention of Ethnicity*; J. M. Yinger (1994), *Ethnicity: Source of Strength? Source of Conflict?*
71. Miller (1995), p. 19. He suggests that the difference is that 'ethnicity is not an essentially political phenomenon in the way that nationality is' Miller (1995), p. 122. For a similar criticism of the ethnic/civic nationalism distinction see also B. Yack (1999), 'The Myth of the Civic Nation', and W. Kymlicka (1999), 'Misunderstanding Nationalism' both in R. Beiner (ed.), *Theorizing Nationalism*. Beiner suggests that 'it might clarify the debate somewhat simply to drop the term "civic nationalism" and replace it with references to citizenship (or Habermas's constitutional patriotism).' R. Beiner (1999), 'Nationalism's Challenge to Political Philosophy', in Beiner (ed.), *Theorizing Nationalism*, pp. 24–5, note 56. What I am proposing here is to reserve civic and ethnic nationalism as terms to describe degrees of cultural nationalism, and to preserve liberal constitutionalism for the position that makes 'nationalism' identical with liberal citizenship.
72. D. Weinstock (1996), 'Is there a Moral Case for Nationalism?', *Journal of Applied Philosophy*, vol. 13 no. 1, pp. 87–100; p. 96.
73. Miller (1995), p. 122.
74. Miller (1995), p. 87.
75. Miller (1995), p. 87.
76. Miller (1995), p. 87.
77. Miller (1995), p. 88.
78. Miller (1995), p. 195.
79. Tamir (1993), p. 139.
80. Miller (1995), p. 100.
81. Miller (1995), p. 100.
82. Miller (1995), pp. 100–1.

Chapter 7

LIBERAL ARGUMENTS

~~~~~~~~~~~~~~~~~~~~

SECTION 1: INTRODUCTION

In moving from liberal nationalist to liberal arguments, we should first
note that there is an element of artificiality in this distinction. It is
not so much the distinction between the two positions itself that is
questionable, but the implication that liberal nationalists base their
arguments for membership controls exclusively on issues of national
and cultural identity, while non-nationalist liberals base their arguments
exclusively upon more 'traditional' concepts as private property, public
order and welfare. The truth is that there is a considerable overlap of
concern in both positions: the nationalist is concerned with public
order and welfare, while emphasising the importance of national identity in maintaining these values; and many non-nationalists appeal to
arguments from culture and identity, again to stress their value for liberal institutions. Perhaps the difference is that the former see national
culture and identity as directly valuable for members of a political
community, separate from their contribution to the maintenance of
other values, while the latter see them only as indirectly valuable, in
terms of their contribution to *liberal* values. Whatever the details of the
distinction, for the sake of clarity in this chapter I examine arguments
that make no reference to issues of culture and identity, and take it that
the problems that arise for direct arguments for the value of national
culture for liberal states that were examined in previous chapters also
apply to the indirect arguments sometimes used by non-nationalist

liberals. The arguments in this chapter, therefore, must distinguish between members and non-members without appeal to differences in cultural identity.

For the sake of the arguments developed in this chapter, I will distinguish between three possible liberal positions on the question of immigration:

1. There is an absolute moral right to immigration; no immigration controls can be justified from a liberal point of view.

2. There is a prima facie moral right to immigration, but that right can be overridden. However, its existence places an obligation upon liberal states to have recognisably liberal immigration policies. There must be a coherence between internal principles that the liberal state applies to its members, and the external principles it applies to non-members. While these need not be the same in content (otherwise there is no members/non-members distinction at all), they must both be liberal in form.

3. There is no moral right to immigration: freedom of entry is at the discretion of the state. In addition, liberal states are under no obligation to have liberal immigration policies. The only relevant concern in judging immigration policy is whether it protects the interests of the state and its members.

The first two positions are concerned to show that there can be a liberal coherence between internal and external principles. The third position, which I examine in the next chapter, argues that there need be no such coherence. It is perfectly reasonable for a liberal polity to have non-liberal, even illiberal, immigration controls if the need arises. The priority for the liberal polity is its survival in a dangerous and unstable international order – a Hobbesian state of nature – and the only rational and therefore ethical response is to do whatever needs to be done to ensure its survival.

In this chapter I am concerned with the second response: that there can be immigration restrictions which maintain liberal coherence. In the previous chapter I argued that liberal nationalism failed to achieve this coherence: for example, Tamir's proposal to 'test' potential immigrants for their ability and willingness to be good liberal citizens violated a fundamental liberal distinction between what is properly the public business of the state and what a citizen has the right to keep private: political beliefs belong in the private realm. Therefore to demand that applicants for membership reveal their political beliefs and intentions is to apply illiberal practices to outsiders. I argue that the liberal arguments I examine in this chapter involve the same breakdown of coherence – while liberal principles are applied within the border, its exterior is policed through illiberal principles and practices. I outline this objection in Section 3. But there is a second objection: that the arguments fail to address the central liberal dilemma over membership. This dilemma becomes apparent when we characterise the membership question as a distribution problem: membership is a good that is to be distributed. One central response to the membership question is to argue that we must regulate immigration strictly according to the assimilative capacities of the receiving state: that is, we can admit a certain number of applicants but must exclude the rest. The real problem for a liberal approach here is how to distinguish between those who are to be admitted and those who are to be excluded. That is, if we decide that we can receive 500 new members and there are 1500 applicants, how do we choose the 500 to admit? The liberal nationalist may feel they have an answer to this problem in that we can choose the 500 on grounds of cultural affinity, but this just seems wishful thinking: why suppose there will be 500 applicants who share cultural affinity with us and 1000 who do not? Even if we attempt to use the cultural test, if we are strictly working with a quota we will, in the end, have to make a distinction at the limit of that quota which is not based on the cultural test.

Setting aside the use of a cultural test, the question then is whether there is a way of drawing a boundary between those who are to be included within the quota and those who are to be excluded which is defensible from a liberal point of view? I explore this question in Section 4, where I use the example of rationing health-care resources as an illustration of the problem. It might be thought that if there is a way of rationing health-care resources which is acceptable from a liberal perspective, it can be transferred to the membership question; and, as opposed to the membership question, the issue of rationing health-care resources *has* received a great deal of attention in liberal theory. However, I conclude that there is one overriding problem which prevents the use of any such model: that one necessary ingredient for an acceptable rationing strategy is the consent of those most affected by it, and such consent is absent when it comes to the membership question.

SECTION 2: THE LIBERAL PUZZLE

Before we look at these arguments, it is worth reminding ourselves of how puzzling membership controls are for the liberal egalitarian. Once the principle of nationality is set aside, or at least given its proper place in the order of things, then surely the principle of humanity takes its place. Yael Tamir certainly thinks that if she is mistaken about the role of nationalism in political theory, then strict universality is the only other legitimate option:

> [A] consistent liberal argument should advocate the removal of restrictions on membership. All those who wish to become members should be accepted, irrespective of the possible deleterious effects of an influx of new members on the welfare of the present ones.[1]

Onora O'Neill is similarly puzzled:

> [H]ow can those who argue for universal principles of justice, or for human rights, endorse structures that entail that the rights people actually have depend on where they are, or more precisely on which place recognizes them as citizen rather than as alien? Would not a consistent account of universal principles of justice reject as unjust the differentiated restrictions on rights that boundaries must entail?[2]

Peter Schuck sums up the bafflement:

> [I]n a truly liberal polity, it would be difficult to justify a restrictive immigration law or perhaps any immigration law at all. National barriers to movement would be anomalous. Criteria of inclusion and exclusion based upon accidents of birth, criteria that label some individuals as insiders and others as outsiders, would be odious. Wealth, security, and freedom would not be allocated on such grounds, especially in a world in which the initial distribution of those goods is so unequal. Instead, individuals would remain free to come and go, to form attachments, and to make choices according to their own aspirations, consistent with the equal right of others to do likewise. No self-defining, self-limiting group could deny to nonmembers the individual freedom of action that liberalism distinctively celebrates.[3]

These declarations display the level of discomfort the membership question provokes for the liberal egalitarian. This discomfort can be illustrated through one of the most important statements of a liberal egalitarian account of social justice, that made by John Rawls.

Rawls pursues the project of arriving at acceptable liberal principles of justice through the strategy of the original position, a thought experiment in which choosers are placed behind a veil of ignorance, and choose a set of principles they believe best represent their interests in a liberal society. A great deal of controversy surrounds what information is placed behind the veil of ignorance, and the most relevant for this discussion is whether the parties know they are all members of the same state; this will determine whether they adopt a local or global perspective. Rawls argues for the local perspective, as the principles he is concerned with are those that govern the basic structure of a particular society;[4] they are not meant to be applied at the more local *or* more global level:

> They may be irrelevant for the various informal conventions and customs of everyday life; they may not elucidate the justice, or perhaps better, the fairness of voluntary cooperative arrangements or procedures for making contractual agreements. The conditions for the law of nations may require different principles arrived at in a somewhat different way. I shall be satisfied if it is possible to formulate a reasonable conception of justice for the basic structure of society conceived for the time being as a closed system isolated from other societies. The significance of this special case is obvious and needs no explanation.[5]

However, Rawls allows himself the conjecture that, once we have worked out the theory for this special case, we can move on to the other levels: 'With suitable modifications such a theory should provide the key for some of these other questions.'[6]

However, the purely local perspective is not secured by stating that the choosers in the original position know they are all members of the same state, because once they arrive at their principles of justice, the question remains what can justify limiting their application within the national border. In the end, for Rawls, the choice of principles rests not on the authority of the choosers in the original position, but upon how we reconcile what we know and believe about the world with those principles in our attempts to reach a condition of reflective equilibrium. Therefore, even if the original position choosers do not concern themselves with people who are not members of their state, we, in revising the principles into a form acceptable to us, have little excuse for a similar level of parochialism.

Frederick G. Whelan argues that the principles themselves seem to rule out national boundaries of distribution, and so force us to think internationally.[7] These principles are the Liberty Principle, that each

person has an equal right to a fully adequate scheme of equal basic
liberties which is compatible with a similar scheme of liberties for all;
the Equality of Opportunity Principle, that social and economic
inequalities are to be attached to offices and positions open to all under
conditions of fair equality of opportunity; and the Difference Principle,
that such inequalities must benefit the least advantaged. Whelan notes
that when it comes to the Liberty Principle, Rawls includes freedom
of movement in the list of basic liberties in earlier versions,[8] but not
in the later versions. For example, it is not listed in *A Theory of Justice*,
although Whelan says 'it may be implicit in the notion of "freedom of
the person"'.[9] Now, if freedom of internal movement is important
to individual liberty, it is hard to see why freedom of international
movement is not:

> Although the existence of reasonably stable, bounded political
> and administrative units, and individuals having a legal domicile,
> may be desirable institutions, there is no special reason why free
> movement across international borders need be more inconsis-
> tent with these institutions than are municipal, county, and US
> state borders with the practice of internally free movement as it
> exists in the United States.[10]

And the lexical priority of the Liberty Principle over the other principles means that freedom of movement cannot be constrained by
appeal to economic consequences; it can only be constrained in order
to protect some other liberty that is equally or more important, or to
strengthen the system of liberty as a whole, and 'it is not obvious how
the exercise of a right to migrate in or out of countries would threaten
the civil liberties of others'.[11]

Under the Equality of Opportunity Principle, the implications are
just as clear: 'Equality of opportunity and freedom of movement have
of course gone closely together in the liberal world.'[12] And so: 'Why
should the parties to the original position not insist that all positions
(jobs) in every society be open to any qualified person, regardless of
international boundaries or the nationality of the applicant?'[13] Assuming
that all parties know they are members of the same state does not rule
out this reasoning; one assumes that they are aware that there are other
states – why would they limit their own opportunities by ruling out
free movement to these states, and why would they dismiss the
possible benefits of allowing others entry into their state? The application of the Difference Principle increases the difficulty: 'If the
would-be immigrants are the worst-off group . . . then the application

of the difference principle would dictate their admission to the extent of the economic-absorption limits of the receiving country, taking into account the robustness of its economy over the long term.'[14]

Even if one does not agree with Rawls' method or principles, the liberal egalitarian perspective which frames his theory also seems to overrule the limits imposed by national borders. What unites liberal egalitarians is the injustice of permitting morally arbitrary factors to determine people's life chances. Rawls says: 'What the theory of justice must regulate is the inequalities in life-prospects between citizens that arise from social starting-positions, natural advantages and historical contingencies.' These are, for Rawls, the fundamental inequalities.[15] Whelan notes that if our concern is to rule out the effects of 'morally arbitrary' features on people's life chances, then national borders must be overridden: 'it seems inescapable that a person's nationality (acquired as it nearly always is by birth), and by extension the restrictions on life chances that are due to exclusive national borders, are just as arbitrary from the perspective of the original position, or of strict moral impartiality'.[16]

And so Whelan concludes that what he describes as 'abstract' liberalism – liberal egalitarianism – gives rise to problems when it comes to justifying membership restrictions:

> [A] moral theory that sets out to attend to the claims of all human beings as such, on an equal basis, is going to have some difficulty in justifying borders that set off groups of people from each other and act as barriers to the free movement of individuals.[17]

This, for Whelan, generates a paradox, as it gives us a result that goes against the liberal political orthodoxy on freedom of movement:

> Nearly everyone rejects it, preferring instead to stand on the established principles of state sovereignty and of protection of the interests of members of one's own nation in preference to (though not necessarily in total disregard of) those of members of foreign communities.[18]

The liberal orthodoxy is that these are 'properly matters of sovereign political choice'; they are 'matters of sovereign discretion'.[19] Our response, for Whelan, should not be to embrace the complete freedom of movement that liberal principles seem to demand, but rather should be 'a certain distrust of (or a failure to achieve "reflective equilibrium" concerning) a paradoxical result of abstract philosophizing'.[20] The way forward is therefore to construct arguments that justify immigration controls but which remain consistent with liberal egalitarianism.

SECTION 3: EGALITARIAN EXCLUSIONS

The arguments I examine in this section are designed to show that the liberal state can impose controls over immigration that preserve coherence between internal and external principles and practices. Joseph H. Carens takes up this challenge, describing his position on migration as liberal egalitarian, and arguing that there can be a coherent liberal justification for some level of immigration control.[21] He offers three such arguments: from national security, the value of liberal institutions and public order.

1. National Security

A liberal democratic state can justifiably exclude invading armies and subversives on grounds of national security. This does not entail 'any real modification' of the principle of free movement, as insiders are equally forbidden to do such things. For Carens, this answers the problem of coherence: in a liberal democratic state there is a strong presumption in favour of freedom of internal movement, and therefore the constraint of international movement looks inconsistent with this presumption; in addition, as we saw in Chapter 3, citizens have complete freedom of entry and exit from the state, while non-citizens have no freedom of entry. A liberal state can justifiably constrain the freedom of movement of invading armies and subversives by preventing this entry, because it would equally constrain the movement of its own citizens if they were mobilising to overthrow the state or engaging in subversive activities. Carens states: 'the principle of free movement does not entitle citizens to organize their own armies to challenge the authority of the state'; and: 'if it is against the law for citizens to try to overthrow the state, that kind of activity would presumably justify refusal of entry to outsiders'. Therefore: 'people who pose a serious threat to national security can legitimately be excluded'.[22]

While the invading army example is difficult to object to, the example of the outsider intent on subversive activity is less straightforward. Indeed, it seems that liberal coherence between internal and external principles breaks down even here – to refuse a person entry because one believes they intend to participate in subversive activity is to treat them illiberally. In the first place, citizens who engage in subversive activities are not deported. Still, the state has a duty to prevent harm to its citizens, and prevention of entry at the border may be on balance the best way to prevent that harm. However, the argument behind Carens' position must run something like this:

1. Doing X will harm the state.
2. If a citizen attempts to do X, then the state has the right to prevent them.
3. Therefore if political authorities believe that an applicant for membership intends to do X, then the state has the right to prevent them.
4. The most effective means of doing this is to refuse them entry into the state.
5. Therefore exclusion is justified in such cases.

The problem, of course, is the gap between propositions (2) and (3), in that citizens are constrained if they *attempt* to do X, while outsiders are constrained if political authorities *believe* that they have the *intention* of attempting to do X. Coherence can only be maintained in two ways. First, outsiders must be allowed entry, and only detained if and when they actually *attempt* to do X; or second, the state can detain its own citizens on suspicion of intent to do X. The latter principle is unacceptable in a liberal state, and therefore Carens' argument, as it stands, has already lost coherence between internal and external principles; outsiders can be treated in ways that would be considered unacceptable if applied to insiders.

2. Liberal Institutions

Carens asks whether liberal democratic states are obliged to admit people who are not committed to liberal institutions and practices.[23] He follows John Rawls in concluding that:

> [L]iberal regimes are obliged to tolerate the intolerant and respect their liberties as long as they do not pose an actual threat to the maintenance of liberal institutions. Where they do pose a threat, however, their liberties may be curtailed in order to preserve the regime.[24]

In applying this to outsiders, the implication is that 'restrictions on non-liberal entrants would be justified only if one had good reason to believe that they would threaten the liberal character of the regime if admitted'.[25] If we set aside the difficulties of making such judgements, which were examined in the previous chapter, then we still face problems of coherence: citizens who pose such a threat are not expelled, but outsiders judged to pose the same threat are refused entry. One could argue that admitting additional members with problematic political commitments will increase the overall number of non-liberals to such a level that liberal institutions become endangered. However, we will not start to deport non-liberals if their numbers grow through other means, whatever threat they pose to liberal institutions; and so it is difficult to see how such an appeal to numbers is justified when it comes to outsiders – unless coherence is abandoned.

And this, in the end, is what Carens does. He argues that 'there is something to the claim of asymmetry'.[26] He states:

> Under many circumstances, the right to leave is much more important than the right to enter any particular place. It is only in the limiting case where there is nowhere to go that the two become equivalent.[27]

And so, 'under many, perhaps most circumstances the right to remain in a country where one is already a member is much more fundamental than the right to get in'.[28] One has connections and ties: a framework of living where one is, which one does not have in a place one is trying to enter. Therefore 'expulsions of members are almost never justified from a liberal egalitarian perspective'.[29] The freedom of movement of illiberal citizens can never be constrained by the liberal state whatever their numbers, while the freedom of movement of illiberal outsiders can be constrained precisely by appeal to their numbers. Coherence between internal and external principles and practices is therefore abandoned, and this breakdown becomes more dramatic if we add the objections outlined in the previous chapter: that the argument from liberal institutions gives us criteria for membership that can only be policed in illiberal ways, by asserting the state's right to know the political beliefs and commitments of prospective members, something which is regarded as importantly private when it comes to members. If the political beliefs and commitments of citizens is irrelevant to their membership, how can they be relevant to the membership of non-citizens?

There is another problem with the argument from liberal institutions which Carens overlooks, but which is made apparent in another version of the argument, outlined by Whelan.[30] Whelan's version of the argument is essentially Hobbesian:

> [A] liberal might, as things stand in the world today, not only

144

uphold the traditional (and admittedly nonliberal) sovereign power over borders and admission to citizenship, but might also support restrictive policies on these matters, insofar as there were good reasons to believe that uncontrolled cross-border movement of people – in particular, the influx of nonliberal people into liberal states – would pose a threat to the survival or perhaps simply to the flourishing and strengthening of liberal commitments and institutions where they exist.[31]

But:

This limit applies only to the migration of nonliberals (as perhaps many of those from non-Western countries would be), because a sudden influx of such people might jeopardize the very system under which they themselves would benefit.[32]

What is made clear here is that, given the assumption which grounds the argument – that liberal institutions are valuable – it must be true that these institutions are valuable to non-members also, even where they are non-liberals. Therefore we face a distribution dilemma, that these goods are being withheld from people who could benefit from them without their consent, and on arbitrary grounds – remember that these goods are being withheld from non-members not because of their illiberal beliefs (illiberal residents receive these goods) but because of where they happen to be (if they had been born as residents they would receive them, whatever their beliefs and commitments).

However, Whelan does face up to this distributive dilemma, and offers a solution to it:

Protectionism with respect to liberal institutions themselves. . . , in contrast to other forms, seems to be justifiable from the universal or impartial viewpoint characteristic of liberal morality itself. The policy is in the interest of humanity as a whole, including those who are not currently so advantaged, if one makes the reasonable assumption that the benefits of liberalism can only be more widely distributed by gradually spreading from a secure base.[33]

Of course, one could reply that if liberalism is secure enough to gain converts through spreading outwards, then surely it is strong enough to convert those who enter. Whelan acknowledges this, and says his argument only justifies immigration controls under certain circum-stances, and under present conditions it may be that western societies are too restrictive: they ought to allow immigration up to their absorptive capacities. 'Every immigrant, being a prospective new convert to liberal principles, represents a step toward the goal of their universal realization.'[34]

The only way to avoid incoherence is therefore to adopt this liberal evangelist viewpoint, and argue that restricted membership is in the interests of the excluded, as it is only through this strategy that we can ensure the spread of liberal institutions across the globe. The argument must look something like this:

1. Liberal institutions are valuable.
2. Liberal institutions are vulnerable.
3. Therefore liberal institutions merit protection.
4. Through this protection, liberal institutions will spread across the globe.
5. Therefore those excluded and therefore denied the benefits of liberal institutions will eventually benefit from them.
6. Therefore control over immigration of non-liberals is justified.

Without propositions (4) and (5) the argument loses its universality, and the distributive dilemma becomes damaging to its coherence. However, while (4) is merely questionable, (5) seems to be false. Under normal circumstances it is highly unlikely that those agents excluded from membership will benefit from the liberal 'revolution' when it eventually reaches their part of the globe. One has to add the suspicion that individuals are being judged to be non-liberal simply because they come from non-liberal states, rather than because of their own individual beliefs: note Whelan's view that potential immigrants from non-western countries are most likely to be non-liberal. And so even Whelan's evangelist version of the argument from liberal institutions fails to save coherence between internal and external principles.

3. Public Order

The public order argument focuses purely upon numbers, and not on cultural or political characteristics and commitments or intentions, and so is perhaps the most 'purely' liberal argument in the sense that it is neutral over which applicants are admitted: its only concern is that a certain number are admitted. Carens argues that: 'the number of those coming might overwhelm the capacity of the society to cope, leading to chaos and a breakdown of public order'. This, he says, 'is a minimalist standard, referring only to the maintenance of law and order'. But it is a standard which retains the coherence between internal and external practices, in that 'the breakdown of public order makes everyone worse off in terms of both liberty and welfare'. Therefore this argument justifies exclusion while at the same time 'respecting every individual as a free and equal moral person'.[35]

However, the argument would only seem to work on the assumption that those who are excluded on these grounds remain no worse off than they would have been had they been admitted. To focus only on the position of those already citizens is to beg the question, unless we can show why present members ought not to be expected to make *any* sacrifice in their levels of welfare and liberty in order to improve the situation of others who are in a worse position for no fault of their own; and this is hardly a view the liberal egalitarian would be anxious to establish. And so the argument seems to be something like this: if we have member P and applicant Q, where P stands at ten units and Q stands at five, then admission is ruled out only if Q's position is worsened.

Such an argument does seem legitimate from a liberal egalitarian perspective, and is actually very radical when we look at the political practices of immigration by liberal democratic states – it certainly has the most radical implications of all the arguments we have examined so far. However, there is still a distribution problem which *any* appeal to numbers faces. Liberal arguments for immigration restrictions never aim to establish total exclusion of new members or of any particular group; they all aim to establish a limit of the numbers of new members or of a group. The crucial boundary is therefore not between members and non-members, but between non-members who will be admitted within the 'quota' and those who will remain excluded. The situation is therefore more like the following: we have member P and applicants Q and R, and three possible outcomes – neither Q nor R are admitted (total exclusion); only Q is admitted (a quota); or both Q and R are admitted (open borders). The usual liberal position is the second outcome. There are therefore three possible distributions:

Total exclusion: P–10, Q–5, R–5
Quota: P–8, Q–7, R–5
Open borders: P–5, Q–3, R–3

Again, from the liberal egalitarian perspective the second distribution is best: it is closer to equality than the first, and although the third is closest to equality everybody is worse off. If it came to preferences, all three would prefer the second distribution over the third, and only P would prefer the first distribution over the second. And so the liberal solution of a quota based purely on a headcount, rather than appeal to cultural or political characteristics, seems fairest, given the public order argument.

But this fails to address the real distributive problem: for the question is not how one chooses between one of the three distributive patterns, but how one chooses between Q and R. As I pointed out in Section 1, this dilemma arises equally for the liberal nationalist, in that they argue that we can admit a certain number of people who do not share our cultural or political characteristics and commitments; therefore they too, at some stage, have to draw a line between prospective members which is based purely on the capacity of the receiving state to take in new members without a breakdown of public order. While this argument can tell us where to draw the line in terms of a partic-ular number, it cannot tell us where to draw the line when it comes to deciding who is to be included in that number. This dimension of the distribution problem is fundamental, and yet is completely overlooked in liberal treatments of the membership question. However there are possible solutions to it based on the idea of rationing: there may be ways of distributing scarce resources which are acceptable from a liberal viewpoint in that they respect moral equality. I will examine the prospects of this strategy in the next section of this chapter.

SECTION 4: RATIONING

We have seen that liberal arguments for membership restrictions do not aim at the total exclusion of outsiders; nor do they aim at the total exclusion of groups they take to be problematic. Rather, they argue that there are no good reasons to exclude new members up to the capacities of the receiving state to absorb them, and this capacity can be measured in a variety of ways: for example, the viability of liberal institutions. If, for the sake of argument, we assume that there are good liberal arguments for such a limit, then I have suggested that there is still a major problem for a liberal viewpoint. Now the crucial boundary is not between members and non-members, but between those non-members who will be included and those who will remain excluded. If we decide that our association can take 500 new members out of 1500 applicants, how are to we distinguish between the included 500 and the excluded 1000 on grounds that are acceptable from a liberal perspective? I also suggested that a liberal nationalist approach faces the same problem, for even where the liberal nationalist argues that we should admit all applicants who share our national identity, they still allow that we should not *exclude* all applicants who do not: a certain number can be admitted; and therefore the liberal nationalist, too, must find a way of drawing a line between the included and the excluded which does not rely on their basic criteria of national identity. One response is that there are other examples of scarce resources where there are acceptable liberal ways to distribute them. One central example is that of scarce health-care resources, where liberal theorists have studied different strategies of rationing in great depth. It may be that a model of rationing can be transferred from health care and applied to the membership question.

At first sight, the distribution debate in health-care ethics only serves to deepen the difficulties over the membership question, for what is central to it is the rejection of the relevance of properties over which the individual has no control, and membership of states is determined by what seem to be paradigm cases of such properties. Tom L. Beauchamp and James F. Childress comment:

> A widely accepted reason why these properties are both irrelevant and discriminatory is that they permit differential treatment of persons, sometimes with devastating effects, because of differences introduced by chance, for which the affected individual is not responsible and which he or she does not deserve.[36]

This suggests that 'differences between persons are relevant in distributional rules only if those persons are responsible for those differences'.[37] Another writer on distribution problems in health care, Julian Le Grand, comments: 'it seems to be regarded as inequitable if individuals receive less than others because of factors *beyond their control*';[38] and so: 'Distributions that are the outcome of factors beyond individual control are generally considered inequitable; distributions that are the outcome of individual choices are not.'[39] We can already see from this how intractable the membership question becomes for liberal theory. What emerges is a fair opportunity rule, which 'attempts to diminish or eradicate unjust forms of distribution'. It states that 'no persons should be granted social benefits on the basis of undeserved advantageous properties'.[40] According to this rule:

> Properties distributed by the lotteries of social and biological life are not grounds for morally acceptable discrimination between persons if they are not properties that people have a fair chance to acquire or overcome.[41]

Still, there is a distinction to be made here – where we *can* judge that a person's situation *is* due to their voluntary actions, then we can hold them responsible for that situation, and they have no claims against us. We can at least apply this to the membership question by making a distinction between voluntary and involuntary migrants, and argue that the latter have a moral claim to membership while the former do not. However, this distinction is not particularly helpful. The voluntary/involuntary distinction is not a rationing strategy at all; its outcome is that all involuntary applicants should be admitted, whatever their number, and then perhaps a quota of voluntary applicants can be admitted. The question of rationing then only applies in the second case, when it comes to choosing between the included and excluded voluntary migrants. Again, if we can take 500 new members and there are 1500 applicants, we cannot credibly imagine that there will be, by extraordinary coincidence, 500 involuntary and 1000 voluntary applicants. Given that there will be no such coincidence, there are two possible responses: either we keep to the 500 limit, and if there are too many involuntary migrants we then have to ration membership among that group, while if there are too few then some 'lucky' voluntary migrants get to fill the empty places (and again we have to ration those places somehow); or we admit all involuntary migrants whatever their number, and apply the quota *only* to voluntary migrants. The problem then is that states have to set a quota for new members, from which new involuntary applicants are exempt, and the obvious temptation will be to build the numbers of the latter into the quota somehow. Whichever strategy we choose, the point remains that the voluntary/involuntary distinction itself plays no role whatsoever in solving the rationing question.

Even worse, there are grounds to suppose that the voluntary/involuntary distinction is itself unsustainable. Beauchamp and Childress make it clear that in applying the distinction to health-care issues we have to be clear that a person's situation is genuinely due to their voluntary actions. This is going to be impossible except in very rare circumstances:

> [I]t is virtually impossible to isolate causal factors for many critical causes of ill health because of the complexity of causal links and the limitations of our knowledge.[42]

There are some cases of risk-taking where it *is* clear where responsibility lies, but these are too rare to help. Even where we conclude that a person's situation is caused by voluntary factors, it is going to be difficult to tell whether they are fully responsible for their situation:

> A denial of a person's right to health care would be unfair if the person could not have acted otherwise, or could have acted otherwise only with great difficulty.[43]

It is therefore going to be very difficult to police the distinction upon which the fair opportunity rule rests:

> To determine accurately the causal conditions of particular health problems and to locate voluntary risk-takers, officials would have to investigate the causes. In the worst-case scenario, those officials would be authorized to invade privacy, break confidentiality, and keep detailed records in order to document health abuses.[44]

And these are all extremely illiberal strategies. Any attempt to distinguish between voluntary and involuntary applicants for membership will face the same problems. Anthony H. Richmond comments:

> More often than not the economic and political pressures to move are so closely linked that a distinction between 'economic migrants' and 'political refugees', or between 'voluntary' and 'involuntary' movements of population, is no longer tenable.[45]

We can see, then, that the example of the distribution of scarce health-care resources only seems to highlight the moral problems that plague the membership question. The features that determine one's membership are clearly arbitrary from a liberal point of view – one has no control over where one is born or who one's parents happen to be. The distinction between voluntary and involuntary applicants for membership does not actually supply a rationing strategy at all, and the distinction itself is questionable. But still, it may be possible to construct a system of rationing which does not appeal to any aspect of the voluntary/involuntary distinction, and again there are examples in health care, such as age-based rationing or random methods such as queueing or lotteries. Michael Loughlin, however, argues that the health-care debate rests on the assumption that there can be a rationing system that is ethically acceptable, and this assumption is groundless.[46] In the end, any system of rationing will deprive persons of needed resources on arbitrary grounds, and that includes random methods of queueing and lotteries, and there is therefore no system of rationing that can measure up to liberal standards of justice. The problem is that even random methods are vulnerable to external factors determining the result: one's place in a queue, for example, will be determined by the resources one has at one's disposal which enabled one to get into the queue in the first place; and to participate in a lottery at all one needs resources to get hold of a 'ticket'. In a sense, to use such 'random' methods to determine who gets to be a member is to surrender any moral responsibility for the outcome, and to allow all the factors we would condemn as morally arbitrary to determine the outcome, but in such a way that we can claim to be 'blind' to them. We, at least, can remain unaware that such factors determined who won and who lost, even though we know that they must have played that role. At a deeper level, even if we devise a lottery which is immune from external factors and so is completely arbitrary, and are sure that all who need membership actually get a 'ticket', there is something deeply disturbing in allowing such an important question to be settled in such a way, and again it carries the suspicion of surrendering moral responsibility. We can, at least, not be blamed for the outcome – it was all a matter of luck. Michael Loughlin is clear that, in the case of health-care resources, there is *no* morally defensible rationing strategy:

> The assumption that there must be a defensible, determinate answer to questions about who should be allowed to suffer and die is false. To take a typical sort of discussion from the rationing debate, not only is it not obvious that we can find an acceptable rational answer to the question: 'should the elderly . . . be sacrificed for the sake of the very young. . . ?' The very idea that we *can* do so is offensive nonsense, and the attempt to construct devices or principles which enable people to make such decisions 'ethically' is an attempt to make a nonsense of ethics.[47]

And:

> Viewed in the right light, phrased in the right language, the brutality and injustice inherent in any rationing procedure can, it seems, become rational and just.[48]

The assumption seems to be, says Loughlin, that the context will not create problems that resist any ethical solution; and yet it may actually be that some contexts do create such problems, and the membership question may be like that, especially given the extensive role played by completely arbitrary, non-rational factors.[49] Loughlin concludes that:

It may well be that if I cannot find the right answer, or if none of the options available seem acceptable, this is not because I am being unreasonable, but because my *world* is being unreasonable, and I am sufficiently sane to have noticed.[50]

And so even though the liberal response to the membership question requires us to fix a boundary between non-members who will be included and those who will remain excluded, we cannot assume that there will be a rational and ethical way of fixing that boundary; and so, if presented with a range of rationing strategies, we are not obliged to choose one.

However, it may be replied that we *are* obliged to choose one. Where a resource is scarce such that some must be excluded from any distribution of it, we have to accept that we must fix upon a rationing strategy, even though there is no strategy that is ethically acceptable. But in that case, what seems essential is consent and consensus. For example, if we have a resource that both agents P and Q need and have an equal claim to, but only one can receive, the only way forward is to fix on a method of distribution which both P and Q accept as fair. We cannot impose a distributive strategy upon them, nor can we impose one which only one of the parties has agreed to. Once we have consent and consensus, then any system of distribution that has been consented to will do. When it comes to community-wide resources, then the solution is that the community itself must reach a consensus upon how those resources are to be rationed. What matters now is not the system of rationing, but that the consensus has been reached through genuinely inclusive and democratic means. The method may remain morally unacceptable, but it is communally accepted.

But there is still a fundamental problem which prevents us from applying this reasoning to the membership question. What is crucial in the case of medical resources is that there is a community-wide consensus, and at the very least all those with an interest in the resource in question have given their consent. But in the case of the membership question, those most affected by the rationing strategy have no say over what form it should take, and so have not given their consent: non-members are excluded from the boundary of legitimation. The rationing solution is therefore only available to the liberal democratic state if those who are to be subjected to it have reached a consensus that rationing is acceptable in this case, and that a particular form of rationing is acceptable. In the absence of this consent, it is difficult to see that the imposition of a form of rationing on any population is legitimate from a liberal perspective, and yet in the case of the membership question this is exactly what is proposed in theory and enacted in practice. Again, we come to the conclusion that liberal principles and practices apply within the borders of the liberal polity, but illiberal principles and practices are used to police those borders.

SECTION 5: PRIVATE PROPERTY

There is one liberal argument for membership control that is remarkable for its absence from any serious discussions of the question, an argument from private property. The argument itself is very straightforward. If one owns an area of private property, one has the moral right to exclude others from entering but not exiting, and there is a clear parallel here with the standard liberal view of the rights of the state – that it has the right to restrict entry but not exit. However, the argument raises difficult questions concerning the relationship between the state and its territory and individual private property which make it far more complex than it may first appear. There are two ways we can take the argument. First, we can take it as an argument from analogy: we should treat the relationship between the state and its territory as though it were like the relationship between an individual and their property. Second, we can take it as claiming that the relationship between the state and its territory *just is* the same as the relationship between an individual and his or her property. If we take it the first way, then it suffers from the same weaknesses as the other arguments from analogy we examined in earlier chapters: why should we think there is any analogy here at all, other than the fact that it enables us to claim that states should have the right to control immigration? The only way to avoid the accusation of question-begging is to show that the relationship between state and territory in fact shares so many features with the relationship between individual and private property that it is reasonable to suppose that it shares this one too.

But if the two relations do share such a range of features – whatever these turn out to be – why treat this as an argument from analogy at all? Why not move straight to the second version of the argument? In this second version, the relationship between state and territory is actually the same as the relationship between individual and property: the state is an individual and the territory is an area of private property. There are two problems here. First, even if we accept that they are the same sort of relationship, they are still very different examples of the same relationship: the differences between them in scale and modes of ownership are so great that there is little reason to suppose that they must share the same rules of inclusion and exclusion. We can call them by the same name if we wish, but this doesn't make the differences between them disappear. Second, to regard the state's territory as its private property has deeply disturbing implications for the relationship between individuals and their property: for ultimately, the true owner of all the individually owned pieces of property within its borders must be the state. This runs against the tradition of liberal political philosophy, which sees individuals as the absolute owners of their property. It has to be said, though, that it is a reasonably accurate representation of English property law which still reflects its feudal roots, where all land was owned by the monarch, and all others were tenants.[51] This is still more or less the legal situation:

> [A]fter some 900 years of development the doctrine of tenure still characterizes the English law of real property. Land is still incapable of ownership by a subject.[52]

Having said that, the accepted view is that individual owners are to be regarded as though they are absolute owners of their property, and so the legal truth of the matter is largely set aside. 'English property law is permeated by a strong sense of "individualism"';[53] and so 'the normal way' in which things are regarded as held is private ownership by individuals.[54] This peculiarity of English property law has caused great difficulty for those who have attempted to reconcile it with liberal theories of property, which carry with them the radical implication of absolute ownership by individuals. Elizabeth V. Mensch sheds interesting light on this difficulty, in an account of the tensions for the British colonialists in north America.[55] Blackstone's solution was to allow that property originated through Lockean natural rights and title by occupancy, but the disorder created by this process resulted in a social contract which created the fiction that the monarch was the sole owner of all property. This gave the system order and stability. Therefore the tension between natural and feudal conceptions of property rights was obscured.[56] For Blackstone, this solved the problem in England, as the English were not terribly concerned with the question of original occupation; but this could not be the case in north America. Colonial thought was a struggle between the two competing views of feudal hierarchy and natural voluntarism. The first view

> assumed the inherent legitimacy of a securely structured and paternalistic political, economic, and ecclesiastical hierarchy, with

a corresponding structure of semi-feudal property relations premised on a divinely ordained inequality.[57]

The second challenged this by

> proclaiming equality and freedom as the only possible foundation for a true republican community and also by regarding actual settlement and use of land as the only legitimate source of title.[58]

And so in the north American colonies:

> [L]iberal lawyers were pressed to formulate a definition of property which avoided both of the extremes they feared: property as the direct extension of royal prerogative authority and property as an extension of the all-too-robust will of an independent republican people.[59]

Whatever the fascinations of the story of English and American property law, the fact is that liberal political theory assumes a picture of absolute ownership, and the point remains that the second version of the argument from property is incompatible with that picture. This may explain why the argument from property is spectacularly absent within liberal treatments of the immigration question.

There is a third way of understanding the argument from property which fits much better with the liberal tradition. One central function of the state within liberal theory is to protect individual property rights. If we regard the national territory as consisting of individually-owned pieces of property, then the state's duty to protect it includes at its core the exclusion of invaders. If individuals do not want outsiders to intrude upon their individual property, then the state has a duty to intervene to protect them. Hans-Hermann Hoppe offers a version of such an argument.[60] However, he starts with an assumption of an anarcho-capitalist society, which is his preferred model.[61] In such a society all land is privately owned, and people can do what they like with their private property as long as they do not harm the property of others. Of course, 'under this scenario there is no such thing as freedom of immigration'[62] – owners can admit or exclude as they wish:

> There will be as much immigration or non-immigration, inclusivity or exclusivity, desegregation or segregation, non–discrimination or discrimination based on racial, ethnic, linguistic, religious, cultural, or whatever other grounds as individual owners or associations of individual owners allow.[63]

Under this situation there is no distinction between 'inlanders' and 'foreigners' – this distinction comes about with the formation of the state.[64]

Hoppe then contrasts a situation where the state territory is its private property, such as a monarchy, with a democracy where the territory is public. He asks how these two different governments would act when it comes to emigration and immigration policy. A monarchy would act so as to enhance the value of the kingdom, and therefore would prevent the emigration of productive subjects, and also expel 'non-productive and destructive subjects'. They would also prevent the immigration of 'all people of inferior productive capacities'.[65] In contrast, a democratic government would 'tend to pursue a distinctly egalitarian – non-discrimination – emigration and immigration policy'.[66] This means that anyone can leave and nobody will be expelled. Therefore little is done '*to expel* those people whose presence within the country constitutes a negative externality (human trash, which drives individual property prices down)'.[67] And immigration would amount to forced integration:

> [T]he forcing of masses of inferior immigrants onto domestic property owners who, if they could have decided for themselves, would have sharply discriminated and chosen very *different* neighbours for themselves.[68]

Hoppe argues for the 'de-democratization of society, and ultimately the abolition of democracy'.[69] And so 'the authority to admit or exclude should be stripped from the hands of the central government and re-assigned to the states, provinces, towns, villages, residential districts, and ultimately to private property owners and their voluntary associations'.[70] Such groups would then be allowed to discriminate as they wished:

> They would post signs regarding entrance requirements to the town, and, once in the town, requirements for entering specific pieces of property, (no beggars or bums or homeless, but also no Moslems or Jews or Catholics, etc.).[71]

If there has to be a national immigration policy, then there should be 'strict discrimination *in favour of the human qualities* of skill, character, and cultural compatibility'.[72] The implication for Hoppe is that:

> [A]ll immigrants must demonstrate through tests not only (English) language proficiency, but all-round superior (above

average) intellectual performance and character structure as well as a compatible system of values – with the predictable result of a systematic pro-European immigration bias.[73]

Whatever else one may want to say about Hoppe's viewpoint, there are two problems of coherence. First, the arguments that allegedly show that the authority to admit and exclude should be taken from central government equally apply to those bodies that Hoppe suggests should take it up. If he consistently applies his own logic, the only body with the legitimate authority to include or exclude is the individual property owner in relation to their individual property, and any voluntary association of individual property owners who contractually agree to the same admissions criteria. Whatever the size of the association, if any individual property owner within it refuses to enter into that contractual obligation, then there can be no overall admissions policy for that area. Second, if there is an overall immigration policy, Hoppe argues that the state must act '*as if* they were the personal owners of the country'.[74] However, if the state can act as if it were the personal owner of its territory in this respect, why not in all respects – and this, as I pointed out above, has disturbing implications for the liberal view of the relationship between individuals and their property.

We could, of course, set aside these particular difficulties and the disturbing implications Hoppe draws from his consideration of the immigration question (for example he has no qualms about the right to expel the 'unproductive'), and still consider the basic model that the state's function is to protect individual property rights, and this includes protection from invaders: we can then argue that this gives the state the right to exercise immigration control. But even this basic model is flawed. First, it requires that the national territory is entirely made up of privately owned spaces in need of such protection: a total absence of any public space. Second, it requires the assumption that all individual property owners have reached a consensus about admissions which can then be acted out at the state level: this is surely a completely unrealistic assumption. If there is variation on this question, then either there cannot be a national immigration policy at all, or some overall policy has to be imposed upon all members of the state, whatever their individual views. Third, the focus upon property can only be used to solve the problem of membership on the assumption that the distribution of property has already been settled as fair and just. If, as egalitarian liberals believe, the distribution of property is a prime example of injustice, then the two questions of property and membership become inextricably entangled, and property itself is to be questioned as much as membership.

Hillel Steiner presents a thoughtful libertarian treatment of the immigration question, in that he acknowledges that it raises the problem of the justice of property distribution.[75] For libertarians, the validity of title to property 'can be generally described as turning on their having a pedigree of successively antecedent valid titles terminating in an ultimately antecedent, or original, valid title'.[76] However, they divide upon what can ground such original titles. Some apply a 'first come, first served' rule,[77] which means that original occupants acquire unencumbered rights over what they occupy. Steiner disagrees, and takes the view that such a division of original property rights is encumbered 'by a proviso designed to render it consistent with each person's self-ownership and/or entitlement to equal liberty'.[78] This proviso is usually something like Locke's 'enough and as good' stipulation,[79] and applies to all subsequent transfers of property, because all persons, wherever they are in time and space, carry the same foundational rights.[80] Crucially, such a view 'poses a serious challenge to any charge of trespassing that landowners might individually or collectively bring against immigrants'.[81]

In the world as it actually stands, rather than in any libertarian utopia, Steiner observes that 'most libertarians strongly oppose legislated restrictions on transnational migration'.[82] Although Hoppe sees immigration restrictions as justified if they protect the value of people's property, Steiner rejects this:

> Since the role of the libertarian state is strictly confined to the enforcement of individuals' moral rights which consist exclusively of property and contractual rights, migration restrictions aimed at protecting the *value* of property rights – let alone broader cultural values are entirely beyond its rightful authority. Protection of such values (the worth of which the libertarian in no way denies) is quintessentially a private concern.[83]

And he agrees that:

> [A]rguments for legal restriction that invoke the danger of socially harmful consequences cannot avoid being question-begging if the population over whom harms and benefits are being summed simply excludes some of those who would be affected by the restriction.[84]

In a libertarian utopia, however, the libertarian has no problem with immigration restrictions, for in such a world there are only individual pieces of private property over which, assuming all questions of justice have been settled, the individual owner has complete control when it comes to admission. All the state can do here is protect my property rights by preventing others from entering against my wishes. However:

> Beyond these considerations . . . there is a conception of transnational migration envisioned by libertarianism that is far more radical than what is commonly entertained in discussions of its restriction.[85]

For what can migrate, for the libertarian, are not only individuals, but their *entire* property bundle, including land – that is, secession.[86]

From these observations we can see why the argument from property has played such a minimal role in liberal arguments concerning immigration restrictions. In one sense it begs the whole question, in that it only works on the assumption that all questions of justice concerning property ownership have been settled, while a major consideration behind the immigration question does in fact concern the distribution of property. However, it also raises difficulties for a liberal theory of property, by posing awkward questions concerning the relation between the state and its territory and individual property owners. The argument from property in fact only has any plausibility in Steiner's libertarian utopia, which is possibly why no welfare liberal uses it. And even there we saw that the immigration question simply reduces to individuals deciding who can enter their property: there are no prospects for an immigration policy at the state-level, and so in that sense the libertarian perspective simply makes the membership problem disappear in a way that offers no satisfaction for the majority of liberal theorists. My own conclusion is, then, that the argument from property is the weakest, most confused and confusing option when it comes to liberal justifications for membership controls.

SECTION 6: CONCLUSION

In this chapter I have examined attempts to solve the membership question which make no appeal to cultural or national characteristics: they are in that sense neutral over prospective applicants. One of the arguments, from liberal institutions, did appeal to the political commitments of applicants, but the other arguments were neutral even on this question. All of them, to be acceptable, had to maintain what I have described as liberal coherence; that the principles used to police membership are consistent with principles applied within the state – they are both recognisably liberal in form. I have argued that none of the arguments succeed in doing this: in all of them, there is a breakdown in coherence, and while liberal principles are applied within the border, illiberal principles and practices are used to police those borders.

I have also highlighted what I take to be the fundamental distribution problem. Where we see membership as a scarce resource, we can treat it as a distribution problem: that is, we can distribute membership to a limited number of applicants. However, the question then is how to distinguish between such applicants without appealing to cultural or political differences between them: the crucial boundary is now not between members and non-members, but between non-members who will be included and those who will remain excluded. This question is unaddressed in liberal arguments about membership, and yet all liberal positions assume that such a boundary can be found. Liberal nationalists allow that a quota of new members who do *not* share 'our' national identity can be admitted, but then have to choose the lucky new members without relying on any of the criteria supplied by the preferred national identity. Non-nationalist liberals, in refusing to appeal to notions of national identity, face this problem immediately. The problem is that even if we accept the legitimacy of any of the arguments which impose an upper limit on the number who can be admitted as new members, the challenge is not so much how to arrive at that number, but to decide who will be included within it.

I suggested that there may be possible solutions to this problem in treatments of rationing of health-care resources. However, there was one major objection here. The legitimacy of any rationing procedure must rest on the consent of those affected by it – without any such consent, it is hard to see how any rationing system can be regarded as legitimate. While it may be possible to achieve a consensus with respect to the distribution of certain kinds of scarce resource, this is not possible when it comes to the membership question. And so liberal treatments of this issue assume that there will be a morally unproblematic way of fixing the boundary between 'lucky' and 'unlucky' applicants for membership: that assumption is, we have seen, groundless. If a system of rationing is simply imposed upon applicants for membership, then we have a clear breakdown of liberal coherence, as such an imposition would never be acceptable *within* the boundaries of the liberal polity.

One final response, however, is that the demand that there be liberal coherence between internal and external principles and practices is misguided. Certainly, a liberal polity is under a clear obligation to treat its own members in terms of liberal principles, but it is under no obligation to treat non-members according to the same standards. The membership question can therefore be easily answered, as now the answer does not have to comply with standards we would expect internally. This, the argument goes, is not to abandon liberal political philosophy at all. I examine the justification for this argument in the next chapter.

NOTES

1. Y. Tamir (1993), *Liberal Nationalism*, p. 127.
2. O. O'Neill (1994), 'Justice and Boundaries', in C. Brown (ed.), *Political Re-structuring in Europe: Ethical Perspectives*, pp. 70–1.
3. P. Schuck (1984), 'The Transformation of Immigration Law', in *Columbia Law Review*, 84, pp. 1–90, pp. 85–6. Quoted from J. A. Scanlan and O. T. Kent (1988), 'The Force of Moral Arguments for a Just Immigration Policy in a Hobbesian Universe: The Contemporary American Example', in M. Gibney (ed.), *Open Borders? Closed Societies? The Ethical and Political Issues*, p. 68.
4. J. Rawls (1972), *A Theory of Justice*, p. 7.
5. Rawls (1972), p. 8.
6. Rawls (1972), p. 8 and see p. 378. Charles R. Beitz is the best-known application of the Rawlsian approach at the international level; see C. R. Beitz (1999), *Political Theory and International Relations*. See especially pp. 129–36.
7. F. G. Whelan (1988), 'Citizenship and Freedom of Movement: An Open Admissions Policy?', in Gibney (ed.), *Open Borders? Closed Societies?*
8. For example in J. Rawls (1963) 'Constitutional Liberty and the Concept of Justice', in C. J. Friedrich and J. W. Chapman (eds), *Justice: Nomos VI*.
9. Whelan (1988), p. 35 note 4; see Rawls (1972), p. 61.
10. Whelan (1988), p. 8.
11. Whelan (1988), p. 8. However, what Whelan is overlooking here is that this lexical priority will only protect freedom of movement from economic objectives under Rawls' 'special' conception of justice: under the 'general' conception of justice there is no lexical priority between the principles, and freedom can be traded against improvements in economic position. Rawls could always argue that, when it comes to international affairs, the general conception of justice applies. The importance of the distinction between the general and special conceptions of justice is often overlooked, as is the distinction itself. See Rawls (1972), pp. 151–2 for the distinction, and see Cole (1998), *The Free, the Unfree and the Excluded*, pp. 129–31 for its significance. However, Whelan could reply that even if there is no lexical priority, as, in his view, none of the three principles

can be coherently constrained within national borders, this makes no difference to his point.

12. Whelan (1988), p. 8.
13. Whelan (1988), pp. 8–9.
14. Whelan (1988), p. 9.
15. Rawls (1978), 'The Basic Structure as Subject', in A. Goldman and J. Kim (eds), *Values and Morals*, p. 56. See Cole (1998), pp. 181–4.
16. Whelan (1988), p. 10.
17. Whelan (1988), p. 7.
18. Whelan (1988), p. 14.
19. Whelan (1988), p. 14.
20. Whelan (1988), p. 16.
21. J. H. Carens (1992), 'Migration and Morality: A Liberal Egalitarian Perspective', in B. Barry and R. E. Goodin (eds), *Free Movement: Ethical Issues in the Transnational Migration of People and of Money*.
22. Carens (1992), p. 28.
23. Carens (1992), p. 28.
24. Carens (1992), p. 28. See Rawls (1972), pp. 216–21.
25. Carens (1992), pp. 28–9.
26. Carens (1992), p. 29.
27. Carens (1992), p. 29.
28. Carens (1992), p. 29.
29. Carens (1992), p. 29.
30. Whelan (1988), pp. 16–23.
31. Whelan (1988), p. 17.
32. Whelan (1988), p. 21.
33. Whelan (1988), p. 22.
34. Whelan (1988), p. 23.
35. Carens (1992), p. 30.
36. T. L. Beauchamp and J. F. Childress (1994), *Principles of Biomedical Ethics*, p. 341.
37. Beauchamp and Childress (1994), p. 341.
38. J. Le Grand (1991), *Equality and Choice: An Essay in Economics and Applied Philosophy*, p. 86.
39. Le Grand (1991), p. 87.
40. Beauchamp and Childress (1994), p. 341.
41. Beauchamp and Childress (1994), p. 342.
42. Beauchamp and Childress (1994), p. 359.
43. Beauchamp and Childress (1994), p. 359.
44. Beauchamp and Childress (1994), p. 359.
45. A. H. Richmond (1994b), 'International Migration and Global Change', in J. H. Ong, K. B. Chan and S. B. Chew (eds), *Crossing Borders: Transmigration in Asia Pacific*, p. 36.
46. M. Loughlin (1998), 'Impossible Problems? The Limits to the Very Idea of Reasoning About the Management of Health Services', in S. Dracopoulou (ed.), *Ethics and Values in Health Care Management*.

47. Loughlin (1998), p. 88.
48. Loughlin (1998), p. 88.
49. Loughlin (1998), p. 91.
50. Loughlin (1998), p. 92.
51. E. H. Burn (1994), *Cheshire and Burn's Modern Law of Real Property*, p. 13.
52. Burn (1994), p. 83.
53. W. T. Murphy and S. Roberts (1994), *Understanding Property Law*, p. 42.
54. Murphy and Roberts (1994), pp. 40–1.
55. E. V. Mensch (1987), 'The Colonial Origins of Liberal Property Rights', in K. L. Hall (ed.), *Land Law and Real Property in American History: Major Historical Interpretations*; originally published in *Buffalo Law Review* 31 (1982), pp. 635–735.
56. Mensch (1987), pp. 427–8.
57. Mensch (1987), p. 421.
58. Mensch (1987), p. 421.
59. Mensch (1987), p. 429.
60. H. Hoppe (1995), 'Free Immigration or Forced Integration?', *The Salisbury Review*, June, pp. 17–20.
61. Hoppe (1995), p. 17.
62. Hoppe (1995), p. 18.
63. Hoppe (1995), p. 18.
64. Hoppe (1995), p. 18.
65. Hoppe (1995), p. 18.
66. Hoppe (1995), p. 19.
67. Hoppe (1995), p. 19
68. Hoppe (1995), p. 19.
69. Hoppe (1995), p. 20.
70. Hoppe (1995), p. 20.
71. Hoppe (1995), p. 20.
72. Hoppe (1995), p. 20.
73. Hoppe (1995), p. 20.
74. Hoppe (1995), p. 20.
75. H. Steiner (1992), 'Libertarianism and the Transnational Migration of People', in Barry and Goodin (eds), *Free Movement*.
76. Steiner (1992), p. 88.
77. Steiner (1992), p. 88.
78. Steiner (1992), p. 89.
79. Steiner (1992), p. 89.
80. Steiner (1992), p. 89.
81. Steiner (1992), p. 90.
82. Steiner (1992), p. 90.
83. Steiner (1992), p. 91.
84. Steiner (1992), p. 91.
85. Steiner (1992), p. 92.
86. Steiner (1992), p. 93.

Chapter 8

THE HOBBESIAN RESPONSE

—⌇⌇⌇⌇⌇◉⌇⌇⌇⌇⌇—

SECTION 1: THE END OF PHILOSOPHY?

In this chapter I examine what I have described as the Hobbesian response to the question of membership. This response has a strong and a weak version. According to the strong version, the international 'order' is a Hobbesian state of nature, in which liberal states are rare and vulnerable and are under constant danger from external and illiberal threats. They therefore have the right to do whatever they consider to be in their best interests when it comes to international affairs, and they are the sole authority on what those interests are and which actions will protect them. Immigration policy falls within this external sphere, and therefore a liberal state is under no external constraints when it comes to fixing such a policy. According to the weak version, the international order is not a Hobbesian state of nature, and it is therefore possible to reach international agreement on particular issues, and so liberal states can be under external constraints when it comes to those issues. However, a policy of open borders would create such a level of instability that liberal institutions would be overwhelmed, and so on this particular question liberal states must have Hobbesian powers.

What both versions share is the belief that, when it comes to immigration, liberal states are under no obligation to maintain a coherence between internal and external principles and practices: they have the right to police their external borders in any way they believe best

165

protects their interests, and this can include the imposition of illiberal principles and practices upon non-members. They remain obliged to adhere to liberal principles when it comes to internal government, but illiberal principles are justifiable at the border. Both these responses also share an assumption concerning sovereignty: that is, the liberal state has unlimited sovereignty and therefore cannot be constrained by any external agency when it comes to its own practices. The strong Hobbesian response claims that the state has unlimited sovereign power over all matters, and so can never be subjected to external limitations. The weak response claims the state has unlimited sovereign power on the question of membership, although it may be subjected to external limitations on other issues.

The Hobbesian response, in either form, is a deeply pessimistic conclusion to the question of membership, and has worrying implications for political philosophy. The unavoidable implication of the strong version is that political philosophy – understood as a normative discourse – comes to an end at this level: it can have nothing to say about state policy in the international sphere. Those who condemn liberal theories of justice for their insularity, in that they confine their principles within the boundaries of a particular polity, have missed the point; such theories are vindicated – liberal justice *does* come to an end at the state border. At that border the liberal polity has the right to do whatever it judges to be in its best interests, and liberal commitments to the moral equality of all human beings have no role to play. In a sense, liberal political philosophy reaches its vanishing point – it comes to an end. If we take the weak version, the conclusion is less universally pessimistic in that certain questions of international justice can be raised; but the question of membership is not one of these – ethical argument has no purchase upon it, and again we have reached the end of political philosophy as a normative discourse. We arrive at the Hobbesian conclusion that, at this level or on this question, there is no morality:

> [N]othing can be Unjust. The notions of Right and Wrong, Justice and Injustice there have no place.[1]

However, the Hobbesian response can be resisted. The strong version, that the international order is a Hobbesian state of nature, is highly questionable, and many theorists of international relations would reject it. Regimes of international rights can be established, and there is no reason why this cannot be achieved for the immigration question. The weak version is less easy to dispose of, with its more limited pessimism, based on the empirical prediction that open borders would lead to catastrophe and therefore states must have Hobbesian powers on this issue. But there are two possible replies to it. First and most radically, we can question the prediction of catastrophe. Second, and less radically, we can accept the pessimistic prediction but reject the pessimistic conclusion: even if completely open borders would bring about catastrophe, this does not show that the only reasonable position is the Hobbesian one. The possibility of a framework of international rights dealing with immigration, setting out principles of justice which all states can be expected to apply in shaping their immigration policies, remains a reasonable alternative to either open borders or Hobbesian powers.

If we put forward such an alternative, the only remaining objection is that states have an inherent *right* to Hobbesian sovereignty, regardless of any empirical prediction, and such an international framework is therefore unacceptable. This sovereignty assumption lies behind many of the arguments we encountered in previous chapters (for example, see Frederick Whelan's comments towards the end of Section 2 of Chapter 7). And yet there are good reasons, from a liberal perspective, to regard this sovereignty assumption with suspicion, even if it is limited to the membership question. If regimes of international rights are considered legitimate in other areas, it is hard to see – apart from the catastrophe prediction – why states should have an inherent right to Hobbesian sovereignty on this particular issue. In other words, if Hobbesian sovereignty is rejected as a general assumption, we would have to find an argument to show why it ought to be retained when it comes to membership. In this chapter I examine the catastrophe prediction and the role it plays in leading us towards the Hobbesian response to the membership question, and I will provide further arguments to show why the sovereignty assumption ought to be rejected. The conclusion is that there are no good reasons why immigration in general should not be subjected to a framework of international rights – even if this falls short of an absolute right of immigration for all, it still radically constrains the power liberal states currently have over immigration policy.

SECTION 2: THE CATASTROPHE PREDICTION

At the heart of the Hobbesian response is a prediction of catastrophic consequences. James Woodward, in replying to James Carens, uses this prediction to reject the claim that 'there is a basic human right to move freely across national borders',[2] and he does not see that liberal egalitarians need to hold such a right. He notes that an unrestricted right of immigration is not to be found in the principles or practices of any liberal democratic state, party or group, and this gives grounds for scepticism about its liberal status. Woodward offers a specific example of the argument from liberal institutions, which we examined in Section 3 of Chapter 7, in that he focuses upon the welfare state: unrestricted immigration would severely damage the sorts of welfare institutions that are central to the liberal egalitarian state. For Woodward, the argument focuses on 'the possible problems such movement may pose for sustaining the institutions, policies and values characteristic of states presently committed to liberal egalitarianism'.[3] He claims that 'there is a serious tension between the demand for anything like open borders and the desire of states to maintain institutions and policies supported by liberal egalitarians within their borders'.[4] There are three specific problems: (1) the effect on the labour market and wage levels; (2) the impact on the provision of social services; and (3) the consequences for the political character of the liberal egalitarian state.

The first problem is that 'competition within the labour market between immigrants and present citizens who are poor or disadvantaged may work to the disadvantage of the latter group and may increase income inequality'.[5] Woodward does concede that what empirical evidence there is shows that immigrants have 'a negligible effect' on non-immigrant wage levels.[6] In Chapter 2 we saw that others took a more positive view: for example, David Held and his co-authors observe:

> Studies of the impact of immigration on overall wage rates in a host economy, and the differential impact of immigration on the wage rates of different class and ethnic groupings in national labour markets, suggest marginal but arguably constructive impacts.[7]

However:

> The impact of migration is clearly dependent on the precise character of the immigration in the first place. Migrants cannot be considered as a homogeneous mass when their economic impact is assessed.[8]

Still, on balance, the impact of migration has had beneficial economic consequences. Evidence from Europe, Canada, Australia and the United States shows that:

As immigrants fill the bottom rungs of the labour market, the native workforce moves into higher paid employment.[9]

In a sense, however, all the empirical evidence on the impact of immigration on the host country is irrelevant to Woodward's argument, as these studies, he points out, 'tell us little about the effects of the much more extensive immigration that would presumably result if we were to adopt anything like an "open borders" policy'.[10] He admits that the impact will, as has been pointed out, depend on the type and level of immigration that would follow the opening of borders, but, he says:

> I assume that there is at least a serious possibility that the effect of such a policy would be to depress incomes among some groups of natives and immigrants from what those levels would be in the absence of extensive immigration.[11]

Therefore 'extensive immigration may exacerbate inequality and further diminish the prospects of the worse off'.[12] Liberal egalitarian states wish to protect the interests and improve the prospects of their least well-off citizens, and therefore there are grounds here for restricting immigration.

The second problem concerns the provision of social services, and 'the direct impact of extensive immigration on social services like public education, health care, and employment, disability and welfare programmes of various kinds'.[13] Again Woodward acknowledges that the empirical evidence here is contradictory, but concludes:

> I think it would be very hard to deny that it is at least a serious possibility that a policy permitting very much higher levels of immigration . . . could have the effect of very seriously overloading many public institutions and social welfare programmes.[14]

Such programmes, he suggests, may not be sustainable at all under these circumstances.

The third problem is the impact upon the political character of the state, 'on the values, attitudes and behaviour of present citizens'.[15] There would be a rise in racial/ethnic tension:

> However much we may deplore the existence of racial and cultural conflict, it remains the case that it is much easier for many people to live peacefully with, care about and identity with people who are ethically and culturally like themselves.[16]

Whatever we think of Woodward's arguments so far – and it is interesting to note that although he is replying to Carens, his arguments cover much the same territory and concerns that Carens raises despite the fact he concludes there is a prima facie moral right to immigration – what I wish to focus on is the next step in his argument. Woodward has presented three concerns for which he acknowledges there is no empirical evidence, and so he expresses them in terms of assumptions and possibilities. Having done this, he then states:

> *These facts* generate further concerns about the consequences of extensive immigration for states with a substantial commitment to egalitarian values.[17]

By his own admission, Woodward has not yet supplied any facts, and yet he proceeds as though he has; because he then builds another layer of predictions upon them, predictions which any liberal egalitarian would agree are deeply undesirable. However, rather than these being predictions based on any empirical facts, as Woodward suggests here, what we have are predictions based on assumptions, for which he has supplied no empirical evidence whatsoever.

Woodward's second set of predictions are catastrophic for the liberal egalitarian. For example, there would be:

> the disruption of the operation of many public institutions or services, such as schools and transportation and recreational facilities, not just because of limitations of fiscal resources, but also because of increasingly sharp cultural and economic differences, and (especially in the case of public schools) because of the breakdown of any cultural consensus regarding the character and goals of such institutions.[18]

Certain groups may turn to private institutions to meet their 'needs', and this would further lead to the kind of society liberal egalitarians would deplore:

> [I]t would be a society in which there are very sharp inequalities in wealth and opportunity, in which important public services are non-existent or greatly underfunded, and in which people make whatever private contractual arrangements they can regarding education, health care and related matters.[19]

And so:

> [G]iven plausible empirical assumptions, there is a serious tension, if not an outright contradiction, between the desire of a state to promote liberal egalitarian policies within its borders, and anything like a policy of open borders.[20]

We are, then, faced with an argument which deals with 'empirical assumptions', which have to be assessed for their plausibility. We cannot, in fact, dispute the empirical evidence in favour of Woodward's case, because he does not present any, and he does not present any because there is none. What we have instead is a set of assumptions about what would happen if there were open borders, and another set of predictions about what would follow from the first set of assumptions.

Again, however, whatever one thinks of Woodward's argument, what is of most interest are his conclusions about liberal egalitarian theory itself. For Woodward, it simply cannot be the case that liberal egalitarianism could embody two such contradictory values as commitment to freedom of movement and to equal welfare. Surely, any formulation of it that presents us with this potential incoherence 'does not really capture liberal egalitarian values'.[21] Part of the problem is the working out of liberal egalitarian values at an abstract level, on the assumption of ideal conditions:

> It is not in general a defensible moral principle that if it is obligatory (or even a good thing) to do P under ideal, utopian circumstances, then it is also obligatory (or even a good thing) to do P under the actual circumstances, no matter how far they may differ from the ideal.[22]

Once we take into account the 'real' world, then the contradictions disappear. While it is true that in a perfect world, the case for immigration control is very weak, if not absent, 'even if the result were radically to undermine distinctive national and cultural identities',[23] in the imperfect world immigration controls 'have the status of non-ideal, second-best solutions to problems of preserving institutions and policies we care about'.[24] It may well be true that the central ideals of, for example, Rawls' theory of justice work against having extensive restrictions on immigration; but Woodward concludes that if this is true then Rawls is not a good representative of liberal egalitarianism. An alternative vision would be that:

> [W]e should see the social welfare policies of the liberal egalitarian states as resting not on the single principle of improving the condition of the worst off but rather as resting on a variety of different rationales . . . , which in many cases are less universalistic and more closely tied to the existence of particular communities and particular patterns of expectation and cooperation than is Rawls' Difference Principle.[25]

And therefore:

> Perhaps we should see the modern welfare state as motivated by
> a concern to eliminate and ameliorate the effects of certain kinds
> of 'moral arbitrariness' . . . , but not as devoted to correcting for
> *all* morally arbitrary differences . . . wherever they occur among
> human beings.[26]

But this is surely to concede too much. The liberal dilemma as I have
presented it is either that we accept that freedom of international
movement is required by the consistent application of liberal values, or
we must completely revise those values. The reply we might expect
from the liberal theorist would be that there is no such dilemma; but
Woodward here concedes that there is, and that we must, therefore,
revise liberal values: they do not have the shape we thought they had.
He concludes:

> To consider seriously these possibilities is to accept that standard
> accounts of liberal egalitarian ideals require some fundamental
> rethinking.[27]

And so in attacking the notion that liberal egalitarianism requires
freedom of international movement, Woodward finishes by concluding
that liberal egalitarianism as we understand it is incoherent, precisely
because it *does* require freedom of international movement.

We can see Woodward's argument as representing the weak
Hobbesian response, in that he is concerned with the internal consequences of open borders, and therefore argues only for Hobbesian
powers over immigration. In Section 3 in Chapter 7 we saw Frederick
Whelan offer a strong version of the response:

> While liberalism itself . . . is a scarce and fragile resource in an
> imperfect world, liberal societies can never be obliged to do what
> might imperil their existence as strongholds of liberalism (even
> imperfect liberalism).[28]

In other words, the external world is a Hobbesian state of nature and
liberal states can do whatever is in their interests to preserve their
existence; there can be no moral limits on their sovereign powers. This
justifies exercising this general power over immigration in particular.
Liberal states can identify an upper limit to new members, which is
the extent to which they can tolerate and assimilate non-liberal
immigrants. Whelan states:

> This limit applies only to the migration of nonliberals (as perhaps many of those from non-Western countries would be), because a sudden influx of such people might jeopardize the very system under which they themselves would benefit.[29]

Whelan makes it clear that this appeals only to 'political or civic assimilation',[30] a thin liberal constitutionalism rather than a thicker liberal nationalism. Whelan's position is that:

> [T]he citizens of liberal regimes must be on their guard; the preservation of liberal institutions where they exist must be the first priority, even if this means restricting some of the operations that liberal principles would have in a more ideal world.[31]

Therefore liberal regimes must 'avoid being "swamped" by immigrants in such numbers or at such a rate that the new residents cannot be assimilated into the liberal system, with the consequence that it is undermined from within'.[32]

There are three questions we can ask of Whelan's version of the Hobbesian argument. First, it assumes a world in which liberal institutions are under severe threat from the 'outside'. We can ask whether this 'outside' is as powerful and threatening to the liberal order as this suggests. Note that Whelan assumes that 'non-Western' immigrants are likely to be non-liberal, but one wonders in what sense he can mean this, given his commitment to a thin liberal constitutional identity rather than anything like a liberal national identity. If this liberal constitutionalism is at stake, then it seems harsh to judge that most of the non-western world is non-liberal in this sense. Second, it can be asked whether 'imperfect' liberalism is sufficient to ground the argument, as one assumes that imperfect liberalism is far more robust and far more widespread than its purer form. But imperfect liberalism is all that *can* ground the argument, because as soon as we appeal to purer forms of liberalism we return to the kind of abstract argument that Whelan mistrusts. Not only that, but it would be extremely harsh to exclude outsiders on the grounds that they pose a threat to pure forms of liberal institutions, when all there are to defend in reality are imperfect liberal institutions in all their robustness.

This brings us to the third, and general, criticism of the Hobbesian response. As it is usually presented, it is a realist rejection of an idealist argument. The idealist argues that there ought to be a universal human right of immigration; the realist replies that this would have catastrophic results for the liberal polity, for example in terms of its impact upon a liberal national identity or liberal institutions. Abstract idealism is rejected in the face of hard-faced realism. What is often missed, however, is that the national identities or institutions that are at stake are most often abstract ideals themselves: for example, as we have seen in previous chapters, a conception of national identity is appealed to which one would never encounter outside of abstract political theory; or liberal polities are posed as free and voluntary associations, the product of the consent of their members; or liberal institutions themselves are examples of these free and voluntary associations, which distribute goods to members taken to be free and equal citizens. And so the realist reply to the immigration case itself relies upon a set of abstract and idealised assumptions which do not stand up to serious scrutiny. If we take the more robust versions of national identity or liberal institutions that do exist in the actual political world, then Whelan's claim that liberalism is a scarce and fragile resource in a dangerous and unstable world order becomes much less plausible.

Robert E. Goodin is certainly sceptical about the role of 'political realism' in political philosophy.[33] Goodin is writing in response specifically to political realism as an approach in political science, rather than to this kind of liberal democratic 'Hobbesian realism', but many of his points have resonance: after all, Terry Nardin points out that political realists are very often 'pessimistic liberal egalitarians'.[34] Goodin says of political realism that 'it is not clear that it constitutes a moral stance at all'.[35] Indeed, political realism seems to reject such a view of itself: reasons of state are not moral reasons. 'The whole point of the political realists, to hear how they tell it, is that the state does what it must or what it can, rather than what it necessarily ideally ought'.[36] But this is not helpful when trying to take a moral perspective of freedom of movement as it can be read as the simple rejection of moral principles as such, and so we have to keep some grip on morality. The problem for Goodin is that political realism has too fragile a grip:

> [D]eviations from the ideal moral order made by those trying to do as much good as can be done, given the immorality of others around them, might well be excused by notions of political realism. But the realism serves as an excuse rather than as a justification for deviations from the moral ideal; and appealing to that excuse imposes a further obligation, namely, to make very certain that the constraints on doing better really are immutable.[37]

Certainly, it is perfectly legitimate to point out that we are not in ideal circumstances, and that it is unreasonable to expect us to act as though we were. There has to be considerable scope in liberal theory for 'second best' reasoning:

> Doing the best we can in the circumstances, even where these circumstances are partly constituted by others doing less well than they could or should, is the most that we might reasonably demand of people. That we should be realistic in this sense – that we should choose our own actions with due regard to what others actually will do (or could be made to do) – is a plausible doctrine, and plausibly a moral one.[38]

But the argument only works if the best option is genuinely not available, and in fact 'there is no need to be quite *so* realistic as many commentators might suggest in acquiescing to constraints on free movement'.[39] First, the threats posed by immigration are often 'baldly overstated'. What we in fact face are 'modest alterations to ongoing practices in our community', which are often undergoing change anyway.[40] Second, the moral argument often focuses upon, for example, the preservation of the nation as an organic community, but states are rarely nations in this sense – we cannot demand a dose of political realism when we ourselves are appealing to abstract ideals. Third, the arguments seem to claim that it is impossible to do what our morality demands in this case, but this is an appeal to a 'peculiar sense of impossibility'.[41] The argument is that greater levels of immigration would impose a cost upon citizens, but the claim then cannot be that it is *impossible* for them to bear this cost; rather it has to be that it is *unreasonable* to demand it of them. Of course, under certain circumstances costs will be prohibitive and therefore unreasonable, but we have to be very clear that the particular problem we are dealing with is one of those cases. Goodin concludes:

> The proper role of politics, in such circumstances, is precisely not to 'be realistic' and accept uncritically people's unwillingness to make morally proper sacrifices. It is, rather, to persuade them that moral ideals are worth pursuing.[42]

We can therefore ask whether those who make the Hobbesian response to the membership question have conceded too much too easily to those who believe that political philosophy as a normative discourse has little role to play in practical politics.

SECTION 3: HOBBES AND INTERNATIONAL RELATIONS

The Hobbesian response has a particular context: that is, a conception of the international order which understands it as equivalent to Thomas Hobbes' natural condition of mankind. That natural condition is such that individual agents are in a constant condition of war, given their inability to guarantee their security against others, and given the absence of a sovereign power that can enforce compliance to agreements. Each person in this state of nature has a natural liberty to do whatever is necessary to ensure their own security:

> [T]he Liberty each man hath, to use his own power, as he will himselfe, for the preservation of his own Nature; that is to say, of his own Life; and consequently, of doing anything, which in his own Judgement, and Reason, hee shall conceive to be the aptest means thereunto.[43]

This means, then, that each person has the right to decide what their interests are, and the right to do whatever they believe best protects those interests. This condition leads to extreme insecurity, and it can only be solved by the existence of a sovereign body powerful enough to enforce compliance; without the existence of that power, any agreements individuals enter into with each other are worthless:

> [T]he Lawes of Nature . . . of themselves, without the terror of some Power, to cause them to be observed, are contrary to our naturall Passions, that carry us to Particularity, Pride, Revenge, and the like. And Covenants, without the Sword, are but Words, and of no strength to secure a man at all.[44]

While Hobbes believes individuals *can* solve this difficulty by establishing the required sovereign power, there is no such solution available to police relations between states, who therefore stay within the 'natural condition':

> [I]n all times, Kings, and Persons of Soveraigne authority, because of their Independency, are in continuall jealousies, and in the state and posture of Gladiators; having their weapons pointing, and their eyes fixed on one another; that is, their Forts, Garrisons, and Guns upon the Frontiers of their Kingdomes; and continuall Spyes upon their neighbours; which is a posture of War.[45]

In this situation, the same logic applies as it did to individual agents:

> So in States, and Common-wealths not dependent on one
> another, every Common-wealth . . . has an absolute Libertie, to
> doe what it shall judge (that is to say, what that Man, or Assemblie
> that representeth it, shall judge) most conducing to their benefit.
> But withall, they live in the condition of a perpetuall war, and
> upon the confines of battel, with their frontiers armed, and
> canons planted against their neighbours round about.[46]

This view of international relations, then, is the context for the
Hobbesian response to the membership question. The international
order is unstable and dangerous, and immigration itself poses a threat
to the internal stability of liberal states. They therefore have the right
to impose any immigration policies they believe protect their interests:
they can be under no moral obligation to preserve coherence between
internal and external principles and practices. Therefore the liberal
egalitarian is saved from any charge of inconsistency on the issue of
immigration even where they defend restrictions that appear to be
illiberal.

   An important issue, therefore, is the extent to which this Hobbesian
view of international relations is itself justifiable. Gordon Graham, in
his discussion of the ethics of international relations, identifies the
prescriptive element of realism here – given the view that the international order is anarchic, the most rational response is protection of
self-interest.[47] And so:

> [R]ealism rejects moralism with respect to international affairs,
> and hence denies that there can be ethics in international affairs
> at all.[48]

However, Graham argues that even though it may be plausible to
argue that representatives should represent national interests when it
comes to negotiations, this does not exclude ethics at the international
level. In the first place, they will be concerned with the welfare of
those they represent, rather than *self*-interested; the national interest
therefore has a recognisably moral element:

> [I]n pursuing the welfare and security of their respective coun-
> tries international representatives are pursuing moral aims, and
> hence are morally motivated.[49]

They are, therefore, not like Hobbesian individuals in the state of
nature, and:

> It is a mistake to think that pursuit of national interest is on the

same level as pursuit of personal interest, because national interest includes the well-being of many and not just of one.[50]

Second, we should not even conclude that international negotiators have to be *national* egoists. While they certainly have *special* duties towards those they represent, 'there is no reason to suppose that the moral claims of others are of absolutely no account'.[51] Once we allow that there must be a moral element to the national interest, then:

> [T]here is no reason to think that moral sensitivity or motivation stops at political boundaries. Why should it? If other people's welfare is a reason for my pursuing certain courses of action, it does not cease to be a reason just because of their geographical location.[52]

This does not mean we should see them as universalist altruists: they have special duties to their own citizens, but it does not follow from this that they *only* have such exclusive duties:

> [T]here is no reason to specify 'the national interest' independently of moral aims and ideals, and having done so there is no good reason to think all such aims and ideals are neutralized at national borders.[53]

We cannot deny that the international order is anarchical, says Graham, but 'to say that international society is anarchical is not to say that it is without order'.[54] We do not have to share Hobbes' conception of anarchy. And so Graham concludes:

> Consider, for instance, the remarkable worldwide co-operation which permits an international postal system, and there is a substantial body of international law which is adopted, interpreted and applied, and even to a degree enforced, by international courts of justice. The world of nation states is anarchical, but it is not Hobbes' state of a perpetual war of all against all.[55]

J. A. Scanlan and O. T. Kent trace the role of the Hobbesian response in the formation of the immigration policy of the United States,[56] claiming that: 'the security-based, Hobbesian conception of the political universe has stood behind much of American immigration law and politics'.[57] Because the Hobbesian view places ultimate authority upon the state to decide what is in its best interests, the issue has been one of sovereignty; the state is under no constraints when it comes to international affairs:

Because sovereign power, at least in immigration cases, has usually been presented as the ultimate political value, the issue of unequal global allocation of resources, which necessarily raises more complex questions about morality and distributive justice, has usually been ignored. National borders, on this view, place a limit on the universalizability of moral principles.[58]

Given the nature of the international sphere, in which states are competing in a Hobbesian state of nature, then:

Immigration from another nation to the United States, at least under some circumstances, should be regarded as the functional equivalent of war, with incoming or intending migrants posing threats to the stability of the state – and hence to the existing government and power structure of the nation – which are similar to those posed by an invading army.[59]

Therefore under such circumstances the power of the state over immigration is identical to its power to wage war, and should be as free from constitutional constraint. Scanlan and Kent note that US courts have been more than willing to appeal to the military analogy and interests of national security when it comes to immigration cases, because of:

[T]he usual willingness of the judiciary – in common with most politicians (and, for that matter, most political theorists) – to presume the general validity of the Hobbesian conception of the political universe.[60]

Graham, however, has given us reason to doubt this Hobbesian conception: there are international systems of human rights and international courts with some powers of enforcement. Scanlan and Kent point out that the notion of human rights has played a central role in the moral and political discourse of the United States, and is beginning to play a role in its dealings with non-citizens. For example, the Refugee Act of 1980 adopted the language of the 1967 United Nations Protocol Relating to the Status of Refugees,[61] which requires states to offer refuge to any person who, 'owing to a well-founded fear of being persecuted for reasons of race, religion, nationality, membership of a particular social group or political opinion, is outside the country of his nationality and is unable, or owing to such fear, is unwilling to avail himself of the protection of that country'.[62] Up until that point, the definition of a refugee in United States law was ideological: anybody fleeing a communist regime.

For Scanlan and Kent:

> For a nation to acknowledge formally that there are universal
> rights and to conform its laws to the standards implicit therewith,
> is not *merely* to bring about a set of legal prescriptions and pro-
> hibitions. It is to bring the law explicitly into a realm wherein
> moral considerations are paramount; it is to commit the nation to
> a moral vocabulary that severely restricts what can count as a
> justification for its actions.[63]

Although they remain sceptical about the United States government's
application of the new refugee policy in practice, the fact remains that
the United Nations protocol has been embodied in the law, and that
'[t]he principles on which the 1980 Refugee Act is based are universal
in scope'.[64] If we reject the strong Hobbesian conception of the
international order, then we believe that international frameworks of
human rights are feasible, and there is no reason to suppose that there
should not be such a framework governing a human right of immigration. One remaining argument against such a framework would
be that it violates a central liberal commitment to the sovereignty of
states, but in the next section we shall see there are grounds to question the role of any such commitment within liberal theory.

SECTION 4: THE SOVEREIGNTY PRINCIPLE

Earlier we noted Frederick Whelan's comments that issues of membership are 'properly matters of sovereign political choice', matters of
'sovereign discretion'[65] – and therefore that we must treat any seemingly liberal arguments for freedom of international movement with
suspicion. This presumption of sovereignty does seem to lie behind
many liberal attempts to justify immigration controls, and it may offer
a last defence against the membership dilemma, once the Hobbesian
response is rejected. The claim would be that, within the tradition of
liberal political philosophy, we find a sovereignty principle: that is,
the liberal state has the right to determine policy on internal issues,
and therefore a right to non-interference. Again, we can distinguish
between a strong and a weak version of this argument. According to
the strong version, liberal states have a general right to sovereignty
when it comes to internal issues; according to the weak version, they
have the right to sovereignty on this particular issue. Either version
claims, then, that the liberal state is entitled to sovereignty on membership policy regardless of any consequential arguments. Before we

consider this response any further, we should note at the start that it is a significantly compromised defence. In effect we are considering two types of constraint upon a liberal state's power over immigration policy. The first is the moral constraint imposed by commitment to liberal principles; the rejection of this constraint would lead us back to Hobbesian sovereignty. The second is the external constraint imposed by international legal frameworks and regimes of human rights; the rejection of this kind of constraint does not lead us to Hobbesian sovereignty, because to argue that liberal states should be free from external interference in the form of international legal constraints is not to argue that they ought to be free of any *moral* constraint at all. We can consistently hold that liberal states have the right to autonomy over this and other issues, and at the same time argue that they must exercise that autonomy within the limits of liberal political morality. The sovereignty principle, then, offers no defence against the liberal dilemma over membership, because this has been expressed in terms of moral principle.

What may lie behind the appeal to the sovereignty principle in this context is an analogy with personal liberty, in that many liberal theorists would argue that an individual is subject to moral constraint when it comes to interactions with others, but in the private sphere there is, in an important sense, *no* liberal morality: the private sphere is free from interference in both the legal *and* moral sense, from a purely liberal point of view. Therefore the autonomous state ought to be similarly free from external legal and moral constraint. But it is clear that any analogy with individual liberty breaks down here: even if we accept that in the individual case there is no liberal morality concerning private matters, and liberal morality only governs interactions with others, when it comes to the state there is no 'private' sphere in this sense. The central concern is how the state interacts with others – its members; and therefore the relationship between state and members is the proper object of a public morality. And so where the sovereignty principle rests on an analogy with liberal arguments for individual freedom and autonomy – and therefore individual rights of non-interference – then that analogy has to be rejected.

Charles Beitz also questions the analogy – between states and persons – which makes the principle intuitively plausible:

> [W]e must ask under what conditions it makes sense to think that states have a right to be respected as sources of ends in the same way as do persons. What is the moral content of the right of state autonomy?[66]

181

The argument faces a set of problems we have encountered in previous chapters concerning similar appeals to analogy. We cannot simply claim that states and individual persons can be regarded as analogous because they both enjoy the right to autonomy, because this simply begs the question. We could argue that states and persons are so much alike that the fact that we believe persons have the right to autonomy should lead us to think the same about states; but it is difficult to accept that states and persons are sufficiently alike for the argument to have any force here. We could argue that the features that lead us to conclude that persons have the right to autonomy *are* present in states: all they need to share are these particular features; but even if we did show that those features are present in states, the difference between states and individuals is so vast that we cannot assume those features can play the same role in both cases. Finally, we can provide independent arguments to show that states have the right to autonomy, in which case we have abandoned the argument from analogy:

> Unless some independent sense can be given to the idea of the state as a moral agent, this view cannot be very persuasive.[67]

A second strategy is to argue, not that the state is *equivalent* to the autonomous individual that lies at the heart of liberal theory, but that it *consists* of such individuals:

> [I]t is the consent of the individual citizens that provides the underpinnings of the state's autonomy and secures the analogy with individual liberty.[68]

And so:

> [T]he autonomy of states would rest on one aspect of the autonomy of persons, namely, their liberty to associate in pursuit of common ends. State governments should not be interfered with because they are, in fact, representatives of persons exercising their freedom of association. The liberty of states is a consequence of the liberty of persons to associate.[69]

But here we face the now familiar problem of consent: 'few, if any, governments can be shown to be morally legitimate by appeal to considerations of actual or tacit consent', and this in effect 'undermines the argument from consent to autonomy'.[70]

And so, while the right to autonomy is a plausible principle when it comes to individuals within liberal theory, it is not obvious that it can be extended as a principle to associations, and to states in particular, without appealing to a completely different set of arguments. The fact remains that the relationship between the state and its members is not the same as the relationship between an individual agent and its self, and therefore the individual's moral right to autonomy within liberal theory cannot be applicable at the state level. The state can plausibly be held to be under constraints of justice in how it treats its members, and therefore the relationship between state and citizens is one that can be the subject of external critical scrutiny.

However, while the sovereignty principle cannot be easily grounded by appealing to familiar liberal arguments concerning individual freedom and autonomy, there is still the response that it is a central element of the tradition of liberal political practice, and so it has to be taken seriously. Unfortunately, as we saw in Section 2 of Chapter 2:

> The right, or ability, of the state apparatus to exercise full authority within its own territorial borders has never been consistently established in practice and has been persistently challenged in theory.[71]

The plausibility of the sovereignty principle has, so far, rested on two intuitions: the first ethical, that there is an important analogy here between liberal commitments to individual freedom and autonomy and how liberal theory ought to view the state; the second historical, that there is a tradition of Westphalian sovereignty within liberal political practice. However, we have seen that neither intuition withstands critical examination, and so neither gives us a convincing reason to stand by the sovereignty principle when it comes to the membership question. But there is a third, important, intuition here: that a commitment to democracy involves a commitment to the sovereignty principle, and Frederick Whelan does provide an argument from democracy to justify immigration controls. The appeal seems justified in that there are sound liberal egalitarian arguments for democracy as the most appropriate form of government, and so we are concerned with the immigration policies of liberal *democratic* states. Whelan argues that the practice of democracy requires the division of people into 'bounded groups that function as more or less independent political units'.[72] A world-state democracy would be very difficult, and majority rule on this scale would not be desirable from a liberal point of view. Therefore, 'democracy requires that *people* be divided into *peoples* . . ., with each unit distinguishing between its own citizens . . . and others, who are regarded as aliens *here*, although (hopefully) citizens somewhere else'.[73] However, this functional argument for democracy – that it cannot function without exclusive membership boundaries – is refuted by the overwhelming evidence provided by local and regional democracy and of federalisation. It seems clear that democratic rights can be confined to a region, with people entering and leaving that region freely and exercising the local democratic rights during their residency.

However, Whelan offers another version of the argument from democracy, which focuses on self-determination, and therefore can be seen as providing a defence of the sovereignty principle: the very idea of self-determination, which lies at the heart of any argument for democracy, includes the right to determine membership itself. The right of self-determination includes the right to determine the public character of the association, and admission of outsiders can effect this public character. 'If power over this matter lay elsewhere than in the hands of the members, if the matter . . . were permanently removed from the agenda, the democracy that existed would be seriously attenuated; it would not amount to self-determination.'[74] Whelan explicitly appeals to Walzer's arguments here, when he notes that a democracy 'bears some resemblance to a club'.[75] Most importantly, in a club 'the present members have the power to determine the future membership, at least regarding the admission of new members'.[76] For Whelan, therefore, self-determination 'appears to imply a power in the present citizen body to control immigration'.[77] In our discussion of Walzer's position we noted that the appeal to a similarity between clubs and states by itself cannot justify membership control at the state level. However, Whelan's argument does not depend upon the club 'analogy' but upon the notion of self-determination. He has, in effect, supplied what was missing from Walzer's version of the argument, a reason why self-determination of membership is important at the state level.

However, there are problems with this version of the argument for democracy. There are good reasons why a liberal egalitarian should reject the view that a group can be completely self-determining. If we believe that the moral equality of persons can act as the basis of a framework of international justice and human rights, then we do believe there are limits to self-determination; some matters can rightly be held to lie beyond the scope of the democratic powers of any body of people. Such limits upon democratic power are familiar within liberal political philosophy, with its emphasis on the protection of individual and minority rights. The idea of the absolute sovereignty of *any* group of people is therefore not one which fits easily within the liberal egalitarian perspective.

It seems, then, that the argument from democracy only works if we move beyond *liberal* democracy towards a much more radical position of unlimited democratic power. However, it could be replied that the argument from democracy can remain a liberal one in that it does not depend on the claim that an association should have absolute sovereignty over its internal conduct, but only over certain aspects of that conduct. What Whelan has supplied is an argument to show that one aspect an association *must* have control over is its membership. But it could be argued that one of the most important matters that should lie *outside* the scope of the self-determining power of an association is its membership: there is something disturbing, from a liberal point of view, about a body of persons determining its own limits. While it may not be impossible to make out a liberal argument for this kind of power, it is at least not obvious that a liberal perspective should welcome it, and Whelan seems to assume that it is a necessary component of liberal democracy. Grounds for supposing that this cannot be true go to the heart of the issue of inclusion and exclusion. The issue of the *constituency* is a central problem for the democratic process, and Whelan's argument from democracy assumes that the constituency question has already been settled in a way that is satisfactory from a liberal perspective, when this is the very question being addressed.

It may be that Whelan's claim that groups should have the right to be self-defining has some intuitive plausibility, but I think this is because there is a hidden assumption lying behind it: that the groups we are considering are voluntary and free associations. From a liberal point of view, it may seem only fair that such associations should have the right to be self-defining, and so the right to sovereignty over membership policy; but this is still a deeply puzzling question. For example, W. Ivor Jennings points out:

> On the surface [self-determination] seemed reasonable: let the people decide. It was in fact ridiculous because the people cannot decide until somebody decides who are the people.[78]

A liberal response to this is of course that 'the people should decide who the people are'; and therefore 'the groups to which self-definition applies are self-defining'.[79] However, says Beitz:

> [T]he idea that groups eligible for self-determination are self-defining is made plausible by the analogy with voluntary associations and by the underlying thought that the right of self-determination is a special case of the right of freedom of association.[80]

There are three reasons why this will not do: two are 'realist' objections;

the third is theoretical. The first objection is that the sorts of groups at issue here are not free and voluntary associations: liberal theories of consent to political authority have consistently failed to deliver an argument which shows that all members of a liberal state can be taken to have consented to its legitimacy, and therefore it remains implausible to characterise liberal states as free and voluntary associations. Second – and this is Beitz's objection – there is a crucial difference between voluntary associations and the kind of group we are concerned with here:

> The crucial difference . . . is that voluntary associations are not *territorial* groups: they do not normally have to live together on a separate territory or to deprive others of the territory they inhabited previously. While the creation of a voluntary association involves a partitioning of some population, it does not involve a partitioning of territory. Typical cases of self-determination, on the other hand, have an essential territorial component.[81]

And so the sort of self-determination Whelan is discussing raises problems that the basic issue of voluntary association does not, 'and hence are invisible when self-determination is understood on that model'.[82]

The third objection is more abstract. Can an association that defines its own limits be regarded as free and voluntary? On the one hand, all members that are included freely consented to their inclusion; but on the other hand, those who applied for membership but are excluded did not freely consent to their exclusion. We might want to say that an association is only free and voluntary when all those who wish to be members are free to be. There is a crucial sense, then, in which any bounded group cannot be regarded as a free association, despite the fact that all members joined freely: this exclusive aspect of them is often unstated, and so remains invisible. This means that whatever liberal intuitions we may have about the right to autonomy for free and voluntary associations, these intuitions do not apply to any group with exclusive membership. It is, therefore, not obvious that a liberal egalitarian should hold that any association should have complete power over determining its membership; such a view assumes the justice of the association's current boundary of membership, when it is that boundary that is being questioned. What is also crucial here is to realise that there are two groups subjected to the laws of the state: its own members, and those non-members who are applying for inclusion. Even if we do arrive at a convincing set of arguments to show that the relationship between the state and its members should not be subjected to external regulation, those arguments do not apply to the relationship between the state and non-members. And so, if we accept the abstract and idealised view of the relationship between state and citizens – which rests on notions of free and voluntary consent – the fact remains that this tells us nothing at all about the nature of the relationship between state and non-citizens; because even on the abstract and idealised view of things, there has been no free and voluntary consent to the laws which control this body of people.

And so of the two arguments from democracy, we have seen that the functional argument – that democracy cannot function without membership controls – is false; and the self-determination argument – that the very idea of self-determination includes the right to determine membership itself – is at least not obviously true, as it is difficult to reconcile with liberal concerns about the limits of legitimate democratic power.

To conclude this argument, the principle of sovereignty – that the liberal state enjoys a right to non-interference in its internal affairs – is questionable both in practice and in theory. The relationship between ruler and ruled has always been a legitimate concern of liberal political theory, with the implication that it can be subjected to external regulation. But even if we operate at the level of abstract and idealised theory, a sphere in which all members of the liberal state have freely, voluntarily and actively consented to its authority and agreed to its laws, the membership question still resists resolution – because those subject to immigration law remain outside of this relationship of consent. The legitimacy of immigration practices can, therefore, depend on external regulation.

SECTION 5: CONCLUSION

This chapter has examined one possible solution to the liberal dilemma of membership. That dilemma consists in the fact that any liberal answer to the membership question must maintain a coherence between the principles that are applied internally to members and those that are applied externally at the membership boundary. In previous chapters I argued that there is no practice of exclusive membership that succeeds in maintaining this coherence, and therefore the liberal position on membership – and the practical issues of immigration and naturalisation – is necessarily incoherent. The solution examined in this chapter is the proposal that liberal states are not obliged to maintain any such coherence, as the internal and external spheres are so separate that different standards apply.[83] The Hobbesian response justifies this 'two-worlds' view. According to the strong version, the international order is a Hobbesian state of nature, such that, externally, liberal states have the right to do anything they judge to be in their best interests: they are under no ethical constraints. According to the weak version, although the international order is not Hobbesian, a policy of open borders would be so catastrophic that Hobbesian power over immigration is justified; liberal states may police their borders in any way they think fit. The need for coherence therefore disappears.

I have argued that the Hobbesian response fails. First, as Charles Beitz argues, there is sufficient empirical evidence to show that the international order is *not* a Hobbesian state of nature,[84] and therefore 'international political theory is possible'.[85] Second, if we take the weaker version of the argument, there is little empirical evidence for its catastrophe prediction; and even if we accept that prediction, it does not follow that liberal states should have Hobbesian powers over immigration; there are other alternatives, such as an international framework of human rights regulating immigration practices.

Neither can it be argued that such a framework of rights violates a central liberal commitment to the sovereignty of states, because there is no such commitment within liberal theory. The liberal dilemma over membership then returns: liberal states are not absolved of moral responsibility in the way they treat non-members; they can rightly be expected to maintain a coherence between internal and external principles and practices, and any immigration policy must therefore comply with liberal moral principles. However, the problem is that if my arguments within the preceding chapters are plausible, there does not seem to be any liberal resolution of the membership question that can maintain this coherence. We are left, then, with an incoherence, which the Hobbesian response fails to justify.

NOTES

1. T. Hobbes (1985), *Leviathan*, p. 188.
2. J. Woodward (1992), 'Commentary: Liberalism and Migration', in B. Barry and R. E. Goodin (eds), *Free Movement: Ethical Issues in the Transnational Migration of People and of Money*, p. 59.
3. Woodward (1992), p. 68.
4. Woodward (1992), p. 68.
5. Woodward (1992), p. 68.
6. Woodward (1992), p. 69.

7. D. Held, A. McGrew, D. Goldblatt and J. Perraton (1999), *Global Transformations: Politics, Economics and Culture*, p. 324.
8. Held, McGrew, Goldblatt and Perraton (1999), p. 324.
9. Held, McGrew, Goldblatt and Perraton (1999), p. 324. See A. Inchino (1993), 'The Economic Impact of Immigration on the Host Country', in G. Luciani (ed.), *Migration Policies in Europe and the United States*.
10. Woodward (1992), p. 69.
11. Woodward (1992), p. 69.
12. Woodward (1992), pp. 69–70.
13. Woodward (1992), p. 68.
14. Woodward (1992), p. 70.
15. Woodward (1992), p. 70.
16. Woodward (1992), p. 70.
17. Woodward (1992), p. 70; my emphasis.
18. Woodward (1992), pp. 70–1.
19. Woodward (1992), p. 71.
20. Woodward (1992), p. 71.
21. Woodward (1992), p. 72.
22. Woodward (1992), p. 77.
23. Woodward (1992), p. 80.
24. Woodward (1992), p. 80.
25. Woodward (1992), p. 81.
26. Woodward (1992), p. 81.
27. Woodward (1992), p. 81.
28. F. G. Whelan (1988), 'Citizenship and Freedom of Movement: An Open Admissions Policy?', in M. Gibney (ed.), *Open Borders? Closed Societies? The Ethical and Political Issues*, p. 21.
29. Whelan (1988), p. 21.
30. Whelan (1988), pp. 21–2.
31. Whelan (1988), p. 22.
32. Whelan (1988), p. 22.
33. R. E. Goodin (1992), 'Commentary: The Political Realism of Free Movement', in Barry and Goodin (eds), *Free Movement*.
34. T. Nardin (1992), 'Alternative Ethical Perspectives on Transnational Migration', in Barry and Goodin (eds), *Free Movement*, p. 272.
35. Goodin (1992), p. 248.
36. Goodin (1992), p. 248.
37. Goodin (1992), p. 249.
38. Goodin (1992), p. 255.
39. Goodin (1992), p. 249.
40. Goodin (1992), p. 251.
41. Goodin (1992), p. 253.
42. Goodin (1992), p. 254.
43. T. Hobbes (1985), *Leviathan*, p. 189.
44. Hobbes (1985), p. 223.
45. Hobbes (1985), pp. 187–8.
46. Hobbes (1985), p. 266.

47. G. Graham (1997), *Ethics and International Relations*, pp. 25–30.
48. Graham (1997), p. 19.
49. Graham (1997), p. 32.
50. Graham (1997), p. 32.
51. Graham (1997), p. 32.
52. Graham (1997), p. 33.
53. Graham (1997), p. 33.
54. Graham (1997), p. 45.
55. Graham (1997), p. 45.
56. J. A. Scanlan and O. T. Kent (1988), 'The Force of Moral Arguments for a Just Immigration Policy in a Hobbesian Universe: The Contemporary American Example', in Gibney (ed.), *Open Borders? Closed Societies?*
57. Scanlan and Kent (1988), p. 68.
58. Scanlan and Kent (1988), p. 69.
59. Scanlan and Kent (1988), p. 69.
60. Scanlan and Kent (1988), p. 71.
61. Scanlan and Kent (1988), p. 84.
62. Taken from Home Office (1998), *Fairer, Faster and Firmer: A Modern Approach to Immigration and Asylum*, p. 7.
63. Scanlan and Kent (1988), p. 84.
64. Scanlan and Kent (1988), p. 88.
65. Whelan (1988), p. 14.
66. C. R. Beitz (1999), *Political Theory and International Relations*, p. 76.
67. Beitz (1999), p. 76.
68. Beitz (1999), p. 77.
69. Beitz (1999), p. 77.
70. Beitz (1999), p. 79.
71. S. D. Krasner (1999), *Sovereignty: Organized Hypocrisy*, p. 51.
72. Whelan (1988), p. 28.
73. Whelan (1988), p. 28.
74. Whelan (1988), pp. 28–9.
75. Whelan (1988), p. 29.
76. Whelan (1988), p. 29.
77. Whelan (1988), p. 29.
78. W. I. Jennings (1956), *The Approach to Self-Government* (Cambridge University Press, Cambridge), p. 56; taken from C. R. Beitz (1999), *Political Theory and International Relations*, p. 106.
79. Beitz (1999), p. 106.
80. Beitz (1999), p. 109.
81. Beitz (1999), p. 109.
82. Beitz (1999), p. 109.
83. This is, if you like, analogous to the Aristotelian view of the physical universe, which believed there to be two distinct realms – the heavenly and the earthly – where two distinct sets of laws applied. In the heavenly realm, perfect mathematical laws applied, such as circular motion; in the imperfect earthly realm, correspondingly imperfect laws applied. By this

analogy, the liberal state is the heavenly realm, while the external world is the realm of earthly imperfection. See E. Grant (1977), *Physical Science in the Middle Ages*, pp. 36–7, and S. Drake (1980), *Galileo*, pp. 8–11. I am proposing something analogous to the 'modern' scientific world view: whatever laws and principles we 'discover' must hold consistently throughout the physical universe.

84. Beitz (1999), p. 47.
85. Beitz (1999), p. 65. Beitz means political theory in a normative sense.

Chapter 9

TOWARDS A PHILOSOPHY
OF BORDERS

SECTION 1: INTRODUCTION

Within the context of liberal political theory, there are three options when it comes to the membership question: (1) that this ought to be left to the sovereign will of the individual states; (2) that there ought to be complete freedom of international movement; or (3) that there ought to be an international framework that governs all immigration and naturalisation regulations, to ensure that they all fall within the bounds of a liberal political morality. We have explored the problems with the first option, and concluded that there is no reason why sovereignty should be emphasised on this particular issue; and indeed to choose this as an answer is to give up the attempt to find a moral solution to the membership problem – from the point of view of sovereignty any solution will do as long as it is the product of the sovereign will of the state. However, given the rejection of the first option, many liberal theorists would prefer to move directly to the third, rather than contemplate complete freedom of international movement. Given that state sovereignty should not prevent us reaching an ethical solution to the question of membership, why not attempt to establish a minimum standard of justice for all prospective migrants, which all states must respect in their immigration regulations and practices (and of course 'minimum' does not mean 'minimal')?

192

Unfortunately, the third option is not available either, and to suppose it is begs the question this book investigates. The problem has been whether there can be a way to justify membership controls that is consistent with the central moral commitments of liberal philosophy. All the third option tells us is that if there is, then it should apply as a minimum international standard – but it does not tell us what it might be. If the arguments of this book are sound, then the conclusion is that there is no strategy of membership control that can be consistent with central liberal principles; any such strategy involves an incoherence between internal and external principles, and the result is that in both theory and practice liberal theorists and states apply non-liberal if not illiberal principles to outsiders.

SECTION 2: PHILOSOPHICAL BOUNDARIES

So far, we have addressed a very narrow question: can there be a consistently liberal solution to the question of membership of political communities? In this chapter I wish to pursue a broader issue, concerning what we can learn about the nature of liberal political philosophy from its failure to address this question. We have seen that liberal theory has traditionally had little to say about borders, and that this has something to do with its claim to universality, that its principles and values apply to all human beings, or at least to all moral agents. At the same time, however, we noted that liberal theory has always operated with moral boundaries: there have always been limits, and those that lie beyond those limits have been held to be beyond the scope of liberalism's principles and values. In some cases those boundaries have been explicit although contested: for example there has been a history of lively debate about whether non-human animals should be included within the boundaries of moral concern. Two things seem to have had a bearing on the answer: first, whether these 'outsiders' are capable of *comprehending* our moral principles and values; and/or second, whether they are capable of *benefiting* from them. In Chapter 5 I described these as the boundaries of *legitimation* and of *distribution*, and argued that within the liberal tradition it has always been far more important that one be included within the boundary of legitimation than the boundary of distribution. Indeed, in the universalist tradition of liberal thought, any moral rule must, in principle, be capable of being justified to *any* moral agent, whether or not they are affected by its application. The boundary of legitimation is, therefore, in principle universal, but boundaries of distribution – of rights, duties, and other goods and values – are limited.

However, liberal theory's boundaries are sometimes concealed from view. Liberal theories of social justice, for example, have in effect taken membership as given: everyone is taken to be a member; there is no category of non-member. Given that there are, in fact, outsiders, the effect of this is to exclude them from both the boundary of distribution *and* of legitimation: their existence being unacknowledged, their assent to principles of distribution is never sought. This exclusion has had to be obscured, because while it would be difficult to show that those excluded by this lack of acknowledgement are not capable of benefiting from the goods governed by the principles of distribution, it is even more difficult to establish that they are incapable of comprehending our moral discourse at all, and are therefore justifiably excluded from the boundaries of legitimation. Liberal theories of social justice have therefore concealed the fact that the goods they seek to distribute end at the border, and that the justification of that distribution also comes to an end at the border, by concealing that border from view.

This has meant that this centrally important body of political theory has a glaring omission: it has nothing to say about the moral relationship between members of the liberal polity and non-members; outsiders are not only excluded from the distribution of goods, they are excluded from the theory itself. Liberal theory therefore has the appearance of universality, in that the goods it distributes are due to everybody, and yet at the same time is highly exclusive in that, for the purposes of distribution, 'everybody' here refers only to members of the liberal polity. More seriously, because there is no 'outside' according to this body of theory, members of the liberal polity have no moral or political obligations whatsoever to those outside its boundaries.

While I criticised liberal nationalism in Chapters 5 and 6, it has to be said that it explicitly acknowledges that the liberal polity has borders, and that moral agents lie beyond those borders who have to be taken into account. A priority is therefore to work out our moral relationship with these outsiders. This version of liberal theory retains the appearance of universality at two levels: first, principles and values apply equally to all members of the polity, therefore making explicit what was always implicit in all liberal treatments of social justice; and, second, there is a set of basic principles that apply to all human beings as such, therefore explicitly extending moral responsibilities beyond the border for the first time. However, as we have seen, the local principles have priority over the global principles, a position that rests on a range of arguments concerned with the value of community and/or national identity or culture. And so outsiders are included within the theory but at the same time remain outside the polity.

However, this body of theory also takes something as given: the boundary between members and non-members itself. Although it recognises that there are insiders and outsiders, and therefore the need for a moral/political relationship between them, it does not ask how the distinction between the inside and the outside is constituted: the boundary itself is taken as given. There is a suspicion here of a kind of 'primordialism' about borders, as if they have always been where they are, and all we have to do now that we have acknowledged their existence is to take them into account in our theorising about social justice; and all that amounts to is the recognition that there will be people on the other side of the border. The borders themselves are never theorised. Liberal nationalism recognises the two categories of member and non-member, but the status of individuals as insiders or outsiders is taken as a given fact about them.

This has serious practical consequences, because as we have seen liberal nationalism reserves a 'thick' universality for members and only a 'thin' and secondary universality for outsiders. In a sense we can read this approach as simply seeking to justify liberal theory's parochialism, its reservation of 'thick' moral principles for its members, by appeal to a set of arguments about community and nationality, while conceding the minimal cost of extending 'thin' moral principles throughout the globe. It therefore makes explicit what was implicit within liberal theory, but attempts to save it from the implication that 'thick' liberal principles must be extended globally by limiting their application within the national community, while at the same time allowing a 'thin' universality in order to save the appearance.

An alternative is to examine critically how the 'inside' and the 'outside' are constituted: rather than simply acknowledge the existence of outsiders and the need for a moral relationship with them, it would question the coherence of the distinction between the inside and the outside. But this raises profound questions for how we are to do political philosophy. As we have seen, liberal theory has traditionally proceeded as if there were no outside, and therefore no outsiders to be concerned about. Its principles and values were taken to be universal, while at the same time being withheld from those that inhabited the hidden 'external' world. But the fact remains that the non-existence of others was 'as if'. Liberal theorists were well aware that others inhabited the globe, and had firm views about their nature; that nature, it was held, was such that it excluded them from the boundary of legitimation, and this in turn excluded them from consideration within political theory. The absence of these others from theory is, therefore, not like that of aliens from another planet. In that case we have no idea whether such aliens exist, or what their nature is like if they do exist, and so we have no choice but to theorise without taking 'them' into account. But in the case of the 'aliens' who shared the same globe as the liberal polity, political theorists knew very well of their existence. Their absence from theory is therefore categorically different from that of aliens from another planet. Although political theory remained silent about them, its very structure signalled their presence. So theories of freedom, of justice, of property, took shape with an apparent universality, but with a structure designed to exclude others: a structure based on liberal theory's view of their essential nature. This was, therefore, an exclusive universality: a universality built around a conception of what full human beings were like, and therefore designed to exclude those human beings who were taken to be unable to meet that conception.

In fact my claim that liberal theory has been silent about the existence of others cannot be right. Earlier versions of the liberal tradition were explicit about this exclusion. European humanity was taken to be universal, such that all non-Europeans failed to qualify for inclusion within the boundary of legitimation: they were incapable of participating in moral discourse. Emmanuel Chukwudi Eze explores this exclusion in the work of Immanuel Kant.[1] According to Kant, argues Eze, non-European peoples:

> [A]re devoid of ethical principles because these people lack the capacity for development of 'character', and they lack character presumably because they lack adequate self-consciousness and rational will.[2]

For Kant:

> [T]he difference in natural gifts between the various nations cannot be completely explained by means of causal [external, physical, climatic] causes but rather must lie in the [moral] nature of Man himself.[3]

Kant concludes that native Americans cannot be educated at all; Africans can be 'trained' as slaves and servants only; and Asians can be educated in the arts but not the sciences: 'They can never achieve the level of abstract concepts.'[4] There are other examples of this explicit exclusion of non-Europeans from humanity: Kant once more in *Observations on the Feeling of the Beautiful and Sublime*,[5] David Hume's essay 'Of National Characters',[6] and John Locke's treatment of the status of native Americans in relationship to private property.[7]

At the centre of western political philosophy stood the ideal of the autonomous subject, capable of self-legislation and therefore to be included within the boundary of legitimation. Outside of this boundary stood the non-European outsider, naturally limited in their capacity for autonomy, and therefore excluded from the process of legitimation not by arbitrary whim but by the natural order of things. The space was therefore open for the practices of slavery and colonialism. Eze comments:

> [S]ince, for the Enlightenment philosophers, European humanity was not only universal, but the embodiment of, and coincident with, humanity *as such*, the framing of the African as being of a different, subhuman, species therefore philosophically and anthropologically sanctioned the exploitation of Africans in barbaric ways that were not allowed for Europeans.[8]

But while the charge of silence over the status of non-Europeans in liberal theory is therefore not literally true, two other charges are. First, that this tradition explicitly excluded non-Europeans from the boundaries of distribution and legitimation of its central principles and commitments. Second, that contemporary liberal political philosophy colludes with that explicit exclusion by making no mention of this aspect of its history; such passages in the work of Locke, Hume, Kant and others are unacknowledged, and therefore their role in the 'moral' justification of colonialism and slavery is passed over. Indeed, as far as we can tell from these contemporary works, colonialism and slavery never occurred at all. Contemporary liberal political philosophy could justifiably be characterised as one vast act of racialised forgetting. Liberal nationalism shares this amnesia. We have seen that this new body of theory recognises the presence of others, that the liberal polity has borders, and therefore that there must be a moral relationship between the inside and the outside, but in such a way that does not reduce the outside to non-humanity. Rather than belonging to the category of non-humanity, outsiders now belong to the category of non-nationality. It is debatable whether this constitutes progress.

In effect, liberal nationalism is arguing that what is wrong with liberal philosophy is simply that it failed to acknowledge the existence of others, and now that we *have* recognised them we can get on with the liberal project. But this is in effect to assume that these others have only just come into existence, or as if they *were* aliens from another planet that have just arrived and whom we could not possibly have known about in advance. Instead, we have seen that these others existed throughout the time that liberal theory 'overlooked' them, and that this body of theory was structured around their exclusion. Liberal nationalism takes the boundary between the inside and the outside as given, without asking how it came about. Because of this primordialism, liberal nationalism continues with the exclusive theorising that went before. Along with more traditional liberal theory, it assumes a history in which colonialism and slavery never occurred – indeed, a history of another planet. If we take the history of *this* planet seriously, then it may be that we need a fundamentally different political philosophy, with radically transformed conceptions of freedom, justice, autonomy and equality.

SECTION 3: THE POSTCOLONIAL CONDITION

To what extent, then, can we draw on the traditions of western political theory in thinking through these issues? Cornel West raises this challenge when he discusses the new political movements he believes must be developed by African-American thinkers and critics if they are to make progress towards greater freedom and democracy. An important issue, he argues, is that this new politics must be built upon 'the rich but deeply flawed Eurocentric traditions'.[9] These traditions were unleashed upon the globe during the Age of Europe, from 1492 to 1945, and included powerful critiques of illegitimate authorities, based upon ideals 'like the dignity of persons (individualism) or the popular accountability of institutions (democracy)'.[10] The expansion of freedom and democracy was at the forefront of these traditions, but there was another aspect of them, based upon brutality, exploitation and the dehumanisation of others. At the same time as the European nations were setting out their own independence and autonomy according to their vision of the dignity of humanity, they destroyed the independence and autonomy of others in the race for colonies and empire, and excluded those others from the boundaries of humanity itself. Eze expresses the bafflement that is experienced when confronted with 'this duplicity at the heart of European modernity':[11]

> How . . . could the same European modernity and Enlightenment that promoted 'precious ideals like the dignity of persons' and

'democracy' also be so intimately and inextricably implicated in slavery and the colonial projects?[12]

It is vitally important, says West, to understand this double nature of the European tradition, because the black diasporan struggle for identity and dignity must take place 'on the ideological, social and cultural terrains of other nonblack people', and this entails 'selective appropriation, incorporation and rearticulation of European ideologies, cultures and institutions alongside an African heritage'.[13] Here, West is implying that we can separate the theory of the Enlightenment from its practice. Eze does not share this optimism:

> [T]o speak of ideals or ideas as universally neutral schemes or models which we historically perfectly or imperfectly implement obscures the fact that these ideals and ideas and models are already part and parcel of – i.e., always already infused with – historical practices and intentions out of which ideals are, in the first place, constituted as such.[14]

European modernity was pursued through the *negation* of the non-European: European order and civilisation were bought at the price of the denigration of the non-European.

> By dialectically *negating* Africa, Europe was able to posit and represent itself and its contingent historicity as the ideal culture, the ideal humanity, and ideal history.[15]

Or as Leela Gandhi expresses it:

> In order for Europe to emerge as the site of civilisational plenitude, the colonised world had to be emptied of meanings.[16]

A political theory that can be applied to the world shaped by the European tradition therefore needs to take a postcolonial perspective, and take into account the way relations between peoples have been shaped by the history of colonialism, especially relations of power. Peter Childs and Patrick Williams point to the scale of the colonial experience: European colonial power lasted, in various forms, from the sixteenth century until the second half of the twentieth century, and 'constitutes an unprecedented phenomenon, and one with global repercussions in the contemporary world'.[17] But the phrase 'postcolonial' cannot be taken to imply that the colonial experience is over: 'there are important ways in which European control is very much present'.[18] They highlight Gayatri Spivak's comment: 'We live in a postcolonial neo-colonized world.'[19] A criticism often aimed at liberal political philosophy is that it assumes the political world consists of ready-made independent and autonomous individuals with equal powers of reason and action. While that accusation is not altogether fair, it may be that there is a similar assumption at the level of political communities: that the political world consists of ready-made independent and autonomous nation-states, again with equal powers of reason and action. The central problem of political philosophy has been to ensure that all are empowered to be independent and autonomous members of those states, and the focus has been on the problem of internal equality and social justice. Although some theorists have questioned this assumption,[20] they see the problem as essentially to do with internal unity in the face of cultural diversity. What is not addressed in any depth is how inequality and diversity between states themselves can be made sense of within political philosophy, and how such relations between states impact on relations between members of those states. This is not simply a question of international relations (and so I am not ignoring the extent and sophistication of international relations theory within the liberal tradition), or of relations between individual members of different states. Rather, what needs to be addressed is how this international dimension affects relations between members of the *same* state. The relations between members of a particular political community can be importantly shaped by the relationships between that community and others. This is especially true in the context of postcolonialism: we must understand how the internal relations between members of a community have been irrevocably shaped by the history of European colonialism. In the United Kingdom, the political, social and economic situation of certain groups is importantly determined by their historical relationship with former British colonies. Therefore any political theory that attempts to 'do justice' to that situation must adopt this postcolonial perspective. The idea of citizenship has to be understood in this context, as it has played a central role in European colonialism in setting the boundary between citizens and others. Bryan Turner observes that citizenship has to be seen in the context of the development of nation-states and their colonial subjects.[21] The expansion of political and social rights at the colonial centre goes alongside the decline of the freedom and autonomy of the colonised. 'National citizenship thus involved a contradictory relationship between principles of inclusion and exclusion.'[22]

The point we have reached, however, is one where colonial history not only shapes the relationships between the 'inside' and the 'outside', but, with the mass migration of peoples, also shapes the internal relationships between members of a political community. Homi Bhabha argues that the crucial moment is the arrival of postcolonial peoples within the territory of the former colonial power; people migrate from the colonial peripheries to the metropolitan centre, and this movement of people must have a profound impact upon how that centre conceives of itself and others. And it *should* therefore have a profound impact upon western political philosophy. Bhabha observes that 'the postcolonial perspective forces us to rethink the profound limitations of a consensual and collusive "liberal" sense of community'.[23] If we take such a postcolonial perspective, the relation between the internal and the 'constitutive outside' becomes the central question for any political theory, with immigration as the point at which the tensions raised by this question are expressed; as a consequence, the notions of citizenship, national identity and nation-state become problematic. One possible response is to shift the focus to something more fluid and flexible, in which it is recognised that communities can be sustained without the rigid boundaries which come with the ideas of 'citizenship' and 'state'. Some writers do conclude that the importance of citizenship attaching itself to nation-states is already in decline. For example, David Jacobson comments:

> Under the impact of the transnational movement of people, and its reforming of the way social and political community is constituted, the nation-state is being 'unpacked'.[24]

The way forward, according to such a view, is first to reconstitute the political community in a way that liberates it from the need for rigid membership practices, and second to increase the scope and power of international, rather than national, codes of human, rather than citizenship, rights: the emergence of an 'international constitutional order based on human rights'.[25]

Of course, such a global approach has to be seen in the context of the much less benign growth in global capitalism and global inequalities, with the decline in national sovereignty, welcomed by Jacobson and others, paralleling a growth in the power of bodies such as the World Trade Organisation, committed to the protection of free trade not human rights. This aspect of globalisation, as David Theo Goldberg observes, has 'deep structural implications' for both the former colonies and for the 'colonizing and dominant geopolitical powers'.[26] However, there is an inevitable attraction to an order in which individuals and groups have their integrity protected by internationally recognised rights, rather than having to depend upon rights conferred

by a nation-state, which, because of its history, may regard them as
alien, dangerous and unwanted.

SECTION 4: CONCLUSION

The question I posed at the beginning of this book, and therefore the
project I have pursued through it, was a very narrow one. I asked
whether liberal political philosophy could answer the membership
question in terms that were consistent with its central moral principles
and commitments, and I have suggested that the answer to this question
is that it cannot. Any solution that has been offered to justify exclusive
membership – and therefore immigration and naturalisation regulations – has given rise to an incoherence between the liberal polity's
internal and external principles: those within its boundaries are subjected to liberal principles and practices, while those at the border are
subjected to illiberal principles and practices. In previous chapters I
have presented arguments to draw out these inconsistencies. In this
chapter, I have tried to be more ambitious, and have attempted to draw
a broader picture, to see what the membership question can tell us
about liberal political philosophy itself.

In a sense, the membership question lies in the space between how
liberal theory imagines itself and the world, and its historical relationship with the Age of Europe that Cornel West and others have
described. Liberal theory therefore cannot address the membership
question without addressing itself, and perhaps cannot answer it without radically transforming itself. Whether it transforms itself into a
more explicitly exclusive form – as with liberal nationalism – or into
a genuinely inclusive and liberatory philosophy that includes all of
humanity within the boundary of its own distribution, is itself a
question that lies beyond the scope of this book to answer. All I can
conclude here is that, as it is presently constituted, liberal theory
cannot provide a justification for membership control and remain a
coherent political philosophy.

This is a somewhat pessimistic conclusion, and it might be thought
an inappropriate one given my criticism of the Hobbesian pessimism
explored in Chapter 8. However, that was a pessimism of a different
order. We saw there that according to the Hobbesian response, the
membership question constituted the end of normative political philosophy as such: there could be no ethical solution to it. The only
appropriate response was for particular states to do whatever they

considered necessary to protect the interests of their members, and there could be no moral limits here. This new pessimism is of a much more limited scope: the membership question constitutes the limit of *liberal* political morality as it currently understands itself, but not political morality as such, or even, perhaps, a transformed liberal politics.

This conclusion may not be sufficiently 'applied' for some. At the beginning of this chapter, I outlined the three options available to liberal politics on the membership issue: (1) that this ought to be left to the sovereign will of the individual states; (2) that there ought to be complete freedom of international movement; or (3) that there ought to be an international framework that governs all immigration and naturalisation regulations, to ensure that they all fall within the bounds of a liberal political morality. The first and the third options involve the inconsistencies and incoherences I have described throughout this book, and so it would seem that the only consistently liberal solution has to be the second option, of complete freedom of international movement. If liberal egalitarians cannot bring themselves to accept this conclusion, then they have to ask themselves what they mean by liberal egalitarianism, taking seriously James Woodward's challenge that:

> To consider seriously these possibilities is to accept that standard accounts of liberal egalitarian ideals require some fundamental rethinking.[27]

At the level of political practice, if we do take seriously the argument that the commitment to the moral equality of humanity is the defining centre of liberal democratic politics, then we are entitled to find that commitment at the heart of the central practices and institutions of states that describe themselves as liberal democracies. That it is *not* present in some of the most important of such practices – immigration and naturalisation – must lead us to question the extent to which the western capitalist states who most jealously claim the title of liberal democracies have any right to it. If T. H. Green is correct in his argument that the degree of recognition that the principle of moral equality applies to others beyond our 'tribe', ultimately to all peoples, is a measure of the historical progress of humanity,[28] then clearly history has not come to an end in western capitalist states, as some have suggested. Indeed, they seem to have a considerable historical distance to travel before they can deserve to be described as liberal democracies. This book has at least demonstrated what distance there is still to travel.

NOTES

1. E. C. Eze (1997a), 'The Color of Reason: The Idea of "Race" in Kant's Anthropology', in E. C. Eze (ed.), *Postcolonial African Philosophy: A Critical Reader*.
2. Eze (1997a), p. 115.
3. Eze (1997a), pp. 115–16; taken from F. C. Starke (ed.) (1831), *Kants Philosophische Anthropologie: Nach Handschriften Vorlesungen*, translated by Eze; see Eze (1997a), p. 131. The text is available in translation as I. Kant (1978), *Anthropology from a Pragmatic Point of View*, trans. V. L. Dowdell.
4. Starke (ed.) (1831), p. 352; Eze (1997a), p. 117.
5. I. Kant (1960), *Observations on the Feeling of the Beautiful and the Sublime*, trans. J. T. Goldthwait. See also I. Kant (1950), 'On the Different Races of Man', in E. W. Count (ed.), *This is Race*.
6. D. Hume (1964), 'Of National Characters', in T. H. Green and T. H. Grose III (eds), *The Philosophical Works*.
7. See H. Lebovics (1991), 'The Uses of America in Locke's Second Treatise of Government', in R. Ashcraft (ed.), *John Locke: Critical Assessments*. Lebovics comments:

   > Locke, even more than we have hitherto realized, captured the essence of his age in his treatment of the relation of property, colonial expansion, and good government. (p. 260)

   And:

   > [H]is political philosophy integrated the reality of colonialism and the beckoning riches of colonial resources into modern political philosophy in a new way. (p. 261)
8. E. C. Eze (1997b), 'Introduction: Philosophy and the (Post)colonial', in E. C. Eze (ed.), *Postcolonial African Philosophy: A Critical Reader*, p. 7.
9. C. West (1993), *Keeping Faith: Philosophy and Race in America*, p. 5.
10. West (1993), p. 6.
11. Eze (1997b), p. 12.
12. Eze (1997b), p. 12.
13. West (1993), p. 16.
14. Eze (1997b), pp. 12–13.
15. Eze (1997b), p. 13.
16. L. Gandhi (1998), *Postcolonial Theory: A Critical Introduction*, p. 15.
17. P. Childs and P. Williams (1997), *An Introduction to Post-Colonial Theory*, p. 2.
18. Childs and Williams (1997), p. 5.
19. Childs and Williams (1997), p. 7. G. C. Spivak (1990), *The Post-Colonial Critic: Interviews, Strategies, Dialogues*, ed. S. Harasym, p. 166.
20. See W. Kymlicka (1995a), *Multicultural Citizenship*.
21. B. Turner (1986), *Citizenship and Capitalism: The Debate over Reformism*, p. 47.
22. Turner (1986), p. 47.
23. H. Bhabha (1990), 'The Third Space: Interview with Homi Bhabha', in Jonathan Rutherford (ed.), *Identity: Community, Culture, Difference*, p. 219.
24. D. Jacobson (1997), *Rights across Borders: Immigration and the Decline of Citizenship*, p. 133.

25. Jacobson (1997), p. 136.
26. D. T. Goldberg (1997), *Racial Subjects: Writing on Race in America*, p. 103.
27. J. Woodward (1992), 'Commentary: Liberalism and Migration', in B. Barry and R. E. Goodin (eds), *Free Movement: Ethical Issues in the Transnational Migration of People and of Money*, p. 81.
28. T. H. Green (1883), *Prolegomena to Ethics*, ed. A. C. Bradley, pp. 217–31.

BIBLIOGRAPHY

Ackerman, Bruce (1980), *Social Justice in the Liberal State* (Yale University Press, New Haven).

Anaya, S. James (1995), 'The Capacity of International Law to Advance Ethnic or Nationality Rights Claims', in Will Kymlicka (ed.), *The Rights of Minority Cultures* (Oxford University Press, Oxford).

Anderson, Benedict (1991), *Imagined Communities* (Verso, London and New York).

Andrews, Geoff (ed.) (1991), *Citizenship* (Lawrence and Wishart Ltd, London).

Archard, David (1996), 'Should Nationalists be Communitarians?', *Journal of Applied Philosophy*, 13, pp. 215–20.

Armstrong, John. A. (1982), *Nations Before Nationalism* (University of North Carolina Press, Chapel Hill).

Aron, Raymond (1970), *Main Currents in Sociological Thought 2* (Penguin, Harmondsworth).

Avineri, Shlomo and Avner de-Shalit (eds) (1992), *Communitarianism and Individualism* (Oxford University Press, Oxford).

Babbitt, Susan and Sue Campbell (eds) (1999), *Racism and Philosophy* (Cornell University Press, Ithaca and London).

Balakrishnan, Gopal (ed.) (1996), *Mapping the Nation* (Verso, London).

Barkan, Elliott Robert (1996), *And Still They Come: Immigrants and American Society 1920 to the 1990s* (Harlan Davidson Inc., Illinois).

Barry, Brian (1992), 'The Quest for Consistency: A Sceptical View', in Brian Barry and Robert E. Goodin (eds), *Free Movement: Ethical Issues in the Transnational Migration of People and of Money* (Harvester Wheatsheaf, London and New York).

Barry, Brian and Robert E. Goodin (eds) (1992), *Free Movement: Ethical Issues in the Transnational Migration of People and of Money* (Harvester Wheatsheaf, London and New York).

Barth, Frederik (ed.) (1969), *Ethnic Groups and Boundaries: The Social Organization of Culture Differences* (Allen and Unwin, London).

Beauchamp, T. L. and J. F. Childress (1994), *Principles of Biomedical Ethics*, 4th edn (Oxford University Press, Oxford and New York).

Beiner, Ronald (1999a), 'Introduction: Nationalism's Challenge to Political Philosophy', in R. Beiner (ed.), *Theorizing Nationalism* (State University of New York Press, Albany).

Beiner, Ronald (ed.) (1999b), *Theorizing Nationalism* (State University of New York Press, Albany).

Beitz, Charles R. (1999), *Political Theory and International Relations* (Princeton University Press, Princeton).

Bell, Daniel (1993), *Communitarianism and its Critics* (Clarendon Press, Oxford).

Bevan, Vaughan (1986), *The Development of British Immigration Law* (Croom Helm, London).

Bhabha, Homi (1990), 'The Third Space: Interview with Homi Bhabha', in Jonathan Rutherford (ed.), *Identity: Community, Culture, Difference* (Lawrence and Wishart, London).

Bottomore, Tom and Patrick Goode (eds) (1978), *Austro-Marxism* (Clarendon Press, Oxford).

Brecher, Bob, Jo Halliday and Klara Kolinska (eds) (1998), *Nationalism and Racism in the Liberal Order* (Ashgate, Aldershot).

Brimelow, Peter (1995), *Alien-nation: Common Sense About America's Immigration Disaster* (Random House, New York).

Buchanan, Allen (1998), 'Community and Communitarianism', in E. Craig (ed.), *Routledge Encyclopedia of Philosophy* (Routledge, London and New York).

Burn, E. H. (1994), *Cheshire and Burn's Modern Law of Real Property*, 15th edn (Butterworths, London, Dublin and Edinburgh).

Calavita, Kitty (1998), 'Immigration, Law, and Marginalization in a Global Economy: Notes from Spain', *Law and Society Review*, vol. 32 no. 3, pp. 529–66.

Caney, Simon (1999), 'Nationality, Distributive Justice and the Use of Force', *Journal of Applied Philosophy*, 16, pp. 123–38.

Canovan, Margaret (1996), *Nationhood and Political Theory* (Edward Elgar, Cheltenham).

Carens, Joseph H. (1992), 'Migration and Morality: A Liberal Egalitarian Perspective', in Brian Barry and Robert E. Goodin (eds), *Free Movement: Ethical Issues in the Transnational Migration of People and of Money* (Harvester Wheatsheaf, London and New York).

Carens, Joseph H. (1995), 'Aliens and Citizens: The Case for Open Borders', in Will Kymlicka (ed.), *The Rights of Minority Cultures* (Oxford University Press, Oxford).

Castles, Stephen and Mark J. Miller (1998), *The Age of Migration: International Population Movements in the Modern World*, 2nd edn (Macmillan Press, Basingstoke).

Childs, Peter and Patrick Williams (1997), *An Introduction to Post-Colonial Theory* (Prentice Hall Harvester Wheatsheaf, London).

Cohen, Robin (1994), *Frontiers of Identity: The British and the Others* (Longman, London and New York).

Cole, Phillip (1994), 'Towards a Citizen's Europe?', in Paul Gilbert and Paul Gregory (eds), *Nations, Cultures and Markets* (Avebury Series in Philosophy, Aldershot).

Cole, Phillip (1998), *The Free, the Unfree and the Excluded: A Treatise on the Conditions of Liberty* (Ashgate, Aldershot).

Coleman, Jules L. and Sarah K. Harding (1995), 'Citizenship, the Demands of Justice, and the Moral Relevance of Political Borders', in W. F. Schwartz (ed.), *Justice in Immigration* (Cambridge University Press, Cambridge).

Coolidge, M. R. (1909), *Chinese Immigration* (Henry Holt and Co., New York).

Dahbour, Oman and Micheline R. Ishay (eds) (1995), *The Nationalism Reader* (Humanities Press, New Jersey).

Doty, Roxanne Lynn (1996), *Imperial Encounters: The Politics of Representation in North-South Relations* (Borderlines volume 5, University of Minnesota Press, Minneapolis and London).

Dowty, Alan (1987), *Closed Borders: The Contemporary Assault on Freedom of Movement* (Yale University Press, New Haven and London).

Drake, Stillman (1980), *Galileo* (Oxford University Press, Oxford).

Dummett, Ann (1992), 'The Transmigration of People seen from within a Natural Law Tradition', in Brian Barry and Robert E. Goodin (eds), *Free Movement: Ethical Issues in the Transnational Migration of People and of Money* (Harvester Wheatsheaf, London and New York).

Dummett, Ann and Andrew Nichol (1990), *Subjects, Citizens, Aliens and Others: Nationality and Immigration Law* (Weidenfeld and Nicholson, London).

Durkheim, Emile (1947), *The Division of Labour in Society*, trans. with introduction by G. Simpson (Macmillan, New York).

Eze, Emmanuel Chukwudi (1997a), 'The Color of Reason: The Idea of "Race" in Kant's Anthropology', in E. C. Eze (ed.), *Postcolonial African Philosophy: A Critical Reader* (Blackwell Publishers Ltd, Oxford and Cambridge, MA).

Eze, Emmanuel Chukwudi (1997b), 'Introduction: Philosophy and the

(Post)colonial', in E. C. Eze (ed.), *Postcolonial African Philosophy: A Critical Reader* (Blackwell Publishers Ltd, Oxford and Cambridge, MA).

Fekete, Liz and Frances Webber (1994), *Inside Racist Europe* (Institute of Race Relations, London).

Fekete, Liz (ed.) (1997), *Europe and the Wages of Racism: Race and Class*, vol. 39, no. 1.

Finnis, John (1992), 'Commentary on Dummett and Wiethman', in Brian Barry and Robert E. Goodin (eds), *Free Movement: Ethical Issues in the Transnational Migration of People and of Money* (Harvester Wheatsheaf, London and New York).

Fisher, J. (ed.) (1993), *International Migration and Nationality Law* (Centre for International Legal Studies, Martinhus Nijhoff, Dordrecht and Boston).

Frazer, Elizabeth (1998), 'Communitarianism', in A. Lent (ed.), *New Political Thought: An Introduction* (Lawrence and Wishart, London).

Freeman, Michael (1994), 'Nation-state and Cosmopolis: A Response to David Miller', *Journal of Applied Philosophy*, 11, pp. 79–87.

Fukuyama, Francis (1992), *The End of History and the Last Man* (Penguin, Harmondsworth).

Gandhi, Leela (1998), *Postcolonial Theory: A Critical Introduction* (Edinburgh University Press, Edinburgh).

Gellner, Ernest (1983), *Nations and Nationalism* (Basil Blackwell, Oxford).

Gibney, M. (ed.) (1988), *Open Borders? Closed Societies? The Ethical and Political Issues* (Greenwood Press, Westport, CT, and London).

Gilbert, Paul (1996–7), 'The Concept of a National Community', in *The Philosophical Forum*, XXVII nos 1–2, fall–winter, pp. 149–66.

Gilbert, Paul (1998), *The Philosophy of Nationalism* (Westview Press, Boulder Colorado).

Gilbert, Paul and Paul Gregory (eds) (1994), *Nations, Cultures and Markets* (Avebury Series in Philosophy, Aldershot).

Gilroy, P. (1987), *There Ain't No Black in the Union Jack* (Hutchinson, London).

Goldberg, David Theo (1993), *Racist Culture* (Blackwell, Oxford).

Goldberg, David Theo (1997), *Racial Subjects: Writing on Race in America* (Routledge, London).

Goodin, Robert E. (1992), 'Alternative Ethical Perspectives on Transnational Migration', in Brian Barry and Robert E. Goodin (eds), *Free Movement: Ethical Issues in the Transnational Migration of People and of Money* (Harvester Wheatsheaf, London and New York).

Gordon, Paul (1989), *Citizenship for Some? Race and Government Policy 1979–1989* (Runnymede Trust, London).

Gould, Stephen Jay (1984), *The Mismeasure of Man* (Penguin Books, Harmondsworth).

Graham, Gordon (1997), *Ethics and International Relations* (Blackwell Publishers Ltd, Oxford).

Grant, E. (1977), *Physical Science in the Middle Ages* (Cambridge University Press, Cambridge).

Gray, John (1986), *Liberalism* (Open University Press, Milton Keynes).

Green, T. H. (1883), *Prolegomena to Ethics* (Clarendon Press, Oxford) ed. A. C. Bradley.

Greenfeld, Liah (1992), *Nationalism: Five Roads to Modernity* (Harvard University Press, Cambridge, MA, and London).

Grossmann, R. (1984), *Phenomenology and Existentialism: An Introduction* (Routledge and Kegan Paul, London).

Gutmann, Amy (1980), *Liberal Equality* (Cambridge University Press, Cambridge).

Gutmann, Amy (ed.) (1994), *Multiculturalism: Examining the Politics of Recognition* (Princeton University Press, Princeton).

Habermas, Jürgen (1992), 'Citizenship and National Identity: Some Reflections on the Future of Europe', *Praxis International*, vol. 12 no. 1, April, pp. 1–19.

Hammar, Tomas (1990), *Democracy and the Nation State: Aliens, Denizens and Citizens in a World of International Migration* (Avebury, Aldershot).

Hammar, Tomas, Grete Brochmann, Kristof Tamas and Thomas Faist (1997), *International Migration, Immobility and Development* (Berg, Oxford and New York).

Held, David, Anthony McGrew, David Goldblatt and Jonathan Perraton (1999), *Global Transformations: Politics, Economics and Culture* (Polity Press, Cambridge).

Hendrickson, David C. (1992), 'Migration in Law and Ethics: A Realist Perspective', in Brian Barry and Robert E. Goodin (eds), *Free Movement: Ethical Issues in the Transnational Migration of People and of Money* (Harvester Wheatsheaf, London and New York).

Hiro, D. (1992), *Black British White British: A History of Race Relations in Britain* (HarperCollins, London).

Hobbes, Thomas (1985), *Leviathan* (Penguin, Harmondsworth).

Hobsbawm, Eric and Terence Ranger (eds) (1983), *The Invention of Tradition* (Cambridge University Press, Cambridge).

Home Office (1998), *Fairer, Faster and Firmer: A Modern Approach to Immigration and Asylum* (The Stationery Office Ltd, London).

Hoppe, Hans-Hermann (1995), 'Free Immigration or Forced Integration?', *The Salisbury Review*, June, pp. 17–20.

Hui, Ong Jin, Chan Kwok Bun and Chew Soon Beng (eds) (1995), *Crossing Borders: Transmigration in Asia Pacific* (Prentice Hall, London).

Hume, David (1964), 'Of National Characters', in T. H. Green and T. H. Grose III (eds), *Philosophical Works* (Scientia Veralg, Aalen, Germany).

Hutchinson, John and Anthony D. Smith (eds) (1994), *Nationalism* (Oxford University Press, Oxford).

Huttenback, Robert A. (1976), *Racism and Empire: White Settlers and Colonial Immigrants in the British Self-Governing Colonies 1830–1910* (Cornell University Press, Ithaca and London).

Inchino, A. (1993), 'The Economic Impact of Immigration on the Host Country', in G. Luciani (ed.), *Migration Policies in Europe and the United States* (Kluwer, Dordrecht).

Ivison, Duncan (1997), 'Postcolonial Political Theory', in Andrew Vincent (ed.), *Political Theory: Tradition, Diversity and Ideology* (Cambridge University Press, Cambridge).

Jacobson, David (1997), *Rights across Borders: Immigration and the Decline of Citizenship* (Johns Hopkins University Press, Baltimore and London).

Jones, Charles (1996), 'A Revenge of the Philosophical Mole: Another Response to David Miller on Nationality', *Journal of Applied Philosophy*, 13, pp. 73–86.

Jupp, James (1998), *Immigration*, 2nd edn (Oxford University Press, Australia, Melbourne).

Kant, Immanuel (1950), 'On the Different Races of Man', in E. W. Count (ed.), *This is Race* (Henry Schuman, New York).

Kant, Immanuel (1960), *Observations on the Feeling of the Beautiful and Sublime*, trans. J. T. Goldthwait (University of California Press, Berkeley).

Kant, Immanuel (1978), *Anthropology from a Pragmatic Point of View*, trans. V. L. Dowdell (Southern Illinois University Press, Carbondale).

Krasner, Stephen D. (1999), *Sovereignty: Organized Hypocrisy* (Princeton University Press, Princeton).

Krieger, Joel (ed.) (1993), *The Oxford Companion to Politics of the World* (Oxford University Press, New York and Oxford).

Kristeva, Julia (1991), *Strangers to Ourselves*, trans. Leon S. Roudiez (Columbia University Press, New York).

Kristeva, Julia (1993), *Nations without Nationalism* (Columbia University Press, New York).

Kuijsten, Anton (1997), 'Immigration and Public Finance: The Case of the Netherlands', in Emek M. Ucarer and Donald J. Puchala (eds), *Immigration into Western Societies: Problems and Policies* (Pinter, London and Washington).

Kymlicka, Will (1990), *Contemporary Political Philosophy: An Introduction* (Clarendon Press, Oxford).

Kymlicka, Will (1995a), *Multicultural Citizenship* (Oxford University Press, Oxford).

Kymlicka, Will (ed.) (1995b), *The Rights of Minority Cultures* (Oxford University Press, Oxford).

Kymlicka, Will (1999), 'Misunderstanding Nationalism', in R. Beiner (ed.),

Theorizing Nationalism (State University of New York Press, Albany).

Kymlicka, Will and Wayne Norman (1994), 'Return of the Citizen: A Survey of Recent Work on Citizenship Theory', *Ethics*, 104 (January), pp. 352–81.

Labour Party (2000), *Britain in the World* (Millbank, London).

Le Grand, Julian (1991), *Equity and Choice: An Essay in Economics and Applied Philosophy* (HarperCollins, London).

Lebovics, H. (1991), 'The Uses of America in Locke's Second Treatise of Government', in R. Ashcraft (ed.), *Locke: Critical Assessments*, vol. 3 (Routledge, London).

Lister, Ruth (1990), *The Exclusive Society – Citizenship and the Poor* (Child Poverty Action Group, London).

Loughlin, Michael (1998), 'Impossible Problems? The Limits to the Very Idea of Reasoning About the Management of Health Services', in S. Dracopoulou (ed.), *Ethics and Values in Health Care Management* (Routledge, London and New York).

McKim, R. and J. McMahan (eds) (1997), *The Morality of Nationalism* (Oxford University Press, Oxford).

McMahan, J. (1997), 'The Limits of National Partiality', in R. McKim and J. McMahan (eds), *The Morality of Nationalism* (Oxford University Press, Oxford).

Manzo, Kathryn A. (1996), *Creating Boundaries – The Politics of Race and Nation* (Lynne Reinner Publishers Inc., London and Boulder Colorado).

Martin, David A. (1997), 'Refugees and Migration', in Christopher C. Joyner (ed.), *The United Nations and International Law* (Cambridge University Press and the American Society of International Law, Cambridge, New York and Melbourne).

Martin, Philip L. (1997), 'The Impact of Immigration on Receiving Countries', in Emek M. Ucarer and Donald J. Puchala (eds), *Immigration into Western Societies: Problems and Policies* (Pinter, London and Washington).

Mayo-Smith, Richard (1890), *Emigration and Immigration: A Study in Social Science* (T. Fisher, London).

Memmi, Albert (1990), *The Colonizer and the Colonized* (Earthscan Publications, London).

Mensch, Elizabeth V. (1987), 'The Colonial Origins of Liberal Property Rights', in K. L. Hall (ed.), *Land Law and Real Property in American History: Major Historical Interpretations* (Garland Publishing Inc., New York and London); originally published in *Buffalo Law Review*, 31 (1982), pp. 635–735.

Miller, David (1988), 'The Ethical Significance of Nationality', *Ethics*, 98, pp. 647–62.

Miller, David (1993), 'In Defence of Nationality', *Journal of Applied*

Philosophy, 10, pp. 3–16.

Miller, David (1995), *On Nationality* (Clarendon Press, Oxford).

Miller, David and Michael Walzer (eds) (1995), *Pluralism, Justice and Equality* (Oxford University Press, Oxford).

Mills, Charles W. (1998), *Blackness Visible: Philosophy and Race* (Cornell University Press, Ithaca and London).

Morison, S. E., H. S. Commager and W. E. Leuchtenburg (1983), *A Concise History of the American Republic*, 2nd edn (Oxford University Press, Oxford and London).

Mulhall, Stephen and Adam Swift (1996), *Liberals and Communitarians*, 2nd edn (Blackwell Publishers Ltd, Oxford).

Murphy, W. T. and S. Roberts (1994), *Understanding Property Law*, 2nd edn (HarperCollins Publishers, London).

Nardin, Terry (1992), 'Alternative Ethical Perspectives on Transnational Migration', in Brian Barry and Robert E. Goodin (eds), *Free Movement: Ethical Issues in the Transnational Migration of People and of Money* (Harvester Wheatsheaf, London and New York).

Newton-Smith, William (1981), *The Rationality of Science* (Routledge and Kegan Paul, London).

O'Neill, John (1994), 'Should Communitarians be Nationalists?', *Journal of Applied Philosophy*, 11, pp. 135–43.

O'Neill, Onora (1994), 'Justice and Boundaries', in C. Brown (ed.), *Political Re-structuring in Europe: Ethical Perspectives* (Routledge, London).

Owers, Anne (1984), *Sheep and Goats: British Nationality Law and its Effects* (Ludo Press, London).

Patten, Alan (1999), 'The Autonomy Argument for Liberal Nationalism', *Nations and Nationalism*, vol. 5 no. 1, pp. 1–17.

Paul, Kathleen (1997), *Whitewashing Britain: Race and Citizenship in the Postwar Era* (Cornell University Press, Ithaca and London).

Plender, Richard (1988), *International Migration Law* (Martinus Nijhoff Publishers, Dordrecht).

Poole, Ross (1992), 'On National Identity: A Response to Jonathan Rée', *Radical Philosophy*, 62, autumn, pp. 14–19.

Prescott, J. R. V. (1987), *Political Frontiers and Boundaries* (Allen and Unwin, London).

Prunier, Gerard (1995), *The Rwanda Crisis 1959–1994: A History of Genocide* (Hurst and Company, London).

Rawls, John (1963), 'Constitutional Liberty and the Concept of Justice', in C. J. Friedrich and J. W. Chapman (eds), *Justice: Nomos VI* (Atherton, New York).

Rawls, John (1972), *A Theory of Justice* (Oxford University Press, Oxford).

Rawls, John (1978), 'The Basic Structure as Subject', in A. Goldman and J. Kim (eds), *Values and Morals* (Reidel, Dordrecht).

Rée, Jonathan (1992), 'Internationality', *Radical Philosophy*, 60, spring, pp. 3–11.

Richmond, Anthony H. (1994a), *Global Apartheid: Refugees, Racism, and the New World Order* (Oxford University Press, Toronto, New York and London).

Richmond, Anthony H. (1994b), 'International Migration and Global Change', in Ong Jin Hui, Chan Kwok Bun and Chew Soon Beng (eds), *Crossing Borders: Transmigration in Asia Pacific* (Prentice Hall, London).

Rutherford, J. (ed.) (1990), *Identity: Community, Culture, Difference* (Lawrence and Wishart, London).

Scanlan, John A. and O. T. Kent (1988), 'The Force of Moral Arguments for a Just Immigration Policy in a Hobbesian Universe: The Contemporary American Example', in M. Gibney (ed.), *Open Borders? Closed Societies? The Ethical and Political Issues* (Greenwood Press, Westport, CT, and London).

Schuck, Peter H. (1984), 'The Transformation of Immigration Law', *Columbia Law Review*, 84, pp. 1–90.

Schuck, Peter H. (1998), *Citizens, Strangers and In-betweens: Essays on Immigration and Citizenship* (Westview Press, Boulder, Colorado).

Schwartz, W. F. (ed.) (1995), *Justice in Immigration* (Cambridge University Press, Cambridge).

Shklar, Judith N. (1991), *American Citizenship: The Quest for Inclusion*, The Tanner Lectures on Human Values (Harvard University Press, Cambridge, MA).

Sidgwick, Henry (1881), *The Elements of Politics* (Macmillan and Co., London).

Simmons, Alan J. (1979), *Moral Principles and Political Obligations* (Princeton University Press, Princeton).

Simon, Julian L. (1989), *The Economic Consequences of Immigration* (Basil Blackwell, Oxford).

Smith, Anthony D. (1991), *National Identity* (Penguin, Harmondsworth).

Sollors, Werner (ed.) (1989), *The Invention of Ethnicity* (Oxford University Press, New York and Oxford).

Spencer, Michael (1990), *1992 And All That: Civil Liberties in the Balance* (Civil Liberties Trust, London).

Spivak, G. C. (1990), *The Post-Colonial Critic: Interviews, Strategies, Dialogues*, ed. S. Harasym (Routledge, London).

Starke, F. C. (ed.) (1831), *Kants Philosophische Anthropologie: Nach Handschriften Vorlesungen* (Leipzig).

Steiner, Hillel (1992), 'Libertarianism and the Transnational Migration of People', in Brian Barry and Robert E. Goodin (eds), *Free Movement: Ethical Issues in the Transnational Migration of People and of Money* (Harvester Wheatsheaf, London and New York).

Stoddard, Lothrop (1927), *The Rising Tide of Color Against White World-Supremacy* (Chapman and Hall, London).

Tamir, Yael (1993), *Liberal Nationalism* (Princeton University Press, Princeton).

Taunton, J., D. McCormack and J. W. Smith (eds) (1996), *Immigration and the Social Contract: The Implosion of Western Societies* (Avebury, Aldershot).

Taylor, Charles (1994), 'The Politics of Recognition', in A. Gutmann (ed.), *Multiculturalism: Examining the Politics of Recognition* (Princeton University Press, Princeton).

Teitelbaum, M. and M. Weiner (eds) (1995), *Threatened Peoples, Threatened Borders: World Migration and US Policy* (W. W. Norten and Co., New York and London).

Tempelman, Sasja (1999), 'Constructions of Cultural Identity: Multiculturalism and Exclusion', *Political Studies*, XLVII, pp. 17–31.

Turner, Bryan S. (1986), *Citizenship and Capitalism: The Debate over Reformism* (Allen and Unwin, London).

Ucarer, Emek M. (1997), 'The Coming of an Era of Human Uprootedness: A Global Challenge', in Emek M. Ucarer and Donald J. Puchala (eds), *Immigration into Western Societies: Problems and Policies* (Pinter, London and Washington).

Van Gunsteren, H. (1987–8), 'Admission to Citizenship', *Ethics*, 98, pp. 731–41.

Viroli, Maurizio (1995), *For Love of Country: An Essay on Patriotism and Nationalism* (Clarendon Press, Oxford).

Walzer, Michael (1981), 'The Distribution of Membership', in P. G. Brown and H. Shue (eds), *Boundaries: National Autonomy and its Limits* (Rowan and Littlefield, Towota, NJ).

Walzer, Michael (1983), *Spheres of Justice: A Defence of Pluralism and Equality* (Martin Robertson, Oxford).

Walzer, Michael (1992), 'The New Tribalism', *Dissent*, spring 1992, pp. 164–71.

Walzer, Michael (ed.) (1995), *Toward a Global Civil Society* (Berghahn Books, Providence and Oxford).

Walzer, Michael (1997), *On Toleration* (Yale University Press, New Haven).

Walzer, Michael, Edward T. Kantowicz, John Higham and Mona Harrington (1982), *The Politics of Ethnicity* (Belknap Press of Harvard University Press, Cambridge, MA).

Webber, Frances (1991), 'From Ethnocentrism to Euro-racism', *Europe: Variations on a Theme of Racism: Race and Class*, vol. 32, no. 3, pp. 11–17.

Weinstock, Daniel M. (1996), 'Is there a Moral Case for Nationalism?' *Journal of Applied Philosophy*, 13, pp. 87–100.

West, Cornel (1993), *Keeping Faith: Philosophy and Race in America* (Routledge, London and New York).

Whelan, Frederick G. (1988), 'Citizenship and Freedom of Movement: An Open Admissions Policy?' in M. Gibney (ed.), *Open Borders? Closed Societies? The Ethical and Political Issues* (Greenwood Press, Westport, CT, and London).

Whelpley, James Davenport (1905), *The Problem of the Immigrant* (Chapman and Hall, London).

Williams, Kevin (1992), 'Something more Important than Truth: Ethical Issues in War Reporting', in Andrew Belsey and Ruth Chadwick (eds), *Ethical Issues in Journalism and the Media* (Routledge, London).

Woodward, James (1992), 'Commentary: Liberalism and Migration', in Brian Barry and Robert E. Goodin (eds), *Free Movement: Ethical Issues in the Transnational Migration of People and of Money* (Harvester Wheatsheaf, London and New York).

Yack, Bernard (1999), 'The Myth of the Civic Nation', in R. Beiner (ed.), *Theorizing Nationalism* (State University of New York Press, Albany).

Yinger, J. Milton (1994), *Ethnicity: Source of Strength? Source of Conflict?* (State University of New York Press, Albany).

Young, Iris Marion (1990), *Justice and the Politics of Difference* (Princeton University Press, Princeton).

Younge, Gary (1998), 'Borders of Hate', *The Guardian*, G2, Wednesday 17 June 1998, pp. 2–4.

Yuval-Davis, Nira (1997), *Gender and Nation* (Sage, London).

INDEX

217